WOMEN
of the
RAJ

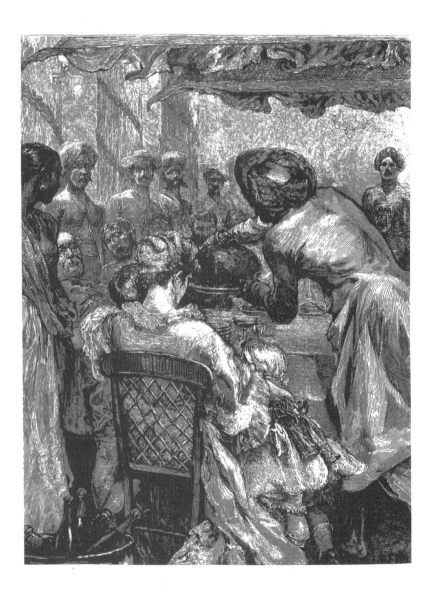

MARGARET MACMILLAN

WOMEN
of the
RAJ

The Mothers, Wives and Daughters of the British Empire in India

New Edition

With 56 illustrations

Thames & Hudson

Frontispiece Christmas at Madras, at the height of the Raj. As the great *punkah* fan swings overhead, the memsahib, flanked by her two young children, is presented with the ceremonial Christmas pudding.

To Bob

First published in hardcover in the United Kingdom in 1988 by Thames & Hudson Ltd, 181A High Holborn, London WC1V 7QX.

This new edition 2018
Reprinted 2018

British Library Cataloguing-in-Publication Data
A catalogue record for this book is available from the British Library

ISBN 978-0-500-29374-4

Printed and bound in Glasgow by MBM Print

To find out about all our publications, please visit
www.thamesandhudson.com.
There you can subscribe to our e-newsletter, browse or download our current catalogue, and buy any titles that are in print.

CONTENTS

PREFACE

Women of the Raj is a historical artefact and I have chosen to leave it pretty much as it was written. I wrote it in the 1980s so it reflects the state of historical investigation as well as my own views and concerns at the time. The history of empire was an old and well-established field, its preoccupations more with the rise and fall of the big western empires than their societies. Women's history was a very new subject of historical inquiry indeed. Since then both fields have expanded and changed and if I were writing my book today it would of course be very different and I would use other terms in places. The book still refers to the Indian Mutiny, for example, where now I would probably write the Great Rebellion or even India's first war of independence. I have made only a few cosmetic changes and added in some of the choicer bits of the new material I have come across.

Yet I hope that what I wrote all those years ago still has something to say to the present. It deals with questions which matter in our globalized world with its marked differences in wealth and status. How do people adapt to living in a different culture? How does power affect the relations between rulers and ruled? How can human beings overcome the stereotypes about each other? And, so I like to think, it helps us to recover voices from the past.

The book, my first, was published almost thirty years ago when global and transnational history, much less cultural history, the history of food, fashion or the body, were yet to be conceived as fields of study at all. I had very few examples to follow as I studied a largely vanished community. Nor could I call, as later historians have done, on the rich insights offered by the explosion in the last years of the twentieth century and the start of the twenty-first in gender and cultural history or the study of the construction of identities or diasporas. When I tried to understand the British women, the *memsahibs*, who made their lives in India, I was largely on my own.

True, the British Empire was still the object of historical study and the ways in which it was studied were slowly changing, from examining the process by which so much of the map of the world came to be coloured

red, to trying to understand why the Empire had melted away so quickly after the Second World War and, increasingly important, what it had meant for those at the receiving end, its millions of subjects around the world. How had the British established their rule? What were the steps by which India had moved to independence? What were the roots of Indian nationalism? Or – and this was a matter of perennial debate – had the British Empire benefited India or had India benefited the British? Important questions but the rise and fall of empires was increasingly out of step with what was happening to the study of history in the 1960s and 1970s. When I went to the University of Toronto, Canada was becoming aware of itself as a nation and that meant breaking the ties to what we had once called the Mother Country. We did not want to dwell on our past as a colony. In Britain, where I did my graduate work at Oxford in the late 1960s and early 1970s, the Empire was a matter for regret if not shame. Or it was simply a joke. Its marks lingered on in the monuments to long-forgotten empire-builders or in the uniforms in the second-hand shops or the chutney in corners of grocery stores. Only a few scholars bothered to look at the copious records that remained.

At the time other fields of history seemed more interesting: revolutions – the French, Russian, Chinese – for example – or the development of the working classes. Historians were moving beyond what had once been considered proper history to explore subjects such as childhood, the family, or disease and society. At my own College, St Antony's, one of the fellows was Theodore Zeldin, who was part way through his monumental history of the French with headings such as Ambition and Love or Anxiety and Hypocrisy. Such new types of inquiry, into social groups, ideas, attitudes or gender, were going to permeate and shake up older established fields such as imperial history where I nevertheless remained. And fashionable or not there was no escaping that Western imperialism and the many and varied responses of the colonized are among the key forces shaping modern history. Forces – the great currents that sweep through history – are only ever part of what I want to consider as a historian. The impact on individuals matters as much to me.

We often choose our subjects – or they choose us – as a result of our own histories. I am a child of the British Empire. In my childhood many Canadians still looked to Britain as the hub of our world. We sang 'God Save the King' and then 'God Save the Queen' in school and before

every performance in the theatre. Both my grandfathers fought in the
First World War for the British Army. Perhaps I did my thesis on the
British in India because I read *Kim* and *The Jungle Book* when I was a
child. Perhaps because one grandfather had been in the Indian Medical
Service, and we as children played with the ragged skin of the tiger he
had shot. My grandmother, who had been a very reluctant memsahib,
told us stories of snakes in the bathtubs and scorpions under the beds and
boredom at the Clubs. My Indian-born mother, who had much fonder
memories from her childhood, talked about the colours and the clash
of bangles on the arms of her beloved Indian nurse. And when I went to
Oxford, where so many of the proconsuls of Empire had been given their
training, there was an Indian Institute, professors who knew much about
the subcontinent, and students from India who were fascinated by their
own history. At our seminars there were elderly men, often, I realized
later, with interesting and distinguished careers who had been in the
Indian Civil Service, the Indian Army, or the Indian Political Service.

For whatever reasons, I decided to write a thesis on the British
community in India in the decades around the turn of the nineteenth
century, when the Raj was at its most pompous and powerful but when
the cracks were starting to appear. I wanted to look at who they were,
how they lived as a tiny community amid millions on the subcontinent,
what assumptions they made about India, and what they thought about
what they were doing there. At that point there were only a few studies
of that ruling group. Although the name later came to refer to Eurasians
they called themselves the Anglo-Indians, which is what I shall use here.
They were of British descent, and proud of it, often born in India but,
when their families could afford it, educated in Britain. As adults they
came back to work and live in India, often generation after generation,
but preferred to retire to what they called Home, a British Isles which
they scarcely knew.

As I made my way through undergraduate and then graduate history
I was also increasingly interested in what it meant to be a woman
in a world where the rules and values were still largely set by men.
The women's movement and women's history was then in its early
stages. Until the 1960s, the study of women's lives, like that of children
or gays, had not been a focus of mainstream history. As undergrad-
uates, we studied political history or economic or military history,

much of it fascinating. We were interested in how people in the past organized themselves, how they made politics or war. We did not care as much as we do today about what they thought or felt or ate or wore. Always, though, when the preoccupations of the present change, we start to ask different questions of the past. In the 1970s and 1980s, the women's movement, the struggle for civil rights, and the challenges to received wisdom and authority helped to put the past under different spotlights. Historians – and this was certainly true in my case – tried to re-evaluate the role of women in history and to re-examine the stereotypes that women were merely minor players or onlookers in the past or pale reflections of men.

So my two interests came together to produce my first book. What, I tried to discover, must it have been like to go as a young, almost certainly apprehensive, woman to a large, ancient and complex land ruled over by a tiny handful of the British? What sort of pressures would there have been to conform? What would happen to those women who defied their own community and its ways? And how did British men see their women as part of the imperial project? How did the women see themselves?

Whether we are looking at people who are not like ourselves or when we write history, the temptation is to shake our fingers, confident in the knowledge that we would never be like that. Yet we should remember that the memsahibs went to India to become part of a community that had a very clear idea of what it was. We like to think we choose our own identities freely, but often they are chosen for us. British women in India were, by and large, a part of the Raj. (There were always exceptions, of course, and they are worth looking at.) For the most part, the British women in India were the daughters, sisters, wives and mothers of the men who worked for the Raj. Their community was the dominant one in India from the beginning of the nineteenth century to the Second World War, and they were expected not to let the side down by questioning the imperial mission or by behaving in ways that would weaken the authority of the Raj. The mission might have been wrong and the expectations imposed by the community absurd, but it would have taken a very strong or desperate women to have said so at the time. And what would they have faced if they fled that community at a time when careers for women were so limited?

Iris Macfarlane, whose family worked and lived in India for generations and who was herself married to a tea planter in the 1930s, published a memoir in 2006 that is highly critical of the world to which she once belonged. Her recollections are suffused with guilt and regret: over the accepted practice that children must be sent back to Britain for their own sake, which damaged relations between parents and children irrevocably, and also that while she and her fellow Anglo-Indians lived for so many years as adults in India, they knew so little about it. She looks back at her younger self and is horrified at how much she took her privilege for granted, how, for example, she sat in comfort in a first-class carriage leaving Assam in the face of a threatened Japanese invasion during the Second World War while desperate Indian refugees banged on the door. And she regrets deeply her casual cruelty to her servants, her incivility: 'Nobody that I can remember ever said thank you. I mourn for all those mannerless years and find little excuse for myself.'

Meeting memsahibs in India – and there were still some left when I was there – also forced me to look beyond the caricatures depicted by novelists, memorably by E. M. Forster in *A Passage to India*, of braying, hard-boiled, thick-skinned harridans. The memsahib I remember best was the wife of one of the last English tea planters in Assam, who invited me to stay on their tea garden. They were both immensely hospitable, and I had a wonderful time. I saw the Burma Road, which ran by their door. I watched elephants dragging logs from the forest. We had a drink at the Club, a simple building with a concrete floor and tin roof, far removed from the glories of the Delhi Gymkhana. They told me that when the Chinese invaded in 1962, the women and children were sent to Calcutta while the husbands stayed. Stories got back to Calcutta that the men were trying to drain the Club cellar before the Chinese armies arrived, and so the women came back.

My memsahib had servants, but while I sat on the verandah and read, she ran her household. There were no shops within miles. The bacon we had at breakfast came from the pigs she had raised and butchered. The bread was baked daily. She was also a nurse and held a daily clinic for everyone on the tea garden. Her husband was often away, and although she had a few friends locally, it was a lonely life. Could I have managed so efficiently and cheerfully? I asked myself. I was not sure of the answer.

I was fortunate in retrospect that I was doing my research before the electronic revolution. Today the Internet means that you need not go to archives nearly as much and, even when it is necessary, you can swoop in for a few days, photograph all the documents you might conceivably need, and retire back to your home campus to pour over them, often far away from the place you are studying. I had to spend a year in the early 1970s living and researching in India and Pakistan. If I had not done so, I doubt that I could have written either my thesis or this book. I learnt what it was to stand out as someone from a minority yet I also had the privileges that still came, even in an independent country, with coming from the former imperial power and from Oxford. Of course my experiences were not an exact mirror of those forgotten British women of the Raj but I like to think they gave me some ability to understand them. I gathered lots of material in archives in Delhi, Calcutta, Bombay and Lahore. Equally important, I got a sense of India, of its extraordinary variety and vitality. I took many train and bus journeys, into arid Rajasthan, where the women were dazzling in their orange and red saris and the men wore huge intricate turbans, to Bengal, so green and lush by comparison. I watched from train windows for what seemed like days on end as the villages on the Ganges plain slipped by. I went up into the foothills of the Himalayas to Simla, once the summer capital of the British. In Lahore, the records office was in an old Mughal tomb. Outside the local museum, the gun that Kim had played on still stood – as it does today – and inside, the labels on the cases were in a clear Victorian hand that had belonged to Lockwood Kipling, father of the author.

The India I saw had many echoes of the Raj. On trains and in hotels, the section of the menu headed 'European' had strange dishes such as Brown Windsor soup and courses called Savouries. In the smaller towns and in the country, I stayed in the *dak* bungalows that British civil servants had used when they went on tour. I visited the lending libraries where the British had once gathered and looked along rows of dusty books by forgotten authors like Dornford Yates. I played tennis at the Delhi Gymkhana, where the members were now largely Indian but the drinks still ran to pink gin and beer. In Simla, I had tea, as so many memsahibs had once done, at Peliti's. In Calcutta, I went to a nightclub in the Great Eastern Hotel where the band played music from the 1930s. And I met some of the British who had stayed on.

It was all what I had expected and yet it was not. I had not expected to feel so overwhelmed by India or feel so far from all that was familiar. I still remember one night in Delhi when I had dengue fever. It was the wedding season, and from a nearby temple, the air was filled with music. It was marvellous, but it was not my music. As I played aimlessly with my shortwave radio, a few bars of Mozart came through, just enough to make me feel desperately homesick. When I recovered and went back to the archives, one of the files I picked up, about a young lieutenant, ended abruptly with the words 'Died of dengue fever'. Such moments made me realize how often the memsahibs must have been lonely and frightened.

Public interest in the Raj began to pick up again in the 1980s. The success of M. M. Kaye's *Far Pavilions*, first published in 1978, and Paul Scott's *Raj Quartet*, which was published in the 1960s but only attracted significant attention in the late 1970s, helped to create an appetite, heavily tinged with nostalgia, for British India throughout the English-speaking world. Films, from *Gandhi* (1982) to *Viceroy's House* (2017), television series such as *The Jewel in the Crown* (1984), made from the *Raj Quartet*, to *Indian Summers* (2015), the success of histories aimed at the general reader such as William Dalrymple's *White Mughals* (2002) or Alex von Tunzelmann's *Indian Summer: The Secret History of the End of an Empire* (2007) demonstrate that the popular enthusiasm for British India remains high.

Starting in the 1970s, scholars such as Christopher Bayley at Cambridge and Thomas Metcalf of the University of California, moved the study of the Raj into new areas such as social communications, imperial architecture or ideologies of empire. Researchers have been exploring new sources, whether diaries and letters which families continue to find in their attics, long-defunct newspapers, or photographs. Much work has gone into trying to recover the voices of the powerless or the marginalized, whether Indian farmers or women, both Indian and British.

Where the British women are concerned, memoirs such as M. M. Kaye's 1990 account of her childhood, *The Sun in the Morning*, as well as the growing document collections in such places as the Cambridge South

Asian Archive, have added to our understanding and helped to fill in the gaps. I always regretted that I could never find out enough about life in the big cities or for lower-middle-class women whose husbands worked on the railways or in offices or at mills. Since I wrote my book, Rumer Godden's *A Time to Dance, No Time to Weep* has appeared to describe the Calcutta of the 1930s where she and her contemporaries lived in flats and went out to nightclubs rather than the world so often depicted of bungalows and the Club. Eugenie Fraser in *A Home by the Hooghly* has shown a community of engineers and managers in the jute business far removed from the more familiar one of Indian Civil Service officers and their wives out in the countryside. I continue to wish that I could find out more about the Eurasian women who longed so much to be seen as British and who were so cruelly dismissed by the British community, but perhaps there are still materials that will surface.

Historians have developed new tools and new avenues to explore as well since I wrote this book. Knowledge – its production and its uses – has been increasingly seen as one of the ways imperialism dominated other societies. Borrowing from literary theory, some imperial historians appeared to argue in the 1990s that language itself was power, that by labelling and defining Indian society the British somehow created its key features from religion to caste. Even the Indian resistance to British rule was, so it was claimed, the product of imperialism and so demonstrated its overarching impact. What happened before the British arrived in India seemed less important and any notion that there was something separate from British rule in India, which had a validity and existence of its own, tended to be dismissed. As a consequence much research into the Raj focused on what the members of the Raj said. The 1980s and 1990s saw a sharp drop in applications for research grants to go to India. Why learn Indian languages or consult archival sources when the texts produced by the British whether Kipling's poems or the writings of ICS officers or Viceroys could be put through 'discourse analysis' without ever leaving home? And there are always new texts to scrutinize. 'Unfortunately', complains a 1998 work that sets out to remedy the problem, 'research on women travellers remains largely uncontaminated by poststructuralist theory.'

The British in India would be amazed to know how their ceremonies, their sports, or their choice of words have been put under scholarly microscopes and their words probed for deeper or contradictory meanings than might appear on the surface. The fancy dress balls, so popular with the British everywhere, are now seen in the Indian context not merely as elaborate social events but rather ways of showing off the powerful links the British have throughout the world, 'symbolically referencing the unimaginable vastness of global knowledge bases'. The Clubs, those social centres for so many of the British throughout India, and the hill stations where they went to escape the heat of the plains, are, no doubt correctly, seen as ways of gathering the rulers into splendid isolation and keeping Indians at bay.

The British family in India has been analysed as a symbol and representation of the Raj in miniature. Durba Ghosh, in her *Sex and the Family in Colonial India: The Making of Empire* (2006), sees the mixed race families of the eighteenth and early nineteenth centuries as the sites in which British anxieties about the purity and dominance of their race in India played themselves out. In her *Empire Families: Britons and Late Imperial India* (2004), Elizabeth Buettner shows how the Anglo-Indian family transmitted the values of the Raj through successive generations and helped to reinforce the solidarity of the ruling minority.

The memsahibs have had their own particular attention: the ways they dealt with giving birth and facing death; their housekeeping; their hats; their novels; and their attitudes towards sex. The clothes worn by Mary Curzon, the beautiful, and rich, American wife of the Viceroy, Lord Curzon, are, so one scholar has argued, visual symbols of the Raj, which appropriated Indian fabrics and techniques while asserting British dominance over India. When Lady Curzon used sari material to make a dress for a pregnancy even this was apparently part of a pattern. 'Mary's wearing of a maternity dress made of sari material, or her adoption of a hybrid European and Indian design evening dress design is indicative of the continuous processes of exchange and appropriation that underscored the colonial experience.'

Although some of the work over the past few years has endeavoured to see British women in India as themselves the victims of imperialism, obliged to adhere to the rules and practices of a world they had not created and in which they did not have power, in general the academic gaze has not been a friendly or sympathetic one. British women in India are often depicted as fervently and unthinkingly upholding the Raj.

That is demonstrated, so a study from 2003 claims, in their household management, which was driven more by the need to uphold imperial dominance than by such mundane quotidian considerations as making sure that meals appeared, clothes were washed, or illnesses avoided. 'The Anglo-Indian woman was not merely engaged in a reactionary rearguard action "to make the bungalow an island of Englishness, secure from a noxious India". The Anglo-Indian bungalow was an important site for cultural appropriation and transformation. But, like the public spectacles of imperialism, such cultural interactions in the private realm did not represent a concession to the demands of the colonized peoples for autonomy and respect. Rather, the hybrid Anglo-Indian domestic culture was intended to demonstrate the colonizers' mastery and dominance in the private arena of the empire as in the public sphere.'

Other scholars are sceptical that there was even such a limited interaction between the British and India. 'To protect their status as rulers and defend British culture in India,' claims one, 'the Anglo-Indians during the 19th century chose racial exclusiveness and altogether rejected Indian goods and dishes.' Yet the evidence suggests a more complicated picture. The cookery books of British India are filled with recipes – no doubt adapted and changed – for curries, spiced soups, or Indian sweets. And was, as the same scholar suggests, the Victorian craze for what they called curry which used imported Indian spices such as turmeric really an imperial appropriation of the cuisine of others? Perhaps it was merely recognition that there were better things to do with the leftover Sunday joint than make Irish stew with it. As Freud famously said, 'Sometimes a pipe is just a pipe.'

When imperial rule is used to explain everything about India, including the British themselves, that process flattens out the varied opinions among both the British and the Indians about what the Raj was for and what it was doing, the rich variety of interactions between the British and the Indians, and the changes which took place over the centuries. Imperialism is seen as a purposive juggernaut with each person involved assigned a role regardless of his or her own desires. And the human parts of the machinery too often are reduced to a collection of pre-programmed attitudes waiting to be decoded by later generations. The ambiguities and the contradictions which we know from our own experience are part of life are lost. The individual memsahibs, like the other participants in British India, are submerged under layers of interpretation.

If I were writing my book today I would certainly benefit from much of the new work but I would also have to go into the undergrowth of theory and run the danger of getting lost. So on balance I was lucky to be researching when I did. And perhaps there is still room for a book like this one that tries to describe what it was like to live back then in India as a European woman and which seeks to understand why they behaved as they did.

If we continue to be fascinated by histories of vanished communities such as those of the British in India, it is partly because they are now so far off and so unlike ours. It is also because they answer our own very present concerns. How do communities with different values and different perceptions of themselves deal with each other? What happens along the frontiers where they meet and intersect? And is there a difference in the way women and men react to others? And because the Raj was the Raj, what happens when one community is in a position of power in relation to the other? These questions matter much to us today, and perhaps those far-off lives described here will provide some ways of answering them. We are aware more than ever today of the difficulties and the benefits that come with the mingling of cultures. We see how diasporas can resist assimilation to a dominant culture and how easily the majority can make assumptions that those who don't look like us, sound like us, eat the same foods or wear the same clothes are alien – the 'Them' as populists like to say. And when the relationship between those of different cultures is shaped by power it is even more difficult for both the rulers and the ruled to approach and understand each other. History offers us many instructive examples that may help us to avoid some of the mistakes, unkindnesses and follies of the past. For me doing history also offers the chance to encounter many different sorts of people and I have told some of their stories here.

INTRODUCTION

Sometimes they were magnificent. Sometimes, on the other hand, they were awful, as only people who are frightened can be. When a conviction of superiority goes with the fear, then the arrogance is heightened and sharpened. The memsahibs (roughly translated 'the masters' women') – even those who know nothing of the history of the British in India have heard of them. They stride through that history in their voluminous clothes which denied the Indian climate, their only concession to the heat the graceless solar helmet, the *topi*, which protected their rose-petal cheeks from the alien sun.

In their photographs they stare back at the photographer, some hapless Indian perhaps, with eyes that looked on the wonders of India and found them rather dull. Over the years, their ringing voices pronounced Indian painting garish, Indian music cacophonous, Indian ways barbaric. The Indian countryside was monotonous – except for those few cherished bits where, just for a moment, one might imagine oneself at Home, on the Sussex Downs perhaps, or among the hills of Scotland. Indians themselves were useful when they were servants – servants who of course had to be treated like wayward children. Otherwise they existed, millions upon millions of them, to serve as extras in the great drama of the Empire. And with what fury and scorn did the memsahibs react when the extras tried to claim speaking parts!

The greatest of all their incivilities was simply to ignore India. Few of the British women who lived there ever bothered to learn any Indian language apart from a few words of 'kitchen Hindustani'. useful for dealing with the servants. And, after years in the country, most knew little more about it than when they arrived. Yet they told each other, and those at Home, that they understood India. It was typical of their carelessness that one of the tips they passed from generation to generation with scandalized giggles was quite wrong. 'Never shake hands with an Indian, my dear,' was the inside information, 'because you never know where his hand has been.' But Indians, as they could have found out very easily, use only their left hands for their ablutions and keep their right hands clean for eating.

To bundle them all up, however, into the stock figure of the mem-sahib is to do to them what they did to the Indians. British women in India certainly behaved badly; they also behaved well. They were brave in ways that are difficult to comprehend today. They might say dreadful things, but their actions were often quite different from their words. They did not, it is true, conduct themselves in India with the patience of saints, the understanding of anthropologists. They were merely, most of them, ordinary middle-class women put into an extraordinary situation.

To begin with, they did not come to India for India's sake. They came, the great majority, to be wives; and they found in existence a tightly knit community which gave them the simple choice of joining or staying outside. It was not much of a choice. Outside meant loneliness or India, and India frightened them.

In any case, Indian society would probably not have accepted them. The caste system, which had originated with the Hindus, permeated the lives of all Indians, whether Hindu, Muslim, Christian, Jew, or Sikh, and caste operated with as many rules and barriers as British society itself. Indeed many more. Caste shaped Indians' lives from the moment of birth: marriage, occupation, friends, the food they ate and the people they could eat with, all were ruled by caste. The India the British had stumbled in on was a collection of thousands of self-contained, self-absorbed little worlds, and those worlds did not easily accept outsiders. The British, like all the other foreign invaders of India, were Untouchables. Strict Hindus dared not eat with them, touch them, barely remain in the same room with them.

If the new arrivals accepted the code of the Anglo-Indians (the name was what the British in India preferred for themselves until the Eurasians appropriated it), they would at least belong somewhere. And the first article in the code was loyalty to the community. By the nine-teenth century, the British were the ruling elite in India and they felt, they *knew*, that the fate of their rule in India – the Raj – rested on the solidarity and will of that tiny elite. They made much of the obstacles to friendship between the races, especially those on the Indian side, because it suited them to do so.

It had been different earlier. The British who had made their way to India in the sixteenth, seventeenth and eighteenth centuries had come as traders, not as conquerors. They had adjusted to Indian customs and coped with the rules of caste. If they wanted to trade, they had little choice. And they came in any case from a society which had few illusions about its own merits. Before the Industrial Revolution changed the balance of power in the world, the British were not vastly stronger than Africans or Asians, and they certainly did not feel that they were a superior race. Of course their constitution and their laws were the best in the world, but then other nations had their own strengths. Sir William Jones, who was a judge on the Calcutta High Court in the 1780s and a renowned Sanskrit scholar, revered Asia as 'the nurse of sciences'.

The British who came to India before the great upheavals of the nineteenth century were sometimes repelled, sometimes attracted by Indian society, but they did not write it off as inferior. Indeed they often compared it favourably with their own. Warren Hastings, the great governor-general who consolidated British power in India in the 1770s, held that Indian learning had achieved 'a higher degree of perfection many ages even before the existence of the earliest writers of the European world'.

The first British to arrive in India were also gamblers, hungry traders who were prepared to risk everything, including their lives, in the search for profit. It was really the fault of the Ottoman Sultan. If he had not made it impossible for the Levant Company to trade with the East through his territories, the merchants of London might never have bothered to establish the sea route to India. The British wanted spices; they *needed* spices to pickle their meat (and to disguise the taste of the rotting bits). They set up trading posts along the Indian coast because there seemed to be no other way of ensuring their supplies. That they ended up building an empire was a matter of accident, good timing, and tenacity.

The East India Company, which was established in 1599 with a charter from Queen Elizabeth I, had a monopoly on the trade between England and the lands east of the Cape of Good Hope. For a long time, the charter was much grander than the reality. The Dutch already controlled much of Europe's seaborne trade with the East and they saw no reason to share it with the British. The East India Company tried – and failed – to establish itself on the spice islands of Indonesia. And it was only after an English ambassador had prostrated himself before the Mughal Emperor in India that the Company managed to get permission to set

up a small trading post at the Indian Ocean port of Surat – an area the
Dutch did not want anyway.

The East India Company did not exactly flourish during the seventeenth century. Its representatives in India managed to wangle another
couple of trading posts – in one case, only after kissing the toe of the
local ruler. Matters improved slightly in the second half of the century
when Charles II married a Portuguese princess who brought as part of
her dowry the island of Bombay. The Portuguese were no longer much
interested in India in any case, and the Dutch, who might have objected
to the slow spread of British influence, were too busy in Indonesia.
The French, who were likely to object to an increase of British power
in any direction, were only just starting to notice the East.

By the beginning of the eighteenth century the British were comfortably established in a series of posts along the coast of India. Here
again, good timing helped them. As their power slowly increased, that
of the Mughals, who ruled most of India, was on the wane. When the
tough and pious old Emperor Aurangzeb died in 1707 he left an impressive empire that covered almost all of India except for the very tip. In
fact, however, that empire was sick to its core. The Indian princes who
had reluctantly accepted Mughal rule were simply waiting for a chance
to throw it off again. Mughal government was corrupt – worse still,
ineffectual. The ruling family was too torn by jealousies and intrigues
to provide good leadership. Aurangzeb had left no clear successor, and
while his sons and grandsons fought among themselves, Mughal power
drained away. A hundred Indian princes took back their independence.

The East India Company now pushed further into India, partly
because it had to in order to protect its trade, partly because there was
no longer a great power to stop it. It made alliances with some princes,
fought others, and step by step became a power to be reckoned with
in Indian politics. The French also saw the opportunities in the chaos
of eighteenth-century India; they too looked for Indian allies. Perhaps
they did not choose as well; perhaps the British were simply lucky again.
There was fighting and the French lost. After 1757, the British had no
European rivals in India. And after the Mahrattas in Western India were
defeated in 1818 and the Sikhs in the northwest in 1849, they had no
Indian ones. By the beginning of the nineteenth century the Company
had moved a long way from being a straightforward trading concern:

it was now a Raj, responsible for ruling ever larger parts of India. The character of its employees started to change as well: the freewheeling traders and soldiers of fortune were replaced by earnest administrators. More British women ventured out and British communities established themselves in the larger cities. It was no longer necessary, or even desirable, to get along with Indian society.

By the nineteenth century, Britain was a different place too. The tremendous expansion in the economy brought by the Industrial Revolution, the dramatic advances in technology, produced a large, self-confident middle class, sober, God-fearing, hardworking – and utterly convinced that Britain was the best country in the world. The British who came to India were largely from that class and they carried its prejudices along with them. India was a stagnant civilization, Indian religions were idolatrous, Indian arts primitive, Indian customs barbaric.

The memsahibs have often been blamed for the gap that opened up between the rulers and the ruled in the nineteenth century. But it was a gap that was produced by circumstance as much as choice – and the men also wanted it. The British, it was felt, were not in India to make friends. They were there as rulers, and – a view that appealed to the Victorians – to do their duty. About half the men worked for the government, as judges, administrators, teachers, doctors, engineers, foresters, agricultural experts, or officers in the Indian Army, but even the non-officials, the planters (as those who ran plantations were called), businessmen, or lawyers, felt that they were part of the great civilizing mission. India needed all the help it could get if it were ever to share in the benefits of Progress.

The men looked forward to going Home when their part in the work was done. What possible reason could they have for going native? They did not want Indian wives; they wanted middle-class British girls who could share the high purpose of Empire. Young brides soon learnt what being a good wife involved. It meant joining the team, chanting its slogans, cheering it on. The men themselves rarely questioned the justice of British rule. How much less likely that their wives should presume to do so.

In Britain, women were also under pressure to conform, but non-conformity was not so serious a crime as it was in India. If a young wife chose not to go to a church bazaar, no one muttered that the

Empire was going to fall. Moreover, women at Home had a chance to escape from their own social circles if they did not find them congenial. County life was boring? In London or a hundred smaller cities and towns one could find quite respectable society where conversation ran to more than hunting and fishing or the latest village gossip. There was little hope of respectable escape in India. From Madras to Bombay, from the Punjab to Bengal, British society was remarkably similar, its preoccupations much the same.

Most of the women, had they stayed in Britain, would have lived unremarkable lives, in a village perhaps or a suburb of London, doing good works and gently bossing the deserving poor. The bolder spirits might have become Bohemians or bluestockings. In India, British women were obliged to match themselves against a narrow definition of a good woman. They became memsahibs. They shared in the glory of the Raj, yet they had too little responsibility for it.

British women, along with their men, were forced onto a stage in India. They had the leading roles in the imperial pageant. As long as they knew their lines and did not falter, the Indians would tolerate their rule. After 1857, everyone knew what could happen if the Indians decided that they had had enough. The tiny white minority that ruled with such apparent ease could equally easily be hunted down. Who could forget the men, women and children who had been hacked to death as they left the church at Meerut or the pathetic bodies in the well at Cawnpore? The Mutiny, as it used to be called, did not by itself drive a wedge between the British and the Indians, but it confirmed and accelerated the change that was already taking place. The memories of that time, of the atrocities committed on both sides, poisoned the relationship between the races until the British Raj finally disappeared in 1947.

The Mutiny was always close to the surface in the consciousness of the British in India. They had to act the part of confident rulers as much for their own sakes as for the Indians'. With fear as the spur, it is not surprising that the gestures grew too large, the reiterated sentiments too coarse. They could not tolerate ambiguities and uncertainties in their approach to India because it was not safe.

Even without the memory of the Mutiny, India was frightening. It still frightens present-day travellers. The country is so big, so old, so confusing. Trying to understand India is like trying to seize hold of the image in a kaleidoscope. For an instant there seems to be a pattern and then, suddenly, the pieces tumble about. Other patterns appear, but never the same ones. India has too many peoples, too many gods, too much past to be grasped in its entirety. And there is the danger, in getting closer to India, of losing one's foothold in one's own culture. Scarcely a traveller has not felt that sudden rush of panic in the face of so much that is incomprehensible, that longing for something, anything, that is familiar.

The British women who went to India knew that feeling. They ignored India in part because it was so alarming. It threatened them and their families physically – with disease, snakes, rabid dogs, or another Mutiny. The heat drained away their children's strength, leaving pale and listless shadows. It stole the colour from their own cheeks.

Worse, perhaps, India threatened the women spiritually. Indians did not value the right things: they worshipped false gods and scarcely had a moral code at all. The memsahibs were products of their own time. They were not cultural relativists. They could not say, as the present day tries to do, that different peoples have different values and leave it at that. They believed in a hierarchy of human societies, with their own at the top of the scale. They were secure in that knowledge; but what worried the women, and their men, was what would happen to them in the midst of a people who were their moral inferiors. Would they become contaminated?

The memsahibs were especially struck by the sensual side of India. To their amazed eyes the country seemed to be positively writhing with eroticism. Sex seemed to permeate every aspect of Indian life; in the very temples, symbols of the male and female sexual organs were at the centre of worship. Revolting, they declared, but they were intrigued nevertheless. British women were not supposed to feel sexual passion, and men busy with empire-building might not give them reason to change their minds. India could have made them wonder whether they were missing anything. (Anglo-Indian novels so often deal in tones of mixed fascination and horror with the theme of the white girl falling into the clutches of the lascivious Indian.)

The women kept India at arm's length because it might have forced them to question their own foundations. They rejected it, too, with the particular fury of those who know themselves to be rejected in turn.

Indians thought British women shameless and depraved: they mingled freely with men who were not relations, they wore low-cut dresses, and they danced in public places. In Indian society only prostitutes and dancing girls did such things.

In their closed community – closed only partly by choice – the memsahibs struggled to keep Britain alive in the midst of India. The struggle was absurd, but there was a sort of heroism in it. They planted English flowers in their gardens and the heat withered them. They covered their furniture with chintz and the white ants chewed their way through. They got patterns for their clothes from Home but the native tailor somehow altered them subtly. They served English food even though half of it had to come out of tins. In a supreme gesture of defiance they reserved the hottest time of the day – between twelve and two – for receiving calls from gentlemen.

In all they did, even their daily routine, there was a most un-British element of self-consciousness. Like the Sun King, but in bungalows instead of Versailles, the people of the Raj lived public lives. They felt obliged to behave like the rulers they were. The Indians, it was argued, expected pomp and gaudy pageantry. (Over the years of the Raj, the British grew to like it too.) In some ways their lives were much grander than they would have been back Home. There were always quantities of servants, servants waiting behind each chair at a dinner party, servants to pull off the sahib's boots, servants to comb the memsahib's hair, servants for each child.

Because of the servants, entertainments in India were on a scale beyond anything at Home except among the rich. Quite ordinary dinner parties had eight or more elaborate courses. Picnics were preceded by trains of servants and ponies bearing stoves, hampers of food, cushions, rugs, anything that was necessary for their masters' comfort. With an unending supply of cheap labour, concerts, amateur theatricals, dinners, balls could succeed each other night after night.

The British in India longed to be amused. They filled their days with visiting and parties – and sports. It was almost impossible to be a true member of the community without liking sports. Some intrepid women hunted; most contented themselves with gentler sports like archery, badminton or tennis. Visitors to India noticed how youthful the British there seemed, how jolly they all were.

What visitors saw, much as posterity does, was the surface. British life in India looked like fun, but it was not as easy as it seemed. There were lots of servants, but they were a necessity in a world without modern conveniences. And the caste rules meant that each servant was unable to do certain jobs: gardeners would only garden, cooks only cook. There was squalor, too, mixed up with the splendour. Few bungalows had plumbing; a servant called a sweeper carried away the masters' wastes. There were discomforts to Indian life which no amount of luxury could mitigate; under their long dresses at dinner parties, for example, women had to tie pillowcases around their ankles to keep the mosquitoes off. Much more serious was the ever-present fear of disease, which, in the India before penicillin and antibiotics, could carry off an apparently healthy person in hours.

All the parties could not make up for the boredom. On the smaller stations, in particular, the same people met day after day to eat the same meals and exchange the same tired conversation. The times when they would gather in their numbers – during Christmas week in the various capitals, or in the summer in the hill stations – did not last forever. There were few who escaped entirely the loneliness and the irritations of life in India.

It was worse for the women than for the men. The men at least had their jobs and the sense that they were doing something worthwhile in India. The women were there to keep house and raise little empire-builders of the future. They were not expected to take too close an interest in India; that would have been unseemly. They did not carry out charitable works among the Indians because that was the sort of thing missionaries – generally regarded with some disdain – did. And the Indians themselves might get upset, which was the last thing the Raj wanted.

The memsahibs found that they had a lot of leisure time. The difficulty was to fill it. They were not great readers; most had been brought up with the notion that only bluestockings read much. They dabbled a bit in painting – genteel watercolours that toned down the Indian scene. They played a little music – if it was not too hot and the termites had not eaten the piano. For the rest, they devised a social round where they could meet and gossip and quarrel, and then meet again.

They were, of course, expected to do certain jobs. They bore children – difficult, dangerous even, but only intermittently time-consuming. They brought up their children, but they were expected to leave most of the actual work to the servants. They supervised the housekeeping, but they dared not do too much themselves lest the servants protest. And they knew, before they had started, that they were bound to fail in part as wives and mothers. Because of the unwritten law that British children must not stay in India after they were seven, women faced the choice of abandoning either their husbands or their children for years on end. This was yet another factor that contributed to the making of the memsahib of the caricature.

Some women, it is true, could not or would not fit into the mould, but they were the sort of forceful characters who could dispense with social approval. They also had to be strong enough to bear the accusation of ruining their husbands' careers. Flora Annie Steel, in the late nineteenth century one of the most popular novelists of British India, paid no more attention to the attempts of the government of India to restrain her than she did to her husband's. (He, quite sensibly, decided to retire early.)

At either end of the social scale there were women who were not bound by the dictates of local society. At the top were the wives of viceroys and governors who had the aristocratic self-confidence to ignore the middle-class mores of the Raj's permanent staff. In any case, since their husbands were appointed in London, they did not have to worry about approval in India. At the other end were the lower-class British women, most of them the wives of soldiers stationed temporarily in India. They belonged to the self-contained world of the British regiment.

Finally there was that small number of women who had come to India not because of their husbands but because they wanted to. Missionaries, some teachers, others doctors, came to serve a higher authority than the Raj. There were women who were attracted by the romance of India, in a few cases by a particular Indian. There was the occasional radical, most notably Annie Besant, who scandalized the establishment by working for India's independence (or was it because she advocated free love and birth control?). The lives and fates of all the out-of-the-ordinary women are worth examining too. They show the range of responses to India possible among British women and they help to illustrate the limits of the standard response.

It is, however, the ordinary memsahibs who will concern us most. There were so many more of them; the impression they left is still the dominant one of British women in India. The complaints about them are true, but not universally so. And, in spite of themselves and their society, they did take something from India. The sad part is that they often did not realize until it was too late how India had seeped into their bones. When they went Home for good, the Home that they had longed for, they found it flat, like a photograph with all its colour drained out. Many of them discovered only then that they had loved India.

So far, most of the story of the British in India has been written in terms of the men. But the women played their part too. It was less flamboyant. Their concerns were less with the Raj and more with the details of everyday life. Like ants, they constructed nest after nest; without them the British would have had quite a different presence. Whether it would have been better or worse is irrelevant. The point is that the women were there and their story is a part of the Raj's history too.

1

THE VOYAGE OUT

Englishwomen – and Welsh and Scots and Irish women – had been going to India for generations by the time the Raj reached its peak in the late nineteenth century. The first to make the voyage may have been a Mrs Hudson and her maid, Frances Webb, who went in 1617 as companions to an Armenian lady who had been born in India. (Frances had a love affair on the voyage, unwittingly setting the pattern for countless women who came after her.) Over the years, India drew a few women looking for work – as milliners, perhaps, or governesses. And some women had a calling to be missionaries. Others simply went because they had been summoned back by their families after an education in Britain.

The great majority, however, went to India because their husbands were there or because they hoped to find husbands for themselves. (To keep them chaste for the marriage market, unmarried women travelled, until well into the twentieth century, under the care of chaperones, usually married women who were making the voyage anyway.) The 'fishing fleet', as it was known unkindly but accurately by the nineteenth century, arrived in India in the autumn at the start of the cold weather. One lady who came out in 1779 divided what she called 'the speculative ladies' into old maids, 'of the shrivelled and dry description', and girls, 'educated merely to cover the surface of their mental deformity'. The odds were that their fishing would meet success: throughout the period of British rule in India, European men outnumbered European women by about three to one.

Understandably, few British women had cared to come to the unsettled India of the seventeenth and early eighteenth centuries; and, what is more, the early charters of the East India Company pointedly forbade women on its posts. Its employees ignored that regulation as they did so many others. They took Indian mistresses; worse, from the point of view of the Company's staunch Protestant directors, they married Catholics, daughters or widows of the Portuguese. To save the souls of its men, the Company, for a time, played matchmaker. In the later part of the seventeenth century it shipped batches of young women from Britain to India. The cargo, divided into 'gentlewomen' and 'others', were given one set of clothes each and were supported for a year – quite long enough, it was thought, for them to find themselves husbands. Some did not; and the Company tried to deny that it had any obligation to look after them further. Most unfairly it also warned them to mind their morals: 'Whereas some of these women are grown scandalous to our nation, religion and Government interest,' said a letter from London to the Deputy Governor of Bombay in 1675, 'we require you to give them fair warning that they do apply themselves to a more sober and Christian conversation.' If that warning did not have the right effect, the women were to be fed on bread and water and shipped back to Britain. The experiment was not a happy one and it must have been with relief that the Company abandoned the practice in the eighteenth century. British women still travelled to India but they came individually.

The voyage was a dreadful one. The wooden sailing vessels, tiny by today's standards, were tossed about in every storm – and the South Atlantic and the Indian Ocean were famous for their storms. The passengers faced at best being thrown about in their cabins, at worst drowning. The Reverend Hobart Caunter recorded one such storm, which took place off the east coast of India in the 1830s. The weather began to turn foul early one morning. 'The only lady among us every now and then expressed her fears, when a sudden gust caused the vessel to lurch with an increased momentum, as if the billows were already commencing a fiercer conflict.' By late afternoon, they were in the midst of a full-blown hurricane. The ship pitched violently and furniture was torn from its fastenings. More dangerously, a cannon got loose and threatened to batter a hole in the side. Even Caunter, a seasoned traveller, found the noise, coupled with the crashing of waves and the howling of the wind, 'painful in the extreme'. Night came on and the storm increased in fury. As Caunter and the captain were in the main cabin, or cuddy, trying to carry on a conversation, 'suddenly, a heavy sea struck her astern, but happily on the quarter, and in an instant carried away the quarter-galley on that side, swamping the cabin into which the poor lady before spoken of had retired for the night. The force of the water was so great, that it dashed open the door of the cabin, and its fair occupant was borne head foremost into the cuddy, dripping like a mermaid, her hair hanging about her shoulders in thin strips, when she was rescued by the captain from further mischief. She was drenched to the skin.'

At its shortest the voyage under sail took under two months; at its longest well over six. Sometimes the winds were so contrary on the west coast of Africa that the ships were blown off course almost to Brazil. The crew and passengers gasped with the heat; then, when they were rounding the Cape of Good Hope, they shivered in the cold. There was the danger of being dashed against the shore by a sudden shift in the winds. Those who survived often ended up in the great slave markets along the east coast of Africa. Occasionally the winds might fail altogether and the unhappy ship would sit becalmed for weeks on end.

Accommodations were cramped and dirty and often had to be shared with huge rats which scurried about, boldly eating any food that was left out and nibbling holes in clothing. Women who could afford it had cabins above decks. Otherwise they were housed below, in stuffy cubby holes, often with walls made of canvas, where they had very little privacy. A bucket of salt water was the closest passengers got to a wash tub; another bucket made do for a toilet. Mrs Sherwood, later famous as a writer of sentimental children's stories, accompanied her army officer husband out to India at the beginning of the nineteenth century; she had to sleep in a hammock strung above a cannon while filthy water from the bilges ran across the floor beneath.

Mrs Eliza Fay, who lived in India in the late eighteenth century, endured the voyage several times. Fortunately she was a woman who faced difficulties (and she had many – from imprisonment by an Indian ruler to her wastrel of a husband) in an optimistic spirit. Her letters to her sister are filled with cheerful gossip and appalling details of shipboard life. On one voyage back to England, she nearly suffocated. 'The port of my cabin being kept almost constantly shut, and the door opening into the steerage; I had neither light nor air but from a scuttle.' On her first voyage the captain was 'overbearing and insolent' and kept his passengers half starved. At meals, Mrs Fay reported proudly, 'the longest arm fared best; and you cannot imagine what a good scrambler I am become'.

When they could, women on the sailing ships escaped from their cabins to the fresh air of the deck, but that depended on both the weather and the mood of the captain. Many of the captains of the East Indiamen were quite charmingly eccentric on dry land; at sea they seemed half mad and one of their more common phobias was women. Ladies were often forced to take their meals in their cabins rather than in the cuddy because the gentlemen drank and swore so dreadfully. Mrs Sherwood confided to her diary that 'those who have not been at sea can never conceive the hundredth part of the horrors of a long voyage to a female in a sailing vessel.'

At the start of the voyage, there might be the luxury of fresh meat, because many ships carried cows and sheep on deck. Sooner or later, rations would get shorter, the preserved meat tougher and saltier. Water would turn the colour of strong tea, with a foul smell and an even fouler taste. Minnie Blane, a happy, sheltered young middle-class girl from Bath, experienced all the unpleasantness of sailing ships when she travelled out to India in 1856 with her husband, an officer in the Indian Army. (They might have taken the shorter route overland via Egypt and enjoyed the relative comfort of steamships but her husband needed to save money.) Minnie, who was pregnant, was sick a good deal of the time and the meals she faced cannot have helped. For weeks on end, after they had rounded the Cape, the only meat was '*Pork*, boiled, roasted, fried, chops, curry (with so much garlic in it, it is quite uneatable), and one leg of mutton, half raw'. The butter was thick with salt and sugar had long since run out. Some food was quite rotten. 'I cannot tell you', wrote Minnie to her mother, 'how sick it made me one day, on cutting open a fig, to see three or four large white maggots lying comfortably inside!' Cautious travellers often took a private stock of food and wine. Many women brought other little comforts along in a brave attempt to make their quarters bearable. They had their own folding chairs, washstands, linen, and even chintz curtains to hang across the door.

Soldiers' wives had the worst time of all. The Army's own troopships were appalling – leaking, dirty, and cramped – and the transports it sometimes had to hire from private contractors were scarcely better. Since the usual class distinctions were rigidly observed at sea, officers' ladies at least got cabins; 'wives of others ranks', as the Army described them, were below decks, often in a corner of the hold next to the horses. There they endured the voyage, sleeping, eating and passing their days in a stench which got worse as the voyage dragged on. Unless they were working for an officer's wife, they had little opportunity of getting on deck.

The military authorities of the eighteenth and early nineteenth centuries did not approve of women and their children accompanying the troops – only a few of the families of the ranks were permitted to go – so they did little to make them comfortable. The Army gave them a pittance for their subsistence but no advice on what to bring with them. Mrs Helen Mackenzie, the strong-minded and pious wife of an officer in a Sikh regiment, was horrified on her first voyage to India in the middle of the nineteeth century to discover a soldier's wife eating the scraps from her plate. The unfortunate woman was 'worse off than a female convict': she did not even have adequate clothing.

Gradually the Army was forced to modify its attitude; by the twentieth century wives usually accompanied their husbands abroad and the troopships, while never luxurious, gave them at least decent food and accommodation. After the First World War, conditions were better still; the Army even provided free baby food on board ship.

It is not surprising that passengers on those early voyages in sailing ships vented their misery and boredom in violent quarrels with each other. The men threatened each other with duels; the women gossiped viciously and absurdly cut each other dead. Every now and then there were more agreeable moments. If it was calm, the passengers danced on the deck under the stars. They celebrated 'crossing the line', when male passengers who had never crossed the equator before were ceremonially shaved by Neptune and his court. The biggest sailors played Mrs Neptune and her daughters. The gentlemen were shaved with a saw and a tar brush and ducked in a tub of salt water while the ladies watched from a safe distance. Mrs Ashmore, the prim wife of an officer, witnessed the merriment when she travelled out to India in 1840, though the scene 'soon became of too riotous a nature to admit of our remaining witnesses to it'. (She retired to her favourite reading – the works of Bishop Berkeley and Volney's *Ruins of Empire*.)

Occasionally (and not always by design) the ships put in briefly to shore. St Helena in the South Atlantic was a popular spot to pick up provisions and water. The passengers could stretch their legs briefly; if they had time they might make a trip to Napoleon's tomb (at least until the bones were restored to the French in 1840). The Cape of Good Hope was another regular stop. The ships tied up at Simonstown, then a pretty little fishing village, and passengers hired carriages to take them to Constantia, where there were excellent local wines, and to Cape Town with its charming houses set in tidy gardens. The Dutch settlers, various ladies noted approvingly, preserved both the simple ways and the hospitality of their ancestors.

There was a much shorter way of getting to India, by boat across the Mediterranean, then by land across the narrow strip of Egypt that divided the Mediterranean from the Red Sea, and finally by boat again across the Indian Ocean. This route was first used in the eighteenth century and was eventually to supplant the one around the Cape. At first it presented as many hazards as the longer route, because Egypt, nominally under the control of the Ottoman Sultan, was quite lawless. Passengers for India gathered in Cairo until they were a large enough party to defy the bandits who lay in wait in the desert. Sometimes they joined forces with Egyptian merchants heading in the same direction. The caravans travelled with an escort of hired Arab soldiers. The men generally rode while the ladies were jolted about in a sort of litter, slung between two camels. In spite of a canopy and blinds, the unfortunate occupants nearly stifled in the heat of the day only to shudder in the sudden chill of the desert night. Mrs Fay, who travelled in one of these in the 1770s, remembered with particular antipathy 'the frequent violent jerks, occasioned by one or other of the poles slipping out of its wretched fastening, so as to bring one end of the litter to the ground'. In later years, men and women bounced together across the desert in crude horse-drawn vans; later still there was a railway.

The journey became much safer and much faster as the nineteenth century wore on. In 1830 the first steamer was put into service between Suez, at the head of the Red Sea, and Bombay. In 1840, the Peninsular and Oriental Steamship Company signed an agreement with the government of India to provide a regular service between Suez and certain Indian ports. The P&O was in time to become almost synonymous with the journey to India, but there were other lines: the Anchor and the Clan Lines, which ran between Liverpool and Bombay, the Calcutta Star Line between Liverpool and Colombo, and (generally considered by the British inferior to all these) the Italian Rubatino Line from Genoa and Naples to Bombay. Steam and the opening of the Suez Canal in 1869 helped to shorten the trip to four weeks and even less and the whole experience became rather enjoyable. The author of *Indian Outfits*, a guide for women published in 1882, was quite rhapsodic. 'To those who like the sea, the voyage is very pleasant; there are generally many nice people on board, and, if troops are carried, sometimes a band, and on fine nights dancing on deck, or singing, glee parties, and so on; very often amateur theatricals are got up, and come off the night before port is reached. There is usually a library on board, and there is no reason why, with so much that is new to interest and with pleasant society, the time should not pass quickly and agreeably.'

The marked improvement in communications between Europe and India meant that more women were able to travel out. By the end of the nineteenth century, the trip had developed its own rules. Old hands booked cabins on the side facing north to avoid the heat of the sun: Port Out, Starboard Home – and so, one explanation goes, 'posh' came into the language. Baggage was labelled 'Baggage Room' (for pieces not needed at all on the voyage), 'Present Use Baggage Room' (where the owners had access every day at a fixed time), and 'Cabin'. The guide-books recommended that ladies' Cabin Baggage include a chintz bag for dirty clothes and a provision basket with such comforts as biscuits, Bovril, whisky or brandy, and a spirit lamp for brewing up cups of tea. (There must have been some accidents because many liners would not allow either spirit lamps or curling tongs.) Passengers should also take a patent medicine such as chlorodyne for aches and pains. And, *Indian Outfits* informed its readers, 'a bottle of essence of Jamaica ginger … is good for sea sickness.' (The P&O line thoughtfully provided grey-and-scarlet cardboard boxes for those passengers whom no remedy helped.) Clothes posed a problem because of the changes in climate. The general rule, said *The Complete Indian Housekeeper and Cook* – compiled in the late nineteenth century by two women of the Raj, Flora Annie Steel (see pp. 242–43) and Grace Gardiner – with an excruciating pun, was a tweed costume for 'Homi-cide' and light dresses for 'Suez-cide'. To get around the difficulties of doing laundry on board, sensible ladies took their oldest underwear and nightdresses along and simply threw them out the portholes when they were soiled.

Most passengers for India travelled the whole distance from Britain by boat, but some, to shorten the journey, went by train across France or down through Italy to catch a steamer to Egypt. The departures, whether from a railway station or dockside, gave those going to India for the first time a preview of British society out there. So small was the British community in India that old hands spotted friends and acquaintances among the crowd; they chatted with each other in an English peppered with strange words. The novices also began to realize the pain that the British Empire in India caused to those who worked for it. There were sad leave-takings, mothers saying goodbye to their children who were staying at Home to be educated, families seeing off, perhaps for years on end, one of their own. 'No one', wrote Pamela Hinkson, a writer who went to India in the 1930s, 'had told me about the cord that goes with one as far as Port Said, seeming to link one with the country and life one has left; stretching as the boat moves on, but always tugging at one's heart as if to prevent one turning one's face forwards, to go on, a free person – East.'

On the way across the Mediterranean, the ships sometimes stopped for twenty-four hours to take on coal at Malta, where 'the coral, silver, and lace shops in the Strada Reale are very tempting', and ladies who were not squeamish could visit the 'pickled monks' – embalmed members of the Carmelite Order. The first really 'oriental' stop on the way was Port Said. Women went ashore carefully escorted, because the city was said to be full of cut-throats of all nationalities. They were followed about by motley crowds of beggars, little boys, fortune-tellers, and locals trying to show them conjuring tricks. In the twentieth century, in a well-known shop run by a Chinese, they could buy embroidery or porcelain or perhaps a pair of japanned vases for their future homes. The famous Simon Arzt stocked everything from topis to Turkish delight to the striped shawls which were to be seen on memsahibs all over India. (Old hands back on board were fond of telling novice travellers that they had paid too much.)

Some travellers took the overland route across Egypt even after the Suez Canal had opened, and they might do some sightseeing in Cairo or Alexandria. *Indian Outfits* recommended hiring a dragoman as guide 'from among the yelling horde who surround you directly on landing'. There was a good deal worth visiting – Pompey's Pillar, for example, and the Khedive's Palace, where 'very good taste is displayed in general'.

The Suez Canal route was less wearing, but not nearly so interesting. The town of Ismailia offered few distractions beyond the 'bumboats' which came out to sell a strangely assorted cargo of shoes, black bread, onions and monkeys. Passengers could amuse themselves by throwing coppers to the boys who ran alongside begging. At the southern end of the Canal was the dreary town of Suez, where the only amusement was donkey rides on beasts with names like 'Lily Langtry' and 'the Archbishop of Canterbury'.

The Red Sea was, surprisingly, a beautiful blue. But, warned the author of *Indian Outfits*, 'In it one is sure to be hot, and if there is any breeze it is sure to be the wrong one.' By now it was getting hotter day by day; the ladies brought out their summer clothing, the gentlemen (in the twentieth century) started to wear shorts, and the staff went into white uniforms. The hot broth served at eleven in the morning disappeared, to be replaced by ices and melons.

As the ship sailed on down the Red Sea, those passengers who were of a religious turn of mind could amuse themselves by trying to pick out the mountains described in the Old Testament. Most were far too busy. Sudden close friendships formed and of course there were romances, watched with amusement or disapproval by the older ladies. 'We felt nervous', reported Pamela Hinkson, 'about some of the young ladies going out to be married. They were divided into two classes, those who sat alone dreaming and those who made the most of their last fling.' Shipboard life after Port Said was an endless round of activity. In the 1930s Dennis Kincaid, who wrote one of the best books on British society in India, heard a lady declare: 'The only way to travel is by British liners, because of the lovely organized games.' When Ethel Savi, the wife of an estate manager in north India and a novelist of Anglo-India, went by the P&O's *Viceroy of India* in 1929, she discovered that the games deck with its shuffle board, quoits, and deck tennis was 'easily the most popular spot on the ship'. Besides the games there were concerts where passengers and crew would give recitations or sing and fancy dress balls with prizes for the best costumes – perhaps a young lady disguised as a plum pudding or a hearty young man as Cupid. The novices found themselves pressured to join in all the jollity, yet another foretaste of life in India.

By this stage, the passengers had sorted themselves out, the hearty enjoying themselves loudly and energetically, the serious-minded talking quietly in corners of the ship. For women who were new to India, shipboard life also revealed that deeply engrained Anglo-Indian love of hierarchy. Within hours of departure, the elites from the Indian Civil

Service and the Indian Army had found each other; planters gathered to drink hard and play hard; and missionaries were shunned by common consent. In the large cabins which several women shared, the senior lady took the best berth.

The last port of call before India was Aden, uncomfortably wild and austere with no green to soften its rocks. And the natives were 'rough, wild-looking creatures, with shocks of red or yellow hair'. After Aden, the weather became hotter still. The Southern Cross now glowed in the sky at night, and the ships left a silver trail of phosphorus in their wake. During the day whales and porpoises raced alongside. When it became unbearably hot, some passengers had their bedding taken out to the decks. The ladies slept on one side of the deck, the men on the other, with a sail rigged up between them for decency's sake; at bedtime and in the mornings, a signal warned the men to avert their eyes while the ladies trooped by.

For those making the journey for the first time, it was all very exciting. Monica Campbell-Martin crossed the Indian Ocean in the 1920s on her way to India with her husband and tiny daughter. She was young and enthusiastic and she was fascinated by the tropics. 'All day long the flying fish swept past like fairy rapiers. Always there was a concerted upsurge of glistening backs, then a cloud of silvery needles shot through the air. Swiftly they pierced the waves again without a splash, only to be followed by another school in gleaming horizontal flight. We slept on deck, for only a salamander could have felt comfortable in the cabins. Going to bed on deck could scarcely be called "sleeping". In the small hours, later arrivals stepped over us or on us. At dawn we were roused by the washing of the decks with powerful jets of water from a hose. But I forgave the tropics their heat for the sake of those magnificent starry nights.'

As they got closer to India, sharp-nosed passengers claimed that they could smell the land. (It was a favourite joke to deceive the new arrivals by rubbing a foul-smelling substance on the rails.) The last night on board was always an uneasy one, as passengers said goodbye to friends or perhaps lovers they had not known a month previously. Some women faced a return mixed with sadness as they thought of the children left behind. For the young girls who had been born in India but educated at Home, there was the sudden sense of familiarity, the rush of recollections that had faded during the long cold years away. And for the women coming out to India for the first time, there was the apprehension of arrival in a strange land. Would they be met? Would they recognize their fiancés? How would they fit in? Shipboard life had given them a taste of the society they were going to meet in India, with its gregariousness, its passion for games, and its strong sense of hierarchy. Now they had to come to terms with India as well.

2

FIRST IMPRESSIONS

Whether they came by sailing ship in the eighteenth century or by steamship in the twentieth, the first impressions the new arrivals had of India were almost always similar. The noise, the smells, the colour – and the people in all their dazzling variety. Women's recollections of that initial encounter also reveal an undercurrent of panic. After the enclosed world of the ships, India was too big, too untidy, too crowded – in fact, too much India.

The smell was the first thing they noticed. Even before they landed, a whiff of India was borne out to them on the breeze. India has a smell so much its own that even the faintest echo of it somewhere else can bring a sudden strong nostalgia. All hot countries have scents unfamiliar to noses from northern countries: garlic, cooking oil, pungent tobaccos. India adds dust and the tang of spices – chilies, turmeric, ginger, cloves; the scent of jasmine and sandalwood; and the acrid smoke of burning cow dung.

From the first, too, the newcomers' eyes were assaulted by the colours, on the people and in the streets. As Pamela Hinkson's P&O liner docked in Bombay in the 1930s, she leaned on the rail and gazed at the pier. 'A group of women in *saris* made one think that they must be colour-blind. Orange, red, yellow, pink, blue and mauve were mixed together, all of the brightest shades.' Mrs Guthrie, an endlessly inquisitive and energetic Englishwoman who visited India in the 1870s, was less censorious. On her first drive through Bombay, she admired Parsee women 'walking about in short satin skirts of the most brilliant hues – an exquisite pale cherry and an emerald green appeared to be their favourite colours – flowers were in their glossy black hair, and they wore quantities of gold lace and handsome ornaments'.

Then there were the noises. The liquid syllables of different Indian languages lapped about the women. Bullock carts, which were everywhere, creaked along on squeaking axles. Horses clattered by with their carriages. The birds known as the seven sisters because they always fly in flocks of seven cackled relentlessly. Often there were snatches of music, alien to the European ear. Late into the evenings, there was a constant bustle as the inhabitants went about their shopping, or simply stood gossiping. Mrs Guthrie arrived in Bombay in the season of marriages: 'We could see the guests, and hear the discordant music. Rockets shot up into the sky, and broke into balls of brilliant colours; crackers exploded in every corner, and Bengal lights tinged all around with their vivid hues.'

Rosamund Lawrence came from generations of British in India (she was descended from Sir Charles Napier, the conqueror of Sind), but she was as awestruck as any new arrival when she first saw India in the years before the First World War: 'There is such a lot of everything.' She never forgot her first drive through the streets of Bombay. 'I had never seen so many people; a mixture of brown faces, and dirty white garments and spotless uniforms, and helmets, mixed up with oxen, mangy dogs, crows, and beggars, and driving through narrow streets between tall colour-washed houses, with vivid trees jammed between them, jingling victorias and bullock carts round you, and parrots shooting across the road over your head, black crows squawking. People. People. People. And your frock stuck to your shoulders.'

The women drove by alleyways where craftsmen worked in brass or leather or precious metals outside their tiny shops. They peered curiously at their first mosques, at the pyramid-shaped Jain temples behind high walls, and at the Hindu temples (where Mrs Guthrie glimpsed 'some hideous copper idol, or figure of stone, daubed with red paint and greasy with libations of butter'). They visited the market to admire the flowers – roses, marigolds, jasmine, tuberoses – heaped carelessly into mounds, the fruit and the vegetables, sometimes unlike any they had ever seen. Mrs Guthrie was particularly taken with the aubergines or eggplants, 'some of them white and smooth like ivory, others resembling balls of gold'. The dashing Lady Falkland (daughter of William IV and the beautiful Irish actress Mrs Jordan), who came to Bombay as wife of the Governor in 1848, loved it all: 'What bits to sketch! What effects here! What colouring there!'

In the west of India, Bombay was the port of entry. Like its rivals in the south and east, Madras and Calcutta, it owed much to the arrival of the British and their trade, but in its situation it was handsomer than either of them. The curving harbour with gentle hills rising behind it was frequently compared to the Bay of Naples, and visitors were impressed by its European buildings along the waterfront. They were also fascinated, perhaps appalled, by the crowded native quarters, with their narrow streets and their ramshackle houses painted in gaudy pinks and yellows.

Travellers bound for eastern parts of India often stopped briefly at Ceylon. Young Emily Metcalfe, who was being brought back to India in 1847 to join her father, the British Resident in Delhi, felt 'intense admiration for everything in Ceylon': 'so beautiful were the trees, and shrubs, and flowers, that I looked upon it as a kind of paradise.' She, like many other travellers both before and since, found Madras an anti-climax, with its flat, monotonous shoreline. When the ships from Europe dropped anchor, they were at once surrounded by a horde of small boats filled with natives clamoring to sell fruit or to take the passengers ashore. The noise and the sight of so many dark skins was enough, said one lady, to make her think she had suddenly visited 'the infernal regions'.

The main thrill of the arrival at Madras, until the end of the nineteenth century when a proper harbour was built, was the trip to shore through the miles of breakers that crashed unceasingly against the coast. With many misgivings, the passengers clambered down into one of the rickety boats (simply rough planks lashed together with twine of coconut fibre). Each boat had eight or so rowers and a steersman who stood at one end. Julia Maitland, a sharp-tongued and observant lady who arrived in the 1830s, was full of praise for the boatmen, 'wonderful people', who sat 'crouched upon their heels, throwing their paddles about very dexterously'. Picturesque catamarans, made of several logs bound together, escorted them in to shore. The catamarans were not there just to add local colour: their job was to pick up passengers if their boats capsized in the surf – assuming, of course, that the sharks which lingered hopefully in the waters did not get them first.

The Madras boatmen were famous not only for their skill but for their rapacity. Their practice was suddenly to demand more money as the boat neared the surf; passengers who refused to pay up often found themselves soaked. Many women were also shocked by their boatmen's appearance – 'naked', said one lady who arrived in 1810, 'all but a turban, and a half handkerchief fastened to the waist by a pack-thread'. The scrap of cloth all too frequently got blown aside: 'a very awkward exhibition this', reported William Hickey, the notorious eighteenth-century nabob and rake, 'for modest girls on their first arrival.... Use, however, soon reconciles them to such sights.' Julia Maitland was more tolerant than most: 'the black skins prevent them from looking so very uncomfortable as Europeans would be in the same *minus* state.'

Sometimes the boatmen, or the occasional gallant gentleman, leaped into the surf and carried the ladies through the rollers to shore. Otherwise the passengers clung to the sides of their boat as it shot through the last waves and crashed roughly down on the sand. It was with relief that they stepped out onto solid land at last and made their way through crowds of curious Indians to their carriages.

When they were composed enough to look about them, the women were struck by the spacious and elegant European parts of Madras and the crowded jumble of the native quarter – Black Town, as it was known. Mrs Ashmore, the serious lady who occupied her 1840 voyage in study, noted approvingly that 'some of the public buildings are very handsome, the roads extremely good and wide and smooth as the finest gravel walk'. Mrs Fay in the 1770s found Madras beautiful and exotic, with its gleaming white buildings 'covered with a sort of shell-lime which takes a polish like marble, and produces a wonderful effect'. And the inhabitants were worthy of their surroundings.

One saw, she reported to her friends in England, 'Asiatic splendour, combined with European taste exhibited around you on every side, under the forms of flowing drapery, stately palanquins, elegant carriages, innumerable servants, and all the pomp and circumstance of luxurious ease, and unbounded wealth'. Madras developed early and then, through the nineteenth century, settled into a stately decline. The British inhabitants of other parts of India thought it a backwater. Trade and industry passed it by in favour of Bombay and Calcutta.

By the nineteenth century, Calcutta had become the pre-eminent port in India and the main gateway for travellers to the east of India. Those who arrived in Calcutta by sea approached the city gradually, along miles of the treacherous Hooghly River as it ran through the lush and green Bengal countryside. This was often the most dangerous part of the voyage: the Hooghly was, and still is, infamous for the shifting shoals and sandbanks which lurk beneath its waters. Countless ships have been lost over the centuries. Emily Metcalfe found that the hazards of her arrival at Madras paled by comparison: 'The excitement was great as the steamer neared Calcutta, because we had to pass the dangerous sandbank, the James and Mary, on which many fine vessels had been stranded and sucked down by the peculiar nature of the quicksands, most of the passengers losing their lives.'

As her boat made its slow way upriver in 1856, Minnie Blane got a taste of both the beauty of India and the horrors it was capable of producing. 'The scenery is getting more beautiful', she wrote to her mother. 'The dates, coconuts and bananas are lovely, and rice has the appearance of corn in the distance, and the trees are lovely today. I saw a dead body on the bank of the river being devoured by Pariah dogs, a horrible sight.'

In the eighteenth century, Calcutta was beautiful enough to rival Madras. Mrs Fay found that 'The banks of the river are as one may say absolutely studded with elegant mansions…. These houses are surrounded by groves and lawns, which descend to the water's edge.' By the nineteenth century, Calcutta was to become more impressive for its docks and warehouses, factories and offices, for its vitality and dynamism, and for the fact that it was the capital of India.

Whichever of the great ports they came to, the women were left with an impression of an India bursting at the seams. After the swirling crowds, the confusion of colour, sound and smell, most found it a relief to get to the uncluttered European quarters, with their spacious bungalows and shady gardens, such a pleasant contrast, wrote Monica Lang in the 1920s, 'to the heat and dust and squalor of the city streets'. Europeans in India, they were to discover, showed their spiritual distance from the country in their physical surroundings. Whereas Indians lived jumbled promiscuously together in houses and tenements that were built to no clear pattern, their rulers lived serenely apart in bungalows (and sometimes in flats) which were laid out tidily in straight lines.

New arrivals quickly realized just how tiny was the minority they belonged to. Anne Wilson, who came out to join her civil servant husband in the 1890s, wrote to a friend in England just after her arrival: 'I honestly confess that the overwhelming crowds of people frightened me…. What were we in the land, I thought, but a handful of Europeans at best, and what was there to prevent these myriads from falling upon and obliterating us, as if we had never existed?' That fear, she was to find, never left her compatriots.

India was frightening, not just because it had so many people, but because there were so many different types and colours. In any of the big ports, one could see fierce Pathan horse-traders from the Northwest Frontier, Bengali baboos (the clerks who kept the Raj running), Parsee businessmen, handsome Rajputs from the dry reaches of Rajasthan, Portuguese-speaking half-castes from Goa, and yellow-skinned peoples from Nepal and the northeast with a Mongol tinge to their features. Indians from the north could be tall with pale skin and light eyes; from the south, they were often short and very dark. There were women in saris, women in trousers, women veiled from head to foot; men in yards of white muslin, men in skirts, men with brilliantly coloured turbans, men in skullcaps. There were alarming holy men, 'horrible objects,' said Mrs Guthrie, 'with their wildly-rolling eyes, long tangled locks, and every bone in their wretched bodies visible'.

Most of the women who came to India had no idea of the diversity that they were going to find. When Monica Campbell-Martin met her first Indian official, she was surprised to learn from a fellow passenger that the marks on his forehead indicated his caste. 'I thought there were only Hindus and Mohammedans', she said. But Indians, as the new arrivals had to learn, are divided and then subdivided in a myriad of ways. Religion, for example. The great distinction was indeed between Hindu and Muslim. (Muslims made up perhaps a fifth of the population.) But there were also Buddhists, Jews and Christians. There were Parsees, followers of Zoroaster, who had come to India from Persia to escape religious persecution. There were Sikhs, the Protestants of Hinduism; they had started out as a movement to purify Hinduism but they had evolved into something more like a separate religion. There were Jains who believed so strongly in the sanctity of all life that they often wore gauze masks lest they inadvertently swallow a tiny insect. And there were a large number of Indians who could not really be slotted into any recognizable religious grouping but who obviously worshipped something. The British administrators lumped them together as Animists.

Within each religion, there were more divisions. Most Indian Muslims were Sunnis, but there were also Shias to represent the other half of the schism that had run through Islam almost from the moment of the Prophet's death. There were newer sects, such as the Wahabis, who wanted to purify Islam; since part of the purification involved war against infidels, they caused the British much trouble in the nineteenth century. Islam at least had only one god. Hinduism had an enormous number, and most gods had their own followers. In Bengal, for example, the most popular was Kali, a terrifying goddess who is often depicted dancing with a tongue dripping with blood and a necklace of human skulls as adornment. On the other side of India, in the Bombay Presidency, the gods most worshipped were male: Shiva, the destroyer, and Vishnu, the preserver. Followers of Shiva might paint three horizontal lines on their foreheads; followers of Vishnu wore their lines vertically. And there were darker, underground sects, which the British looked at with a fascinated repugnance: the Thugs, for example, who (before the British finally put a stop to their activities in the nineteenth century) had sought to please Kali by strangling travellers.

Then, just to complicate the Indian jigsaw puzzle further, there were the castes, which were originally tied up with Hinduism but had spilled over into India's other religious groups. Muslims, Christians, Indian Jews all had high and low castes. So too did Sikhs, in spite of the fact that Sikhism had originally been impelled by a reaction against the caste system.

Castes are a bit like Scottish clans – belonging to them is a matter of birth, not of choice – but they have far more power over their members. Violation of caste rules is punishable, in extreme cases, by expulsion from the caste. The family of the outcaste no longer dare have anything to do with him. The boundaries which mark off one caste from another are enforced by a fear of pollution, a fear so deeply ingrained in Indian society that only the very bravest dare ignore it. Pollution comes from contact with those from lower castes. Most dangerous were the Untouchables, who did the jobs that all other Hindus considered too dirty, such as skinning dead animals or washing clothes or handling corpses; in some parts of south India there were castes so lowly that the mere sight of them was polluting to the highest castes. In theory, there were four main castes, but what really counted for Indians were the sub-castes, and at the beginning of the twentieth century there were well over two thousand of them. It was at this point that many newcomers despaired of learning anything of India at all – and some never did. As Isabelle Fane, the daughter of the Commander-in-Chief in India in the 1830s, said dismissively, 'All mosques are so much alike that, excepting some are larger than others, having seen one you have seen them all, I think.' (To be fair, she adopted the same tone with virtually everyone she met and everything she saw: the Eden sisters stank like 'polecats', the preacher at her church was 'detestable', the widely admired beauty Mrs Thoby Prinsep was 'odious'.)

From the early nineteenth century onwards few women lingered long in the ports. They fanned out to join one of the British enclaves that were spreading across India with the growing power of the Raj. Before the middle of the nineteenth century, there were few railways and travel was slow and generally very uncomfortable. The pleasant-est way to go was by boat. Emily Metcalfe travelled from Calcutta up the Ganges towards Delhi in a style befitting a Resident's daughter. 'The progress was slow against the stream, but the life was most enjoy-able and peaceful. It was one continual picnic from morning to night, and for the whole of the month that we were on board we all spent the day on deck under an awning, reading, working or writing letters. We had our meals on deck, and in the evenings when we were moored to the bank, we went on shore for a walk, and then returned again to the deck to spend the evening in pleasant conversation before going to bed.' It was the best of introductions to India. From the decks the women could see the country at a safe distance, and appreciate its beauty without feeling threatened by its immensity and its strangeness. Honoria Lawrence, who was married to the great administrator Henry Lawrence in the first half of the nineteenth century, saw, as she put it, 'the fair face of nature'. She described the scene along the Ganges for a friend in England: 'The banks have been a good deal varied but their present clothing is *moonge* or *jeplassee*, a tall coarse grass ten or twelve feet high with a feathery head of white downy seed, presenting in places a surface so unbroken, so unspotted as to look like a heavy fall of snow. Balsam, purple, white, red and variegated abound in the hedges, and are planted around temples and tombs. The blossoms are laid as offerings on the shrines, and are afterwards thrown into the river, which I have seen quite enamelled with them.'

Most women had to travel by land, and that was quite a different matter. Before trains, they jolted along in carriages or in litters carried by bearers. When Minnie Blane made her first journey in India she was six months pregnant. Her husband reassured her anxious mother in England that she was really very comfortable: 'She travels in a palanquin up to Jhelum, a sort of bed carried by four bearers who run barefoot and frequently change places with accompanying relief men.'

By the end of the nineteenth century the palanquin had disappeared, but carriages or humbler carts remained necessary in those parts beyond the railway network. When Julia Curtis arrived to visit her planter brother in south India in the 1890s she travelled up into the hills in a rough open cart pulled by bullocks. There was a cover of woven date mats to protect her from the weather. She could not sleep because of 'the jolting and bumping, the creak, creak of unoiled wheels, the incessant shouts of my driver urging on his bullocks, and the dreadful smell of rancid oil with which that individual's body was anointed'. A breakfast of mutton chops, curry puffs and kidneys on toast did little to cheer her up. But as the cart made its slow way up, she began to realize that India had its compensations: 'Lovely blue hills loomed ahead of us, and belts of jungle and tall forest trees and vividly green vegetation.'

For most women by that time, the train was to provide their first extended contact with India. They travelled in compartments reserved for Europeans, so that they did not actually meet many Indians, but as they gazed out the train windows they got an inkling of the size and complexity of the country.

As they travelled to their ultimate destinations, the women encountered widely different Indias: an India of green paddy fields and palm trees, as in large parts of the south, or an India of dusty sun-baked plains, as in much of the north. Parts of India – much of Rajasthan, for example – were desert; but others, like Bengal, were wet and lush. There were hills where the air was cool, almost like Home, and to the north lay the great wall of the Himalayas.

For some women India was to be the spare and dedicated life on the Northwest Frontier, where they dared not stir too far from the station without an armed escort. Others were going to know the loneliness of the tea garden or coffee plantation. Some were to spend their years in India in small out-of-the-way places, while others, especially if they married businessmen, were to live in the bustle of the big cities where there were enough other Europeans and enough amenities to give them the illusion that they were not really in India at all.

Monica Lang, as a young girl on her way to marry a planter in the 1920s, remembered thinking at her first sight of an Indian railway station that 'it would take me a lifetime to get anywhere near an understanding of this strange country with its dramatic contrasts of wealth and abject poverty, beauty and squalor, intangible mysticism and downright cruelty'. The new arrivals were also deeply impressed by the apparent miraculous ability of the British to rule such a country and such a people. That first trip imbued women with a sense of reverence for the Raj and for their humble share in it which they rarely lost. Indian trains were like the Raj itself, chugging steadily onwards with their countrymen firmly in control. The newcomers also became aware, perhaps for the first time, of the shell of privilege which encased them in India. They were shielded from unwanted contact with Indians, but also treated with a deference that was intoxicating. If they were short of money, their credit was good simply because of their race. When Monica Campbell-Martin and her husband travelled north from Madras, an Indian stationmaster helped them out of an awkward situation. As she later wrote, 'Mr. Das at Kargpur had never seen us before. He was never to meet us again, but he advanced us money, with only our word for it that the name we gave him and our address a thousand miles away were correct.' In a memoir she wrote long after India had become independent, Iris Macfarlane wondered at how easily her younger self took her privileged position for granted. When she fled Assam in the face of a threatened Japanese invasion during the Second World War she and her newborn child sat in a first-class carriage while desperate Indians banged on the doors hoping, in vain, to get in.

Privilege eased their introduction, but the women still had to learn the basic rules of survival in India. They had to learn how to ward off the diseases which were endemic in India. They had to cope with the climate. They had to remember always to wear their topis in the sun, not just for protection but because wearing a topi was a badge of the ruling race. They also had to unlearn some of what they had been taught at Home. In the 1930s old hands told Pamela Hinkson, for example, that because of the heat 'one may put one's fish to one's nose before one eats it, even at a dinner party, and if one is suspicious one may warn one's host, as one might be shy to do at home'. They had to get used to less privacy than at Home; the rooms in their new houses sometimes had no doors, and in any case the barefoot servants came and went without knocking.

Above all they had to learn to remember that they were part of the Raj with all the obligations and privileges that that brought. Even the wives of the ordinary soldiers who came out on the strength of their husbands' regiments were expected to behave themselves. For the embryo memsahibs, which is what most of the British women who came to India were going to be, there was much to learn. They were helped by the senior ladies, who often took their duties with enthusiasm, sometimes mixed with kindness, sometimes with bullying. The new arrivals were to discover that the most important things they had to learn were not about India at all but about British society in India.

3

THE SOCIETY OF THE EXILES

After the shock of India, the insular little society of their compatriots was a welcome refuge to the women. It took them a while to realize that 'learning the ropes' was not always as easy as it seemed. That jolly, open surface hid reefs of convention; if the newcomers were not careful they could come to grief. Sometimes the community tolerated those who flouted its unwritten rules; more often it did not.

British society in India even had its own vocabulary, with words borrowed over the years from the Indian languages or with English words which were used in quite a different sense from the way they were at Home. The *mofussil* was anywhere in India outside the cities, and 'station' meant any spot where Europeans lived. When they got up in the morning they had *chota hazri*, in the middle of the day they ate *tiffin*, and in the evening they might go to the Club and have a 'peg' – but only a little one, a *chota* peg, because sahibs and memsahibs were not supposed to drink too much.

It was a world in which there were few Indians. In the great majority of their memoirs and novels, the British draw an India dotted with their bungalows and Clubs, echoing to the sound of their bustle and their gossip. By the mid-nineteenth century, India had dwindled in their consciousness into a mere backdrop to real life. Indians appear silently, as servants or as picturesque decoration. *The Pioneer*, a newspaper printed in Allahabad which was widely read by the British, once inadvertently supplied the perfect image. Its Calcutta correspondent was describing the Christmas races of 1881: 'most of the élite were present. Outside the enclosure the Native and Eurasian public were to be seen in their thousands.'

To their compatriots, as the women were to discover, other Anglo-Indians (they used the term, of course, only to refer to those of unmixed European blood) were the most important inhabitants of India. They were, most of them at least, within the charmed enclosure of the Raj. It comes as a shock, therefore, to realize just how few of them there were, even at the height of British power. In 1881, when the first India-wide census was taken, the authorities counted 145,000 Europeans out of a total population of 250,000,000. Forty years later, there were still only 165,000 Europeans in the whole of India. (There are probably more than that living there today.) The Census Commissioners always paid a good deal of attention to that tiny minority; as one said in 1881, 'they are the ruling race and … as such all information in respect to them has an importance quite out of proportion to their numerical strength.' It was difficult to get an accurate count. Much time was spent debating the tricky question of whether Armenians were Europeans or Asians. And the Eurasians muddled things by trying to scramble up into the ruling race, claiming first that they were Anglo-Indians and, when that term finally came to stand for those of mixed race by the time of the First World War, that they were Europeans. (Their claim on 'Anglo-Indian' caused much confusion, and annoyed the original Anglo-Indians.) They in turn were being pressed hotly by the native Christians, who saw no reason why they should not share more than just the imperial religion.

Probably about half the Europeans in India lived in the cities and larger towns. In Calcutta and Bombay, there were substantial communities of between 10,000 and 12,000. Madras had half that number. By the beginning of the twentieth century, Karachi, which was rapidly becoming an important port, and Delhi, the capital of India after 1911, were developing as centres of British life. There were also concentrations of Europeans in the military camps and cantonments, especially those in northwestern India. In such centres, homesick women could find European shops, restaurants, Clubs, even theatres, and, by the twentieth century, cinemas.

Other women faced a lonelier – but perhaps more interesting – life. Beyond the major centres, there were pockets of Europeans scattered across India, along the railway lines, in the smaller towns and the hill stations. Further out in the *mofussil* were assorted planters, missionaries, forestry experts and policemen, and their families, who often lived miles from their nearest British neighbours. Europeans were also sprinkled here and there throughout the princely states (such states had Indian rulers and a nominal independence). Some were sent by the government of India to keep an eye on the princes; others were employed by the princes themselves. In the Rajputana Agency in western India, for example, the government discovered in 1894 the following Europeans: a gardener, a lady teacher, a music master, and a Mr F. H. Sandys, who was in charge of the princely 'Tricycles and other light vehicles'.

Many women experienced both sorts of life because few exiles (as they called themselves in their moments of self-pity) spent all their time in India in one spot. Men were moved about by their regiments, their firms, their departments; and their wives packed up the household and followed them. If they were lucky, they stayed in the same area; if not, they were posted to an entirely new part of India where their painfully acquired smattering of the local language and customs was no use at all.

In spite of the restless existence of most of the British community, they themselves insisted that there were distinct regional types among them. The British inhabitants of south India were generally agreed to be sleepy and old-fashioned by their peers in the north. Bengalis (the European kind) believed themselves to be at the hub of the Raj. It was in Bengal that India had been won for Britain, and Calcutta was not only the country's commercial and industrial hub but also, until 1911, the capital. If the British from Bengal felt themselves to be an elite, Punjabis, as the British in the Punjab liked to call themselves, knew they were. The Punjab had been the last piece of India to be conquered and its reputation as a wild frontier land that required a special type of men and women to deal with it lived on.

Bombay Presidency was much more lively; its inhabitants, especially those from Bombay City and Poona, considered themselves to be energetic and modern. They also prided themselves on being less excitable and more tolerant of the Indians than their compatriots in Bengal or the Punjab. In Bombay the relations between the races were markedly better than they were elsewhere in British India. That may have reflected history: British rule over Bombay had been established with relatively less violence than in Bengal, for example. It may also have been a result of greater economic co-operation between British and Indian businessmen. Finally it may have had something to do with the existence of a large Parsee community which acted as a bridge between British and Indians. Nora Scott, the wife of a judge who lived in Bombay in the 1880s, kept a journal for her family in England in which she describes frequent meetings with Parsee lawyers and their families. Her comments on their personalities, their customs, or their clothes are not condescending but interested and sympathetic. (Indeed she comments on her fellow Anglo-Indians in much the same way.) When Sir Jamsetjee Jeejeebhoy, a leader of the Parsee community, takes her and her husband to the Towers of Silence (where the Parsees leave their dead for the vultures) she notes, 'We came away feeling that much of the horror that we had felt before in looking up at the Towers of Silence was gone, and that there was a solemn, religious and wise respect for the living, and for the dead, in the custom that had endured for 6000 years.' And when she is invited to the ceremony when a Parsee child is being given the symbols of its religion, she tells her family, 'It seems to me the najote is to Parsees very much what confirmation is to us.'

The frequent moves left their mark on all the British in India. They were rarely in any one place long enough to establish a sense of belonging. Perhaps they would not have wanted to in any case; their creed was that they were all going Home in the end. It meant, however, that they could not develop close friendships and they could not cultivate family ties. Rumer Godden, herself part of that world in the first part of the twentieth century, thought that the impermanence of their society had a bad effect on them all. She compared Europeans in India to 'cut flowers; that is why most of them wither and grow sterile, they cannot live without their roots, and so few of them take root'.

It was hardest of all on the women who had to dismantle their carefully constructed nests and build them again miles away. (One skill they rapidly acquired was packing, for there were few professional movers in India.) There was little point, as they soon discovered, in hoping to take all the pieces with them. *The Complete Indian Housekeeper and Cook*, that indispensable guide for so many memsahibs, said firmly, 'People are here to-day, gone to-morrow, and so solidities and fragilities of all sorts are a sheer nuisance.'

Honoria Lawrence, for one, paid the penalty for being married to a rising civil servant. Henry Lawrence was so admired for his administrative and diplomatic abilities that the authorities were constantly changing their minds about where to use him. In 1843, the Lawrences moved three times; at the end of it, Henry Lawrence was posted to Nepal as British Resident. As a tremendous concession on the part of the Nepalese, Honoria was allowed to accompany him, thus becoming the first European woman to set foot in that isolated Himalayan kingdom. It was a dubious privilege because in those days the journey to Kathmandu, the capital, was long and laborious. Even she, generally so cheerful, complained to a friend in England about 'trying to carry some few household goods, the vexation of their arriving smashed, cracked, rubbed, bruised, drenched after jolting on miserable *hackeries* over unutterably bad roads, being dragged through streams of all imaginable depths and regaled with alternate showers of dust and rain'.

The coming of the railways did not always make much difference; goods went astray, boxcars caught fire, packing cases fell off the carts taking them to and from the stations. Women resigned themselves to these difficulties. When a family left a station, the large furniture and sometimes the china and glass were sold off. The new station would undoubtedly have a merchant who could rent or sell them whatever they needed. They took with them small things to re-create a feeling of Home. The author of *Indian Outfits* advised that 'by dint of hanging up photographs, pictures, brackets for odds and ends of china, Japanese scrolls, having books and papers about, and a piano, which you can hire in most stations, a room can be made fairly pretty.'

Their wanderings made the British all the more conscious of the need to stick together. There were a few who did not get caught up by what Edward Thompson, one of the more thoughtful of the British missionaries, called 'the compulsory sociability of the United English nation', but they were eccentrics, like the Scot found living in the hills of North Arcot as the elder of a tribe of hillsmen. Sociability was part of belonging to the ruling race. The British felt that any weakening of the team spirit would lead to a weakening of the Raj itself, and so they clung to each other with determination. Their hospitality, particularly in remote stations, always amazed visitors from Britain. They thought nothing of inviting complete strangers to lunch, to supper, to stay a night, a week, a month. Anne Wilson, whose husband was a District Commissioner in the Punjab in the early 1900s, wrote to a friend from her husband's post that she kept an eye out for new arrivals at the *dak* bungalow (where Europeans on tour stayed); if one fell sick, she sent down food from her kitchen.

As the wife of a junior manager at a jute mill near Calcutta, Eugenie Fraser also knew that solidarity which came with being part of a small community surrounded by peoples of another culture. Her India was largely life on a compound with about a dozen other Anglo-Indian managers, overseers, engineers and mechanics, with a few other wives for companionship and advice. The company provided the bungalows they lived in, or in the case of the bachelors, the quarters, the tennis courts, swimming pool and gardens. In other respects, however, her life was different from that of Anne Wilson. The jute *wallahs* did not go to the hills in the hot weather because they could not afford it. And she knew that she and her world were near the bottom of the hierarchy of British India. 'I saw it like some high ladder stretching away to the skies at the top of which was the heaven-born ruling body of the ICS (Indian Civil Service), followed by the army – guardians of the realm. Far down this social ladder were the box wallahs, the businessmen, Indian and European ...'

No matter how isolated their lives, most British found it inconceivable that they should look to their Indian neighbours for company or friendship. As a consequence, life on the smaller stations was often extremely dreary. An anonymous poet, again in *The Pioneer*, described it well:

> For whist a doubtful three;
> And two of us are cuts, and all
> Agreed to disagree.
> Save now and then when t'other four
> Combine to bully me.
> And nobody's cheroots will draw,
> The soda water's dead:
> And everybody's jokes are old
> And all the books are read:
> And she alone worth talking to
> Is huffed and gone to bed.

The men at least had the diversion of their work; most women did not even have that.

Men and women alike preferred being bored to the risk of going native. It was considered extremely important to keep as much of Home alive as possible. They waited eagerly each week for the post from Europe with its letters and months-old newspapers and magazines. But Home *was* rather a long way off. The exiles were hurt when visitors from Britain found them old-fashioned, and annoyed when wits repeated the old joke about ideas taking years to make the journey to India – but they were secretly afraid that they were out of touch. Perhaps, too, India had more effect on them than they realized; when they did finally go Home they found it cold and somehow confusing.

The exiles' society could never really hope to be a miniature version of British society. It was such a strange hybrid, with its body in one country and its heart in another. In the end it never quite belonged to either India or Britain. Moreover, it was an incomplete society. It had few old people because its members came to India to work and retired back to Britain. It had young children but those in their teens were usually off in schools at Home. The result, in the words of an old civil servant, was 'a hard, practical, rather uniform society, uninspired by the imagination of youth nor softened by the sentiment of old age'.

It was also a largely middle-class society. Few aristocrats came to India; they usually did not need to. India was for those who had to make their own living. Pay was good for both officials and non-officials and it stretched further than it did at Home. (So did modest abilities, the unkind said.) Officers of the Indian Army were able to live on their pay, whereas their counterparts in the British Army almost always needed private incomes. To middle-class women, India offered better chances of finding a husband than did Britain. The other component of British society largely missing in India was the working class. Some of its representatives came with the units of the British Army that were stationed for limited periods in India; otherwise few had the money or the incentive to make the long journey. Indians were cheaper for most labouring jobs, and only occasionally was it necessary to import skilled workers, for the railways perhaps or the mines. (It is said that miners in Assam still sing the hymns of the Welsh miners who taught their ancestors to mine for coal.)

The British community in India was not quite Britain in miniature; nor was it a colonial society. Neither the East India Company nor the government of India had wanted a white settler group to complicate the task of ruling India. The British who chose to stay on were mainly from the lower levels of society, often retired soldiers, who got jobs on the railways. They married girls who called themselves European but who were widely suspected of being Eurasian.

By the beginning of the twentieth century, there were several tens of thousands of what the government of India called the Domiciled Europeans and Eurasians (the distinction was between those of pure European blood and those of mixed descent). They all insisted that they were European; most British assumed that they were largely Eurasian. They were a sad group, not wanting to be Indian yet not accepted fully as part of the ruling race. Respectable British society laughed at them, at their sing-song 'chee-chee' accent, at the way they said 'Pleased to meet you' and 'Cheerio', at the names – Blossom, Hyacinth, Honeydew – they gave their daughters, and at the way they talked of a 'Home' they had never seen. They were not asked to join the Clubs or invited to the best parties; and English nannies, those bastions of snobbery, refused to mix socially with their Eurasian or Domiciled colleagues. The girls, who were often very beautiful, tried to obliterate any hint of Indian blood with powder and patent preparations which promised 'Four shades whiter in four weeks!' Their dream was to marry a British husband and go Home.

The Domiciled Europeans and Eurasians marked the lower edge of British society; the Viceroy in his lonely magnificence marked the top. In between were minute gradations of rank almost invisible to outsiders but of the utmost importance to the British themselves. Social status depended almost entirely on what one did, or, in the case of married women, on what one's husband did. The *burra* ('great') *memsahib*, the social leader of the station, was the lady whose husband occupied the most senior post. Because roughly half the men in British India were employed by the government, official rankings were the ones that counted socially.

The elite were the members of the Indian Civil Service, or ICS, who were the backbone of the Raj. They filled such posts as district officer, judge, governor, member of the Viceroy's Council (and were also a prize catch for mothers with marriageable daughters). The Indian Political Service, whose members looked after princely India and the frontier peoples, had almost as much prestige; the Indian Medical Service and the upper levels of the Public Works Department were not far behind. Indian Army officers (entirely European until the 1920s) also ranked well; they too were promising material for husbands, especially if they came from certain regiments, for example the Gurkhas. The Education Department was rather looked down upon and, as 'Social Pariah' complained in a letter to *The Pioneer* in 1885, subordinate civil servants were on the outer edge of respectable society. (There were also large numbers of British troops, but since they were in India temporarily and since they lived largely in a self-contained world, they were not really considered part of the resident British community.)

Occupations that were respected in Britain were not necessarily valued in India: clergymen, for example, complained that they were invariably given an unimportant lady to take in to dinner. Non-officials, as all those not fortunate enough to work for the government were known, were an inferior category altogether. There were, however, businessmen and planters so rich that they could not be entirely ignored. In Calcutta the Bengal Club, which had been founded exclusively for the members of the bench, the bar, the clergy or the services, always had important merchants among its members. Merchants and their families were acceptable, but those in the retail trade, no matter how rich, were not. The rules tended to be more inflexible in the big cities and towns; on the smaller stations, people were forced to mix more freely with each other.

Over the years, British society in India came to be governed by a rigid etiquette and what one official called 'the demon of precedence'. Precedence determined the order in which you went in to dinner, where you sat, and the order in which you left at the end of the evening. Women, perhaps because they managed social life, took it all very seriously. In the ladies' side at the Club, the best sofa was reserved by unspoken agreement for the senior memsahibs. In badminton, it was considered polite to serve the first shuttlecock to the senior lady on the other side of the net. Even the siege of Lucknow during the Mutiny did not destroy the memsahibs' respect for rank: a lady who was there told William Howard Russell, the famous correspondent for the London *Times*, that 'there was a good deal of etiquette about visiting and speaking'.

The government of India published what was intended to be a guide to the position of government servants on official occasions, the Warrant of Precedence, which became the bible of every hostess from the middle of the nineteenth century onwards. It did not, alas, provide for all contingencies: in 1896 the government itself spent considerable time trying to determine whether a new arrival from Home should be ranked in his capacity as a major-general or as a peer. The question of what to do about non-officials was never entirely settled; the government, however, discussed it quite often, because, as a member of the Viceroy's Council said, 'of the importance attached to it by many worthy people'.

The British in India also took their jobs very seriously. Work, after all, was the main reason why they were there. Action was prized; idleness and reflection (which was regarded as much the same thing) were not. The missionary Edward Thompson described this society in his 1927 novel, *An Indian Day*: 'If you went into the engine-room you found each stripped and toiling; there was no room for art or scholarship or any sort of intellectual interest.' It was perhaps typical that during a pause in a concert one lady was heard to ask her neighbour, 'How much do you pay for your mutton in Calcutta?'

Visitors may have whispered the word 'philistine' but most of the residents were proud of their reputation. Rudyard Kipling, born in India in 1865, was able to express the prejudices of his own community from his vantage point as a journalist with the *Civil and Military Gazette* in Lahore, even if he did not entirely share them. One of his crueller stories, written in 1887, is of the downfall of Aurelian McGoggin, who joined the ICS with his head filled with the latest social and political theories. 'They fermented in his head, and he came out to India with a rarefied religion over and above his head.' His punishment – and Kipling suggests that it is just that – comes when his mind breaks down and he can no longer speak intelligibly. 'The climate and the work are against playing bricks with words.'

To be fair, there were quite a few scholars among the British in India, who produced learned papers on such areas as Indian history, philology and ethnology. Their work, it was admitted by the rest of the community, could be useful. Denzil Ibbetson, one of the best scholars in the ICS at the end of the nineteenth century, wrote in his pioneering census report on the Punjab in 1881, 'Our ignorance of the customs and beliefs of the people among whom we dwell is surely in some respects a reproach to us; for not only does that ignorance deprive European science of material which it greatly needs, but it also involves a distinct loss of administrative power to ourselves.' Even members of the ICS had to be careful about the conclusions they drew from their studies of India. In 1917, for example, the Chief Secretary of the government of Bombay recommended that a young officer, C. A. Kincaid, not be allowed to publish his history of the Maratha people because it contained too favourable a portrait of the great seventeenth-century hero Shivaji. And Sir Malcolm Darling, the friend of the Bloomsbury group who had a most distinguished career in the ICS early in the twentieth century, was once known as a 'red-hot radical' for suggesting that Indians might one day be capable of ruling themselves.

Among most British in India, as Isabel Savory (who visited the country before the First World War) noticed with disapproval, 'to affect deep interest in things native is incorrect'. J. R. Ackerley, for many years literary editor of *The Listener*, spent some months in India in 1923–24 as secretary to a maharajah. The local memsahibs found him odd from the start. When he walked through the native city, '"What on earth do you want to do that for?" asked Mrs Montgomery as I set out. "You're sure to catch something – if it's only a flea."' He tried to take notes at the performance of an Indian play: 'What are you writing down all this rubbish for?'

In the heyday of the Raj it was also bad form to display religious fervour. Ruby Madden, who visited India from Australia in the early 1900s, was startled to find that Sundays were treated much like any other day: 'Posts and papers come and go just the same.' Since their congregations came to church as a gesture of solidarity with the Raj rather than with God, clergymen soon learnt to keep their sermons short.

It is not surprising that outsiders found local society rather dull – 'The most difficult', complained Lady Dufferin, whose husband was Viceroy in the 1880s, 'of all the societies I have ever had to do with.' It was impolite to talk about politics or literature or the arts. 'One scarcely ever hears any topic of general interest except steam navigation.' It was all right to talk about careers, sport, servants and children. Lady Falkland, in Bombay in the 1840s as the Governor's wife, gave a reception for the local ladies where the conversation was 'not lively': 'Our topics were dusty roads, cool houses, the reviving climate of the Deccan (which seemed, from all accounts, to be a kind of paradise), healthy and unhealthy stations, and the coming monsoon.' The other great subject of conversation was gossip: who was going to be promoted and who had been passed over; who had been seen flirting with whom; who was getting married and who had been jilted. 'It is a wonder', said the author of the comic sketches *The Chronicles of Budgepore*, published in the 1870s, 'that the blistered tongue has never been set down in the list of Indian diseases.' Visitors to India found it disconcerting that the locals always tried to listen to several conversations at once lest they miss some titbit.

Its defenders praised their society for its openness. Certainly, as Anne Wilson noticed at the turn of the century, it was easy to make friends very quickly: 'At railway restaurants, in hotels, in dak bungalows, in clubs, strangers talk to one another with a frankness which is more characteristic of other races than taciturn Britons.' New arrivals were expected to label themselves with enough details of background, schools, profession to enable the locals to slot them into their proper niche. It was almost impossible to keep secrets: people usually had a very good idea of each other's income and expenditures.

One particular quality that was valued in both men and women was being a good sport. An old soldier looking back on his life said nostalgically, 'India is the land of practical jokes.' Visitors from Home were always struck by the playfulness that the locals permitted themselves. Was it the heat of India that melted their reserve? Or was it the considerable amounts of drink they all seemed to put away? (A French visitor to India in the 1840s, Captain Edouard de Warren, was amazed at the 'enormous quantity of beer and wine absorbed by young English women, so pale and delicate in appearance …') Whatever the cause, the middle-aged were quite extrovert and youthful compared to their contemporaries in Britain. Anne Wilson once ran into a couple from England who had been transformed by India. The wife, whom she remembered as a quiet, dowdy creature, was holding court as Queen of the Fairies at a Fairy Ball.

Being a good sport meant, of course, loving sport itself. Many of the memoirs, by both men and women – with titles like *Gold, Sport and Coffee Planting in Mysore* (1899), *A Sportswoman in India* (1900), or *Work and Sport in the Old ICS* (1928) – describe an India made up almost exclusively of polo fields, duck blinds and racecourses, and peopled by game, beaters and the sports lovers themselves. The new arrival who did not show an enthusiasm for sport was widely regarded as being 'unsound' (another favourite local word). In the Indian Army, sport was considered to produce exactly the qualities an officer needed; polo players especially tended to get the best appointments.

Before the middle of the nineteenth century, sport had been almost exclusively for men. Women had been expected to be rather languid.

'The real Indian ladies', reported Julia Maitland in 1843, 'lie on a sofa, and, if they drop their handkerchief, they just lower their voices and say "Boy!" in a very gentle tone, and then creeps in, perhaps, some old wizen, skinny brownie, looking like a superannuated thread-paper ...' By the end of the century, however, women in India, like those at Home, were busy with archery, badminton, and later with tennis and golf.

For the most part the British had to make their own entertainment. Paper chases or treasure hunts, on horseback, were considered great fun. Amateur theatricals were part of any season; in Simla, as befitted the pre-eminent hill station, the performers had a real theatre, but on the smaller stations they had to make do with someone's drawing room. There were balls, as many as could be organized: regimental balls, bachelors' balls, fancy dress balls. (An earnest lady tried to bring a more serious note to a viceregal fancy dress ball in the Simla of the 1880s by appearing as a Bulgarian Atrocity. She did not win a prize.)

The exiles were great joiners – of the local dramatic society, the gymkhana or sports club, the Masonic lodge, even the humble 'mutton club', which existed to bring fresh meat to remote stations. Above all, they joined the Club. At one extreme were the modest Railway Institutes; at the other, the Bengal Club, which occupied Lord Macaulay's old house in Calcutta. The Club was where the British met their friends, played their games, carried on their flirtations. And it was where they read the books and magazines that kept them, however tenuously, in touch with Home. (The occasional Club library still survives today, its bound volumes of *Punch* and *Tatler*, its rows of Ethel M. Dell and Rider Haggard novels slowly decomposing; but India is swallowing up these monuments of the Raj just as it has swallowed up the marks of earlier conquerors.)

On the smaller stations especially, the Club was the main focus of social life; every evening its members would gather for games and gossip. Rosamund Lawrence, writing after Independence, recalled her first evening years earlier: 'Women in muslins, women in riding habits and tennis kit. Men everywhere. How am I ever to remember all these people? People sitting at tables eating chip potatoes, and dipping their fingers into parched gram, and drinking immense tumblers of very weak whisky and soda, or tiny glasses of milk punch.' Iris Macfarlane, who had lived in Assam as the wife of a tea planter, wondered how her younger self had endured the many hours at the local Club.

1

Arriving in Bombay in 1928 by liner (1), this family might be apprehensive, but they were at least composed. Landing at Madras ninety years earlier (2) had been quite a different affair, as the East Indiamen anchored offshore and passengers were carried through the surf towards the gleaming classical buildings (see pp. 43–45).

2

3

The destination might be an outpost with only one or two British families to show the flag (3). If you were lucky, it might be a fine house with a croquet lawn (4), and you might enjoy the social life of a little station, with straight streets, bungalows and a steepled church, as drawn by Captain G. F. Atkinson in the 1850s (5).

4

5

6   Keeping cool old style involved wrapping the house in *khus-khus tatties*, screens of fragrant grass, which were kept damp; Government House at Mahableshwar was so cocooned as late as 1937 (6). Four years earlier, this electric fan (7) was on offer from the Army and Navy Stores in Bombay.

7

THE ARMY & NAVY

KEEP KOOL

HOT, DRY, DUSTY AIR   104°   85°   COOL, CLEAR, FRESH AIR

THE "KEEP KOOL" ELECTRIC FAN

WILL BRING COOL, HILL-STATION AIR TO YOUR HOME IN THE PLAINS.

Printed by The Army & Navy Stores, Bombay.

But coolness began with the design of the house. The bungalow's thick thatch and spreading eaves (8) insulated and shaded the rooms within, and the verandah (9) provided a breezy place to sit. If the breeze failed, there was the *punkah*, a long fan hanging from the ceiling. Note also, in these two photographs of the same bungalow, the plants in pots, the hunt trophies, and the white-clad servants grouped outside at the far right.

9

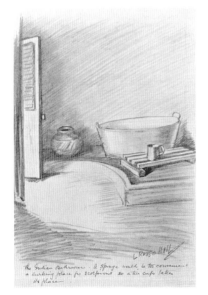

The Indian Bathroom. A sponge would be too convenient a lurking place for scorpions so a tin cup takes its place

Inside, the house was foreign too. In the bedroom of Percy Brown's house in Calcutta c. 1927 (10) the bed stood away from the wall to eliminate hiding places for insects and also for coolness, though there was an electric fan; at night the mosquito netting was let down, and the cloth across the top also caught any lizards or insects that might drop from the open rafters. The bathroom (11) was a shock; a tin cup replaced the sponge, which, Leonard Raven-Hill explained in his 1903 drawing, 'would be too convenient a lurking place for scorpions'.

Colonel Egerton's lady filled her drawing room (12) at Sialkot in 1895 with exotic fabrics and plants; the room's high ceiling, plain walls, and French doors hung with curtains mark it unmistakably as Indian.

The verandah (13) was an outdoor room. Percy Brown's had the usual blinds, cane furniture and potted plants.

12

13

14

Strangeness and danger faced the women in India. On tour through a Mysore town (14) with the deputy superintendent (husband? brother? father?), as their path is cleared of a cow and pariah dog, two ladies stand out in self-conscious isolation.

Neither moving house nor pregnancy was easy or necessarily safe. Ellen Beames, who had already had one miscarriage, was sketched by her husband, John, as they moved by river in 1861 (15); their son was born three months later and, thanks to the attentions of a half-drunk army doctor, lived only a week.

15

'If there is a hell for me it'll be an endless day in a club in the North Indian state of Assam; a day of staring through dazzling dust at men galloping about on polo grounds; of sitting in sterile circles drinking gin with their wives; of bouncing stickily round an unsprung dance floor, clutched their soggy shirts; of finally being driven home at night by one of them peering woozily over the wheel, tipping old villagers in bullock carts into the ditch.'

When the Club first began to assume a central position, in the nineteenth century, women were not allowed to use it except on special occasions. By the twentieth century, however, most had capitulated and accepted women as members, a recognition perhaps of their role in supporting the Raj. And it was a supporting role. In their copious memoirs, with a few exceptions, the men say far more about favourite horses and dogs than about their wives. General Greaves, who spent many years in India, recounted a life of shooting and fishing, and horses and dogs. He mentions his wife only once: 'Ranee [his dog] took to her at once, I am glad to say, so there were no complications.' Where *did* women fit into such a busy masculine society? The common wisdom was that their main function was to marry the simple, manly servants of the Empire and to keep the supply coming. Unmarried girls should be innocent but fun-loving, perhaps even boyish. Captain Edouard de Warren found two equally unappealing characters assumed by British girls in India: 'One is the affectation of an impossible innocence, especially in view of the fact that an unexpurgated Bible is placed in her hands from infancy. The other is that of a coquette and romp.' Married women were allowed to be experienced in the ways of the world, but they always had to remain ladies (which meant, at least before the First World War, not wearing imitation jewelry, perfume, or make-up). Their ambition should be to further their husbands' careers: the old joke among the men was that the only way to get on was to make yourself useful to other men's wives or to have a wife who was useful to other men.

Women were brought up to be good wives and mothers; the idea that they could be anything else, which was starting to circulate in Europe by the end of the nineteenth century, was one that took even longer than usual to make the journey out. In 1909 Maud Diver, who wrote a series of successful novels about British life in India, commented on 'the extreme backwardness of Anglo-Indian society in recognizing the modern advance in the intellectual and social position of women'. New arrivals learnt that very quickly: Evelyn Bell, a pert and high-spirited girl who came out to marry a professor in the 1920s, was given useful advice by an older woman: 'Don't try and be too clever in India. It doesn't go down.' Lady Frances Smyth, who had the benefit of being brought up in India at the beginning of the twentieth century, knew without being told that being clever was a flaw in a woman: 'If by any conceivable chance anybody was they kept it pretty dark.' Some women could not or would not conform. Margaret Smith was so appalled at the role she was expected to play as the wife of a tea planter in the 1920s that she left her husband and became a militant feminist in Britain.

Femininity was associated with weakness; women had to be protected because they could not protect themselves. They should be discouraged, for example, wrote two old hands in a guide to life in India, from drinking alcohol: 'they become sooner the creatures of impulse, and less able to resist the seductive influence of alcohol.' In return for being protected, women were to remember their duty to the Raj. In one of Maud Diver's novels, her hero Captain Desmond (V.C. of course) shouts at his wife as they stand together on a raft in the middle of a raging river: 'Remember that you're an Englishwoman in a boat full of natives and our women are *not cowards.*' Adultery was never condoned, but some kinds were worse than others. In 1918 *The Englishman*, another popular Anglo-Indian newspaper, reported a messy divorce case involving a member of the Bengal Police and his faithless wife; 'I remonstrated with her', he told the judge, 'for being so low as to misconduct herself with a native.'

One group of women whose existence particularly worried the British were the European prostitutes. Although a speaker at a meeting on 'Social Evil' in Bombay in 1891 congratulated himself that there was not a single English girl among them, it was feared that Indians might not be able to see the distinction. Not surprisingly, there was also concern in official and unofficial circles over pornography that involved European women. In the 1880s the authorities were worried by the activities of something called the Calcutta Phrenological Institute, whose catalogue, which included titles like 'What Every Young Man Should Know About Marriage' and 'One Hundred Ribald Rhymes', had been sent to a lady missionary in Allahabad by mistake. Photography brought fresh dangers; a member of the ICS warned the government of India to act at once or 'the result will be that obscene photos of all kinds including very numerous photos of stark naked white women will be common in India'. The new medium of cinema was a problem, too. In 1917, the European Association warned the government against a film called *The Serpentine Dance*, which 'was certainly calculated to bring the white men and women into low esteem in the Indian mind'.

What was perhaps the greatest challenge to the white woman's reputation in India came just before the First World War. The British were already edgy over the growth of Indian nationalism; when word got out that the music hall star Maud Allen was planning to tour the country, they reacted as though a second Mutiny were about to break out. Miss Allen was going to perform her interpretative dances, including, it was feared, her version of the Dance of the Seven Veils. The worst of it was that Indians would be able to buy tickets to see her. Petitions poured in to the Viceroy: from the Young Women's Christian Association of India, Burma and Ceylon, from the Men and Women of Ootacamund, from the Women of Jubbulpore, from the Church of England Men's Society in Lahore. The Women's Christian Temperance Union of India, which claimed 2,500 members, told the Viceroy: 'Not only do we think that contumely to womanhood generally will accrue from such exhibitions but we actually fear that a diminution of prestige to the Government of the Empire will also result.'

In the end in spite of all the government of India and the India Office in London could do, Maud Allen did make her tour. The Raj survived. The British were to continue in their self-confident way for another generation at least. And the women were going to press on with their daily tasks, creating homes for their men, bringing up their children, and trying always to live the life of an English gentlewoman in the midst of an alien people.

4

THE LAND OF EXILE

It took little time for most of the women who came out to India at the height of the Raj to become memsahibs. They assumed their new community's prejudices and habits, and they stuck to its rules. They adapted so well, in fact, that they struck an acquaintance of Anne Wilson's as having less individuality than their contemporaries at Home. 'They all seemed to be of the same age, to have the same social pursuits, to live as it were outside of themselves, to be without a background or shadow.'

Did they have much choice but to conform? They had been trained, after all, to be good wives and mothers and in India that also meant being part of the team. If they rebelled (and some did), the alternatives were not appealing. There were not many jobs open to them, and few were prepared to abandon all hope of respectability – unlike the young and beautiful Mrs James, who was the toast of Simla in 1839. She left her husband, a lieutenant in the Indian Army, and made a name for herself as Lola Montez, dancer and mistress to, among others, King Ludwig I of Bavaria.

There were compensations for accepting their ready-made role. They had the psychological security of knowing where they belonged. Their community had its class distinctions, but right down to the wives of the railway workers, they were all members of the ruling race. They travelled in reserved compartments on the trains and stayed, if they wished, in government bungalows reserved for Europeans only. If they fell sick, they could usually be cared for by doctors from the Indian Medical Service (who were invariably European until the twentieth century). If they could not afford to send their children back to England for their education, there were special schools, on which the government of India spent considerably more per capita than it did on schools for Indian children. If they got involved with the law, they could generally expect to be treated leniently by the European juries and magistrates. If they were unfortunate enough to be convicted, they were sent to jails for Europeans in the cooler air of the Hills.

Among the lessons that the fledgling memsahibs learnt was that it was not necessary to know much of India or of the Indians. The views of a lady in Madras in the 1830s were firm but not untypical. 'I asked', wrote Julia Maitland, 'what she had seen of the country and the natives since she had been in India. "Oh, nothing!", said she: "thank goodness, I know nothing at all about them, nor I don't wish to: really I think the less one sees and knows of them the better!"' In the twentieth century the Indian Army tried to encourage wives of its officers to learn Indian languages by giving them a grant for passing a test in, say, elementary Urdu. 'But it wasn't done amongst the wives', said one. 'They thought it was rather sort of – how shall I describe it? – well, just not done.' Even if women did learn a smattering of a language, they usually did not pick up the polite forms for speaking to their social equals.

The British themselves blamed cultural differences for the gulf that opened between the races as the Raj grew stronger. They did not always recognize that their own attitudes had changed as the position of Britain in India and of Europe in the world had changed. A conviction of superiority is not, after all, a good beginning for friendship. In the eighteenth century, the British would not have drawn themselves back so firmly from contact with Indians. Until the start of the nineteenth century, the East India Company was only one power among several and its representatives had to deal with Indians who were their equals, if not their superiors, in power. There were independent and powerful Indian princes; the British were rather in awe of them. What is more, the 'exiles' normally expected that they would spend the rest of their days in India, and that, coupled with the fact that their own society was very small, meant that they were thrown into closer contact with India and Indians. Since European society in India was chronically short of women, the men, through necessity as much as choice, took Indian mistresses and wives. They were not ostracized as they would have been a century later. Even as late as 1848, Emily Metcalfe, staying with her father in Delhi, where he was the senior British official, saw nothing strange in calling on families with a good deal of Indian blood. She described one such visit in her journal, with amusement, certainly, but not condescension: 'Both Mrs Foster and her sister Mrs Fuller were enormously stout people, and being half-castes, were dark in complexion and spoke English with a very curious accent. And as both were dressed in white cotton dresses made very like bedgowns, they presented a curious spectacle to a newcomer. They were, however, excellent old ladies, and their sons and daughters were all connected with the British Army in India.'

British women often made friends with Indian women as a matter of course. They did not find anything odd about going into the *zenana*, or women's quarters, and since they often spoke an Indian language fluently they were able to have real conversations. Mrs Major Clemons, who spent fourteen years in Madras at the beginning of the nineteenth century, wrote of Indian women: 'The society, in the highest ranks, is entertaining, and anything but insipid: the natural gentleness of their manners, and their easy politeness, make them pleasing companions, and their remarks are just and pertinent.' Lady Login and her husband, who was doctor to the court in Lucknow before the Mutiny, spent their honeymoon in a palace lent by the King of Oudh and made many friends among the royal household. Lady Login, who spoke the polished Urdu of the court, found the royal women highly cultivated and intelligent: 'We used to discuss all sorts of subjects.' Indians simply had different customs, sometimes indeed better ones. Mrs Fanny Parks, who was an enthusiastic explorer of India in the early part of the nineteenth century, found that Indian women were 'remarkably graceful' in their saris where her compatriots with their stays were 'as stiff as a lobster in its shell'. Mrs Maria Graham, who travelled in India in the early 1800s, discovered support for the Enlightenment's belief that virtue was not synonymous with Christianity: 'Everywhere in the ancient Hindu books we find the maxims of that pure and sound morality which is founded on the nature of man as a rational and social being.'

The Industrial Revolution, which made Europe vastly more powerful than the rest of the world, helped to put a stop to that easy intercourse. Their success led Europeans to consider the pleasing possibility that they were not only stronger than the rest of the world but inherently superior as well. It came to be widely assumed that human societies evolved much like natural species and that it was possible to assign rankings to them on the scale of evolution. Europe was evidently at the forefront of human development (although there was some bickering over the relative rankings of the separate European nations).

The belief that Western civilization was somehow better than all others fitted in conveniently with what was happening to the British position in India. By the beginning of the nineteenth century, the Mughal empire had shrunk to the outskirts of Delhi. One by one, the independent princes of west and south India had been brought under Company control. With the defeat of the Sikhs in the 1840s, the British were left alone as the paramount power in the country. The Mutiny in 1857 left them more than ever convinced that the Indians were not fit to rule themselves. The only part of India, significantly enough, where relations between Europeans and Indians kept something of the old equality was the rich and important princely state of Hyderabad.

British society in India was turning in on itself. The opening of the Suez Canal in 1869, together with faster and safer communications between Britain and India, meant that the exiles could keep closer ties with Home. By the 1860s, the practice of taking Indians as wives or mistresses was frowned upon by government and condemned by society. (Only the planters, on their lonely gardens, kept up the old custom, but their little weakness was never discussed in polite circles.) The exiles took to referring to themselves as 'white Brahmins', at the pinnacle of the caste system. Mrs Leopold Paget, who came to India in the 1860s with her husband's regiment, remarked that the British treated Indians with 'a pride and contempt, as of a lower order of beings'.

One of the more awkward discoveries of the nineteenth century was that Indians were largely Aryan, part therefore of that great human family which had also populated northern Europe. Yet surely dark skins must indicate that an inferior blood had been mixed with the Aryan, or, at the very least, that the Indian environment had left its visible mark of inferiority? And if Indians were lesser versions of themselves, the British concluded, that was true also of all aspects of Indian civilization. That conclusion led to the equally satisfying one that Europeans had a duty to take the less advanced peoples under their wing and civilize them. Lord Curzon, Viceroy from 1899 to 1905, told a British audience at the Byculla Club in Bombay in his schoolmasterly tones: 'the Almighty has placed your hand on the greatest of His ploughs, in whose furrows the nations of the future are germinating and taking shape, to drive the blade a little forward in your time, and to feel that somewhere among these millions you have left a little justice or happiness or prosperity, a sense of manliness or moral dignity, a spring of patriotism, a dawn of intellectual enlightenment or a stirring of duty where it did not exist before – that is enough, that is the Englishman's justification in India.'

There were those who argued pessimistically that the Indians were so far behind in the race that they would never catch up, but in general the British in India held that the great work of civilizing them could be done – with immeasurable time and effort. Before the First World War not even the most radical could have imagined that the Raj would disappear in 1947. Indeed, one official wrote in the confident years before 1914, 'as Great Britain gets to closer quarters with her task, its magnitude appalls many of weaker hearts'.

Indians could not be treated as equals as long as they had such extraordinarily backward ways. Take – and the British frequently did – the caste system. What was it but the ossified relic of a primitive form of society which had disappeared centuries ago in Europe? Since all peoples outside the caste system were considered Untouchable, its existence was also galling; the British were the conquerors of India, the representatives of the most advanced society in the world, yet most of their subjects could not bring themselves to eat at the same table with them. New arrivals had to be warned never to shake a Brahmin by the hand; the pollution would be so great that the Brahmin would have to undergo extensive, and expensive, purification ceremonies.

The longer the British ruled India, the more irritated they felt at being lumped together with sweepers and other Untouchables. They reacted by declaring that, if Indians would not eat with them, then there could be no social intercourse of any sort. The novelist Ethel Savi described it in her memoirs as 'a species of tit-for-tat'. A few British saw the absurdity of the argument. As Henry Cotton, a rare liberal in the ICS at the end of the nineteenth century, pointed out, Hindus and Muslims managed to make friends with each other without ever sharing food. In 1881, Annette Beveridge, the high-minded and unconventional wife of a Bengal civil servant, showed what could be done when she held an 'International Evening Party' in Bankipur; there were separate food tents for Hindus, Muslims and Europeans.

The other great obstacle to friendship, according to the British, was the way Indians behaved towards women. An anonymous correspondent in *The Pioneer* explained in 1885 that natives regarded women as possessions, while for the British they were 'the delicacy and purity of nature in the concrete'. Indian men did not always avoid improper subjects in conversation. This so worried a professor of English literature from Calcutta that he published a little book called *English Etiquette for Indian Gentlemen* in 1915. When talking to British ladies, he advised, Indian men should not use words such as stomach, adultery, fornication, childbirth or miscarriage. 'It is well', he added, 'to avoid topics (as, for instance, Sanitation) which may lead to the introduction of words or expressions such as may offend the ears of the company.' (He also begged them to make sure that their *dhotis* – those voluminous lengths of cloth that many Indians wore instead of trousers – were long enough to cover their legs properly and that they did not become disarranged in the presence of ladies.)

Indians, whether Hindu or Muslim, treated their own women badly by British standards. A woman who bore sons was doing her duty; one who had nothing but daughters was a failure. Female infanticide, indeed, was a popular method of birth control. At the basis of Hindu custom were the Laws of Manu, which stated, among other things, that 'a husband must constantly be worshipped as a god by a faithful wife'. The Koran sanctioned similar treatment of women; what is more, it allowed polygamy. And in Hinduism, the highest virtue a widow could show was to immolate herself with her husband's body. (In 1829 the British abolished *sati*, as the practice was known, but instances have continued up to the present day.) The majority, who chose life, did not have much of an existence: widows were supposed to shave their heads, wear the plainest white saris, undertake frequent fasts, and give up all food except the blandest.

Over the centuries, strict rules of behaviour had developed for women, to keep them chaste and modest. When the Muslims invaded India, they brought the further refinement of *purdah*. Families that could afford it kept their women in separate quarters, moved them in enclosed vehicles, and covered them whenever necessary with veils from head to foot. The practice spread to Hindus as well. By the time the British arrived in India, only the lowest castes and the primitive tribal peoples let their women go with unveiled faces.

How could there be true friendship between the British and a people with such an attitude to women? How could there be any social intercourse when respectable Indian women could not go to the dinner parties, the balls, the evening receptions, which were such a standard feature of British life in India? The more conservative sahibs retaliated by not allowing their women to meet Indian men. Anne Wilson explained in a letter to a friend in the early 1900s: 'You must understand that some Europeans of the old school would not allow a lady to accept an Indian gentleman's proferred hospitality. They would not permit her to drive through an Indian town, be a spectator of tent-pegging, or receive an Indian as visitor, far less dine with him. They would, in short, prefer her to be as wholly absent from every kind of Indian society as are the inmates of zenanas. Their argument is that until an Indian gentleman will allow them to meet his wife, they will not allow him to meet an English lady.'

By the second half of the nineteenth century, there was little social contact between British women and Indians. Men met each other in a business setting and occasionally shared sports, but the only Indians women met regularly were their servants. Missionaries often complained that British women did little to meet or help Indian women. Maud Diver in *The Englishwoman in India* (1909), intended as an apologia for her countrywomen, pointed to the formidable obstacles in their way: 'a death-dealing sun, a hazy knowledge of facts, a lurking uncertainty as to how her advances would be received, the probable discouragement of her husband ...' Perhaps, too, they were quite simply afraid of the unknown.

Certainly there were difficulties involved in meeting Indian women, especially if they were in *purdah*. *Purdah* women could not be seen by any men except their close relations, so they had either to be visited in their own quarters or all sorts of special measures had to be taken by their hosts. Such meetings, arranged out of a sense of duty, were awkward and generally disliked by both sides. Since few memsahibs could speak an Indian language easily, they usually talked through an interpreter. The conversation tended to revolve around safe subjects like children and jewels. Different notions of courtesy caused much embarrassment: the British felt that the Indians were being impertinent for asking personal questions; the Indians felt they were rude for not asking them. The British women often grumbled at the Indian custom of putting scent on the handkerchiefs of honoured guests and they took off as soon as they decently could the garlands of flowers they had been given in yet another mark of politeness. In most of the memsahibs' descriptions the

Indian women appear as picturesque types, more interesting for their dress than for themselves. Isabel Savory, in India in the late nineteenth century, called on the Maharani of Mysore and remembered only 'a small, dark individual with wonderful jewels and embroidered garments'. Such visits were exotic the first few times, then simply tedious. Occasionally there were amusing moments when the Indian ladies tried to speak English and got it wrong or when their children sang an English song which they had carefully learnt for the occasion. (Tara Ali Baig, who grew up in a conservative part of Bengal in the twentieth century, saw the reaction in the *zenana* to European visitors. 'Look at those white arms; they look as if they haven't been cooked. And why do they wear those peculiar things on their heads?') It was a great relief, no doubt to both sets of women, when the visit came to an end.

Only a few women of the Raj managed or chose to get past the barriers. At the top of the social scale, there were those such as Rosamund Lawrence with enough assurance to be unconventional. Lower down it was more difficult, but still the occasional woman like Lillian Luker Ashby enjoyed her visits to women in *purdah*. When she lived in a remote part of Bihar at the turn of the nineteenth century, she frequently visited the wife of a Muslim official to smoke a hookah and gossip. She did not object to personal questions because she knew that the Indian women were being polite, 'such interrogation indicating a genuine interest in us'. In Bombay in the 1880s Nora Scott frequently visited women in *purdah* and invited Indian women back to her home, taking care that they should have the right sort of food and ensuring that all men of the household from her husband to the servants stayed out of the way. And she did not take offence when the Hindu wife of a judge from Ceylon could not eat her food but only drink a cup of tea. As Scott reported sympathetically to her family, her guest had said 'she should not mind herself eating our food, but her family and friends would object, but that when she went to England, she should eat anything'.

For the most part the races did not make much attempt to understand each other. That frequently led to awkward moments on social occasions where both British and Indians were present. C. C. Dyson went to a party at a house in Calcutta before the First World War where the Indian host had provided entertainment in the form of dancing girls; 'I am sorry to say that some English women were rude enough to laugh in the faces of these poor women.' On the other hand, when British women danced publicly at balls with men who were not their husbands, Indians assumed they were women of loose morals. (Indeed, at their own entertainments, Indians got much amusement out of imitations of British men and women dancing together.) When the King of Oudh was invited to a European ball in the happier days before the Mutiny, he took the ladies on the dance floor for dancing girls, and not particularly good ones at that. 'That will do,' he said impatiently, 'let them leave off.' In 1881 the Madras correspondent of *The Pioneer* explained why the annual ball to mark the Queen's birthday, which had once been attended by people from both races, was now exclusively for Europeans: 'We began to see ourselves as our Aryan brethren see us – in the matter of decolletés gowns, and dancing matrons to wit.'

When Indian nationalism began to increase before the First World War, the authorities made a belated attempt to mend fences. On the assumption that closer exposure to the gracious ways of their rulers would bind upper-class Indians to the Raj, they encouraged social intercourse. A few carefully chosen Indian men joined Clubs. Wives of high officials held '*purdah* parties' and formed '*purdah* clubs'. Edith Tottenham, who worked for the Maharani of Baroda in the 1930s, went to a *purdah* party at the local Residency where the Indian ladies were set down uncomfortably in a row to watch some bad tennis and badminton and then offered refreshments which bore the inviting label 'The milk used for these ices is not guaranteed.' 'Bridge parties' were arranged at which Indian women who had been bold enough to come out of *purdah* and their husbands were supposed to mingle freely with the British; these were not treated as anything but duty. Iris Portal, born in Simla in 1906 into a distinguished civil service family, was one of the few memsahibs who wanted to be genuinely friendly, but even she found it difficult: 'Sometimes one tried too hard and became unnatural.'

The British women who were arriving in India in increasing numbers after the Mutiny were often blamed for the distance between the races. Wilfred Scawen Blunt, anti-imperialist, poet, and traveller, who usually liked women, could not bear the memsahibs. He toured extensively in India at the beginning of the 1880s and found nothing to say in their favour: 'Englishwomen in India look upon the land of their exile unaffectedly as a house of bondage, on its inhabitants as outside the pale of their humanity …' He held them responsible for at least 'half the bitter feelings' between the races.

His view, which has become the accepted one over the years, was not entirely fair. Times had changed in India and the sort of man who was attracted there was changing too. The early years of the British presence had called for adventurers, if not scoundrels; by the nineteenth century, administrators were needed. As H. G. Keene, himself a civil servant, put it in 1882, 'We do not want heroes to preside over drainage committees.' The nabobs, the William Hickeys with their spectacular drinking parties and their Indian households, disappeared; the empire builders, the Henry Lawrences with their prayers and their sense of mission, took their place. A contributor to the *Calcutta Review* – the most intellectual of the Anglo-Indian journals – explained in the 1880s that 'Many Englishmen have an insuperable objection to the ladies of their families having intercourse of any kind with the natives.' British men, in other words, were getting the wives they wanted – and deserved.

Few women were as openly rude as the one Annette Beveridge overheard in 1873 at a function at the Governor's palace in Bengal saying to a friend, 'Let us sit on the verandah to get out of the natives.' More wounding, perhaps, to Indian sensibilities, the British women simply repeated the same old clichés. With few exceptions, the novels and memoirs written by memsahibs from the middle of the nineteenth century show a superficial knowledge of the country in which they lived. They paint Indians in the broadest of terms: the patient, fatalistic Indian, the childlike Indian, or perhaps the excitable Indian. Muslims were manly and brave; Sikhs were also a people with admirable qualities ('more like us in their habits', as Minnie Blane wrote to her mother). Parsees were a sensible people: 'among other English customs they have adopted', said the wife of a Collector approvingly, 'is cricket.'

The writers reserved their severest words for Hindus. The Hindu, wrote Maud Diver in one of her short stories, has 'an innate love of the horrible and grim'. In the 1920s Evelyn Bell, who, with a husband in the Education Service, had more opportunities than most to meet educated Indians, and might therefore have been expected to have a more discriminating view, was just as sweeping: 'the Hindu, even if reserved, is naturally excitable … most of them are sensitive like children.' Worse still, given British values, Hindus were not 'manly'. The good Indians in fiction are the touchingly faithful servants or the simple sturdy peasants. In a number of novels, Indians who behave with unexpected nobility turn out to be Europeans in disguise. *The White Dove of Amritzir*, for example, a nineteenth-century novel about the Mutiny by Eliza Pollard, has as its heroine a beautiful, blue-eyed girl, ostensibly the daughter of a Sikh. The White Dove is as good and as brave as she is beautiful and the hero, Sir Hubert Pennington (romantic novelists loved titles), falls in love with her. Much to everyone's relief, a potentially awkward situation is resolved when she is revealed, after many twists of the plot, to be the long-lost child of a Colonel Melville.

Villains are usually Indian. If they are European, more often than not the explanation for their wickedness is that they have Indian blood. A novel written by Mrs Milne Rae just before the First World War exploits this particular theme to the full. *A Bottle in the Smoke* features Hester Rayner, married to Alfred, a barrister in Madras. He has an obsessive hatred for what he calls 'those vile half-castes', and when the upright and manly Mark Cheveril of the ICS is discovered to be the son of an Indian princess and an English lieutenant, Alfred leads the chorus of disapproval. As it happens, Alfred himself is not above reproach: he is exposed as both a swindler and, worse, a half-caste himself. He goes rapidly downhill and sensibly gets himself killed. Mark, on the other hand, turns out to be pure European after all. Hester, conveniently free, can marry him.

The views that the memsahibs' books reveal about Indian civilization are equally simple-minded. Religion? Islam and Sikhism were moving in the right direction; at least they had only one god. Hinduism was sheer paganism. You could tell the difference, according to the pious Helen Mackenzie in 1854, merely by looking at Muslim and Hindu architecture: 'The former is as majestic as perhaps man in his fallen state is capable of conceiving; the latter is wholly devoid of this quality, and in spite of the beauty of some minor details, the effect of the whole is grotesque confusion.' The arts? Anne Wilson at first found Indian music 'only another name for discord' – though she later changed her mind. C. C. Dyson was amazed to meet an Indian family with what she considered to be a genuine appreciation of painting: 'The Mullick family are unique in India as possessing aesthetic and artistic talent. Most natives of India will look at a picture or photograph upside down, and not perceive the difference.'

Were the memsahibs racist? Certainly they often sounded so. It is dangerous, however, to judge the words of earlier generations by the standards of today. The Victorians and Edwardians used the word 'race' where we generally speak of 'culture' or 'ethnic characteristics' when we want to generalize about a group. They used terms which seem outrageous today, but those were what everyone used. (It should be remembered that they talked about their own lower classes with the same unflattering generalizations.) And always there was a gap between what the British women said and what they did. The very women who complained about the Indians in general often had close relations of mutual trust and affection with their Indian servants, even with Indian friends. The same Mrs Sherwood who believed firmly that the 'black people' of India were miserable, degraded heathens said of her meeting on the banks of the Ganges with her son's old *ayah*, 'There are moments of intense feeling, in which all distinctions of nations, colours, and castes disappear, and in their place there only remains between two human beings one abiding sense of common nature.'

Even while the Raj was at its strongest, there were women who approached India with curiosity and enthusiasm. They set themselves to learn a language, perhaps, like Annette Beveridge, who ended by translating the memoirs of the Emperor Babur from the Persian; or they explored India's culture, like Anne Wilson, who made a serious study of Indian music. Mrs King was in many ways the typical *burra memsahib* – her husband was in the ICS in north India in the last part of the nineteenth century – yet she had little but praise for the Indian character: Indians were naturally gentle, unlike her fellow Europeans, and they never wantonly destroyed or caused pain. And, as we shall see, there were women who paid no attention at all to the shibboleths and restrictions of their own society.

At the opposite extreme – and they are the ones who helped to give memsahibs such a bad name – were women who never came to terms with India's strangeness. Sometimes they worked on their husbands until, for the sake of peace, the men agreed to throw up their careers in India and go Home. Sometimes their despair was so great that it overwhelmed them. On one of Rosamund Lawrence's first stations in the inter-war years there was a young bride who hated everything about India; 'she is terrified at being alone in the bungalow, but equally terrified, and moreover repelled by her Indian servants.' Rosamund Lawrence recorded her decline in her diary. The bride grew listless. She stopped caring about her health; greatest of sins, she would not wear her topi. 'It is clear she is eating her heart out for an English suburban villa with H and C laid on.' The end came, as ends often did in India, very quickly. The diary entries are brief:

> Day before yesterday Dr Fisher told me she had dysentery.
> Yesterday that she was dead.
> Today she is to be buried.

Most memsahibs did not have strong views on India; they simply ignored it where they could. Unthinkingly they echoed the prejudices of their community so vociferously that they became the symbol both to Indian nationalists and to critics of the Empire at Home of all that was wrong with the Raj. Yet if they cannot always be excused they can at least be explained. The majority came to India when they were very young. As they grew older, they looked back, as people do, to the golden years of their youth, when the world seemed a better place. In their nostalgia they compared their idealized memories of Home with the reality of India. Inevitably India came off second best. Honoria Lawrence, who was in her late twenties in 1837 when she first came to India, wrote, 'I daily see the benefit of not having quitted home so young as most ladies who come to India do. Leaving England before they have had much experience of life there, they persuade themselves that the annoyances, which arise from the fact of ourselves and those around us being only human beings, are exclusively Indian.'

The new arrivals were unformed; all they knew was that they were very far from Home in a very strange country. What more natural than that they should cling to the community that reminded them of what was familiar and that they should look to the older ladies to replace the mothers they had left behind? And the community took its responsibility to instruct its newest members seriously. They must learn the ropes partly for the sake of the Raj and partly for their own sakes. Learning the ropes was the way to safety; ignoring them was perilous. Most of us, in a similar position, would probably have chosen safety.

5

FACTS OF LIFE

Most of the women became useful members of the team. They learnt their lessons well: to keep Indians at arm's length, to look inward to their own community for friendship and amusement and protection. Yet, for all the efforts the British made, they could not shut India out entirely. The women had to come to terms with it in almost every detail of their daily lives.

Even before they left Home, women heading for India were given a taste of what lay in store by the old India hands. The advice poured in on them, much of it contradictory. Always wear a topi in the sun – but never linen undergarments. Wool next to the skin prevents disease; flannel is better. Don't exercise in the hot weather; you *must* keep fit or you will sink and decline without a doubt. Take everything you need from Home; wait to get your lighter clothes in India. Remember that cloves keep moths away.

It was all very confusing and most of it rolled over the recipients, who retained only scraps here and there which they added to the images of the maharajahs, palm trees, and tigers already forming their wildly distorted picture of India.

By the middle of the nineteenth century there were books of advice for the novice memsahibs. (They had to be used with caution because they almost always referred to the north of India only.) The authors, usually women themselves, thoughtfully gave lists, of enormous length, of items which should be brought out from Home. In the days of leisurely travel by sea, it was possible to take quantities of baggage; first-class passengers on P&O liners were allowed 336 pounds (152 kg) each at the end of the nineteenth century.

Most of the lists – and much of the baggage – were taken up with clothes. The sheer number and variety seem staggering today. The anony-mous author of *Real Life in India* (1847) recommended, among many other things, thirty-six calico nightgowns and thirty-six nightcaps. At the turn of the century, Flora Annie Steel and Grace Gardiner,

in *The Complete Indian Housekeeper and Cook*, gave the following to be
taken as the bare minimum for a year on the Plains in India:

6 Calico nightgowns.
6 Silk or wool „ (For hot weather)
6 Calico combinations.
6 Silk or wool „
6 Merino vests.
6 Spun silk „
  Calico slip bodices.
6 Trimmed muslin bodices.
12 Pairs tan stockings.
12 „ Lisle thread stockings.
6 Strong white petticoats.
6 Trimmed petticoats.
2 Warm   „
4 Flannel   „
36 Pocket-handkerchiefs.
4 Pairs stays.
4 Fine calico trimmed combinations for evening.

2 Winter morning dresses.
2 Winter afternoon dresses.
2   „   tennis   „
? Evening dresses (to taste).
6 Summer tea gowns.
4   „   tennis gowns.
2   „   afternoon gowns.
1 Riding-habit, with lighter jacket.

1 Ulster.
1 Handsome wrap.
1 Umbrella.
2 Sunshades.
1 Evening wrap.
1 Mackintosh.

2 Pairs walking shoes.

2 "   boots.

1 "   tennis shoes.

? Evening shoes.

4 Pairs house shoes.

2 "   strong house shoes.

Styles changed in the twentieth century and there were certain additions – the new sanitary napkins, for example, which were not always easy to obtain in India. The principle, however, remained the same: wherever possible it was advisable to bring out a large wardrobe from Home.

There were some sensible reasons for this. The social round, coupled with the Indian climate (especially the hot weather), meant that it was necessary to change one's garments several times a day. The servants who looked after washing and pressing, the *dhobis*, were so notoriously rough that clothes often disintegrated under their ministrations – making it all the more necessary to take an ample supply. Moreover, it was not easy to get European clothes in India. Indian tailors, the *durzis*, could not always be relied upon to understand the mysteries of European tailoring. By the end of the nineteenth century, there were a number of substantial mail-order houses in the big cities, including branches of the invaluable Army and Navy Stores, but even then their stocks, and, more important, their styles, were rather limited.

British ladies in India were nagged by the fear that they were out-of-date. When a new arrival reached a station, especially a small one, it was not only her character and appearance that were dissected by the local ladies but also her clothes – sometimes literally, as they were borrowed to show to a *durzi* for copying. The memsahibs made heroic efforts to keep up with European fashion, subscribing to magazines, getting patterns sent out by their families, begging in their letters to their sisters, mothers, friends for the latest word on what the fashion was. In 1858 Minnie Blane sent an annoyed message through her mother to her sister, who was failing in this important task: 'Tell Cissy she never answers my questions nor tells me how she does her hair and all the things I long to hear.'

Dressing well, in fashions approximating those at Home, was almost a duty owed to the prestige of the Raj. Perhaps, in this as well, women were more influenced by India with its tradition of pomp and ceremony than they realized. Visitors from Home always noticed that they dressed in a more elaborate way than their contemporaries. What Sophia Goldborne, heroine of *Hartley House*, a novel about Calcutta life in the 1780s, remarked then was equally true later: describing ladies' fashion in Calcutta, she wrote to a friend, 'I shall refer you to the fashions in England in their highest and most expensive state of ornament and decoration.' A hundred years later, Steel and Gardiner were urging that their readers take 'really smart' evening dresses with them 'as people dress more in India than they do at home'.

Their clothes were also a visible symbol that the women were not going native. Although it might not be convenient and was certainly not comfortable, the women of the Raj kept firmly to their corsets well into the twentieth century even after they had passed out of fashion at Home. In the nineteenth century they had insisted on crinolines and bustles. (As a result some credulous Indians believed that European women had tails.) Unconventionality in dress, as in anything else, was not admired in the community. One of the lively Misses Wallace-Dunlop (who toured India in 1856, missing the Mutiny by a hair's breadth) was much criticized for not wearing her hat while she was being carried in a litter in a hill station. Both sisters thought the criticism absurd but they took to carrying hats with them in case they met other Europeans.

When women did compromise slightly with the reality of India, they were apologetic. The young Thornhill sisters had to make a hot and uncomfortable journey up to the Hills in 1867 in a post-carriage. Greatly daring, they took off their crinolines and wore the lightest clothes they could get away with (a dressing gown and jacket, with a chemise and two petticoats). 'We looked like such rag bags', wrote one to a friend. Steel and Gardiner warned severely that, during the hot weather, 'We do not advocate any sloppiness in dress; on the contrary, we would inveigh against any yielding to the lassitude and indifference which comes over the most energetic in tropical heat.'

There was one article of clothing that was essential, and that was the sun hat. In the cold weather one might wear merely the 'double terai', which was made out of two layers of heavy felt. Safer, and absolutely essential for the hot weather, was the topi, which came into general use in the first part of the nineteenth century. Made of layers of pith, it was believed to protect European brains against being fried by the vicious Indian sun. Topis came in a variety of shapes; in the nineteenth century there was a dashing Meerut version covered with pelican skin and feathers, which gave its wearer, according to Fanny Parks, who always noticed everything, 'a demented air'. There were the helmet shape and the quilted beehive, sold in London to neophytes, and the inverted soup plate stocked by Simon Arzt in Port Said. All brought amusement to the old hands. British residents of India preferred styles like the Cawnpore Tent Club (khaki-coloured) or the Curzon (a pale grey). There were still others – the Lamington or the Minto, for example, last reminders of retired proconsuls. Eurasians, anxious as always to show that they belonged to the ruling race, wore particularly enormous ones. Ladies did their best to make necessity tolerable by covering topis with cotton or silk, piling them with white muslin for riding, adding bits of trim, a few feathers perhaps or some lace. One enterprising milliner advertised a feminine model in a 'popular sailor shape, with a slight mushroom droop, covered with any colour straw flat velvet, birds, and fancy wool finish'. No wonder one of the reasons why women liked going to the Hills was that they could wear proper hats for a change.

The advice on outfits, well-meaning as it was, must sometimes have been a bit chilling to those who had never been to India. 'The best cholera belt for night wear', said *The Complete Indian Housekeeper and Cook*, 'is an ordinary silk or woollen *pugree* [a sort of scarf] wound several times round the body outside the nightdress.' Take a stick, warned *Indian Outfits* in 1882: 'you may get lame and require one.' Shoes should always be loose, 'as your feet swell in India in the hot weather'. Ladies should have boots for outdoor wear as protection against the insects and, of course, must remember to 'shake any boot or shoe, before putting it on that is, if it has been standing out, as scorpions, centipedes, and similar small pests often make snug hiding places for themselves in such retreats.'

While they were advised to take as many clothes as possible, women new to India were at the same time urged to take only a limited amount of household goods. The damage caused by frequent moves in India meant that it made sense to take only those things that could be packed easily. It was silly to take expensive china, folly to take fragile or bulky furniture. (Monica Lang, up in Assam between the wars, lost her piano when wild elephants stepped on a packing case.) It was sensible, though, to take a good supply of household linen, and some cheerful material from Home to brighten one's bungalow; and photographs to remind the exiles of Home, and little knick-knacks – small tables, revolving book-stands and ornaments to go on them, or papier-mâché trays, or whatever was the latest fashion from Home (in the 1890s that might mean tambourines and milking stools). Carpets from Home were not recommended; prisoners in the local jails in India could be relied upon to produce good cheap ones with stripes of blue and grey or a more dashing orange and red.

Again, it was enough to give the nervous second thoughts about going to India. '*Do not buy linen sheeting for Indian use*', warned the author of *Indian Outfits* sternly: 'it is apt to give a sudden chill to the body by checking its natural moisture, and is therefore dangerous.' Footstools will be useful, wrote the author of a mid-Victorian guide, who described herself as a Lady Resident, 'as they keep the feet out of the way of scorpions, centipedes, etc.'

For all the words of advice, the warnings, the encouragements, the women still had to find out for themselves how to live in India. They had to learn, to begin with, how to travel because they were going to have to take long journeys, sometimes on their own. Travel was, like so much else in the lives of the British in India, a mixture of discomfort and privilege. They were privileged because they had an access to government services which Indians did not. When the British had become rulers of India they had revived the old Indian system of *daks* – relays of horses or bearers – and they built *dak* bungalows. No one passed a law saying that only European travellers could use these, but everyone knew that that was the case. When railways were built, it was accepted that Europeans must travel first or second class. Anything lower was not only dangerous – there were vague but alarming references to Indian crowds and Indian germs – but bad for the Raj. Furthermore, railway employees, who at the higher levels were invariably European or Eurasian, knew that Europeans must not be asked to share compartments with Indians. As late as 1920 a high court in the United Provinces of Agra and Oudh ruled against an Indian traveller who had refused to leave the compartment which he felt his ticket entitled him to. The court argued, perhaps not very convincingly, that the segregation was for the greater convenience of travellers of different races.

Travel was glamorous only from a distance. The reality, for all the privilege, was generally slow, dirty, uncomfortable and sometimes dangerous. There were few paved roads in India until the beginning of the twentieth century; most were simply dirt tracks which in the dry weather were deeply rutted and in the wet quagmires. Unlike men, women did not usually ride on long journeys; instead, they bounced about and rattled from side to side in anything from a bullock-drawn cart to a horse-drawn carriage. The standard vehicle, which in the eighteenth century had the imposing name of 'Equirotal Carriage' (it had four wheels of equal size), was known to later generations simply as the *dak-garry*, literally 'post-carriage'. It was nothing very elaborate, merely a wooden box on wheels. There were no springs, because the Indian roads were too rough. For travel at night, which was the common practice in the hot weather, the occupants stretched out on boards laid between the seats. It was usually more comfortable and certainly safer to stay sitting up; carriages were always turning over or breaking axles. There was also something called a *palki-garry* – a horse-drawn litter on wheels.

If the women needed special care, or if there were no roads at all, they travelled in a palanquin, a litter with sliding doors or curtains, carried by four to six men, usually in relays. As Honoria Lawrence found, 'The bearers vary much in their mode of carriage, some keeping step and running smooth; others have a dreadful pace. Fancy yourself in a sieve shaken to try to send you through it, and occasionally receiving a smart jog to facilitate the process. Had it been possible to be ground small enough at first, I am sure I should have been sifted out on the road the first stage.' In addition, there were often undignified disputes with the bearers, who would dump the palanquin on the ground to enforce their demands for more money or longer rests. It was perhaps better for women that palanquin travel became rare after the middle of the nineteenth century.

Whether they were in litters or in carriages, the unfortunate women were jolted, dropped, tipped over almost as a matter of course. There were other hazards too. Lady Login, who lived in Lucknow for some years before the Mutiny, remembered crossing a swollen river in the middle of the night; her litter was tied to inflated skins and she was floated across as the waters lapped around her feet. Although they were not in as much danger, the Misses Wallace-Dunlop had a shock when their *garries* were suddenly picked up and carried across a river by 'a swarm of yelling, screaming, black coolies'.

Women might find themselves stuck for days on end in one place when horses or bearers could not be found because the stately progress of an important official had drained districts for miles around. There was trouble, too, with baggage. It might be dropped, lost, or misplaced; travellers often arrived at their destination to find that their servants and their possessions had apparently vanished. The larger the party, the greater the chance for confusion.

Experienced travellers learnt to take plenty of supplies with them. In most carts, there was a net stretched over the passengers' heads for light things and in the corners were leather cases to hold bottles and food. Honoria Lawrence listed for a friend in England the essentials for a day's march – 'a box of tea, cannister of sugar, ditto sago, teapot, plate, cup, saucer, knife, fork, spoon. A loaf of bread, cold fowl, pepper and salt, two pints of beer, a cork screw and metal tumbler, a candlestick and some wax candles.' It was considered sensible to carry a medicine chest as well.

Dak bungalows were not necessarily welcoming to the weary travellers. Although they were only meant to stay for a very few nights, those in possession sometimes refused to move out and there were unfortunate scenes. The bungalows themselves were spartan: two, perhaps three bedrooms with simple frame beds, a few shelves of rough planks, a couple of rickety chairs and a table. The busier ones had a servant attached to them who could produce an indifferent meal, which usually featured a tough chicken. Many travellers camped out, but that brought its own problems. Tents might not arrive with their owners. Moreover, tents were vulnerable to the skilled Indian thieves, who crept in naked and glistening with oil so that even if the inhabitants woke up it was almost impossible to catch them.

Boat travel was generally better but it too had its drawbacks. Journeys up and down the coast were dangerous and even on India's rivers violent storms could blow up suddenly. When Honoria Lawrence first arrived in 1837, she and her husband went most of the way by river from Calcutta to his post at Gorakhpur in northern India. The boat was quite large,

55 feet (17 m) long, with two masts. In case the wind failed, there were also sixteen rowers. Honoria and Henry Lawrence had two large cabins on the top deck. During the day, blinds were let down to keep the heat out. Their servants were on the lower decks. On small *budgerows* there was not enough room for all the servants and the kitchen and so a little craft was towed behind the main one. That sometimes caused problems when a puff of wind or a sudden change in the current carried off the servants, pots, food and all.

The boats themselves were often squalid. In the 1830s, Mrs Postans, a generally sympathetic observer of the Indian scene who was married to an officer in the Bombay Army, travelled north along the west coast in a local boat. 'The whole scene', she recorded severely, 'is one of filth and confusion; fowl coops, cocoa-nuts, cooking vessels, coir ropes, and passengers mingled together, and surrounded by every ill savour that bilgewater and native cookery can produce.'

Army wives seem to have had a particularly difficult time travelling in India, possibly because the Army resented the presence of women at all. Very little attempt, at least in the nineteenth century, seems to have been made to ensure that they were fed and housed. Florence Marryat – who spent seven years in India in the mid-nineteenth century as the wife of an officer – had to endure a most uncomfortable night on a troopship with her children and servants. It was hot and humid and their baggage had not yet been brought aboard. When she asked the steward for some food, she was told that, according to Army regulations, he could do nothing for her until the following morning. She passed the night listening to the happy revelry of the officers of the regiment in their mess.

By the second half of the nineteenth century, as railways and steamships spread across India, travel, at least between main centres, was faster and easier. Steamers were the best way of all to travel because they were not crowded and noisy like the trains. On the major rivers of India, the Ganges, for example, or the Brahmaputra, which led up into Assam, there were lines which ran until the British left India. Europeans almost always travelled first class on the upper decks, where there was a large saloon surrounded by cabins. The Godden sisters remembered eating their meals in state: 'The tables were covered with starched white cloths, the china and silver marked with the Company's crest; there was a huge carved sideboard, and chairs and settees with fawn linen covers.'

Trains, while efficient, did not have the same leisurely charm. The compartments had leather-covered benches which at night were made up into four beds. Each compartment had a washroom attached to it with a shower which drained away through a hole in the floor. In the hot weather, in the early days of train travel, a roll of matting was kept revolving in front of the window through a tray of iced water. Further refinements – electric fans and electric lights with green flannel caps – were added in the twentieth century. The train windows were extremely complicated: there were usually three sets – one of glass, one of a sort of Venetian blind to keep the sun and the dust out, and one of netting against mosquitoes. Often there were bars as a further deterrent to thieves, who responded to the challenge by learning how to jump on the train when it was moving slowly and force the windows and hook passengers' possessions out between the bars with special sticks. Some skilled thieves had long secateurs for cutting off jewelry; others specialized in filching bags and leaving substitute ones filled with rags. Women travelling alone were put into Ladies Only compartments; these were a favourite target of the thieves.

Women soon learnt to take their own bedding rolled up in a canvas cover, their own towels and soap neatly packed in basins with canvas covers, and usually their own servants for their train journeys. (On some lines first-class compartments had a small servants' room attached.) If they were sensible they took ample supplies of food and drink with them because not all Indian trains had dining cars and the water could never be trusted. Careful memsahibs supplied themselves with a disinfectant for swabbing down the floors and the toilet. Some also took a small stove so that they could brew up comforting cups of tea or Bovril. On certain lines, the train stopped for an hour at mealtimes so that passengers could get off and go to the station restaurant. Large stations had ladies' waiting rooms as well, with baths and an *ayah* (or maid) in attendance. If passengers felt like staying in their compartments, their servants fetched meals for them, each plate neatly tied up in a napkin. Few women had much good to say for the food; Mary Frances Billington, an English journalist who was in India at the end of the nineteenth century, described the standard railway breakfast as consisting of 'tough mutton chops, eggs, and very salt bacon, and the bones of aged fowls disguised under the name of curry'.

Train travel was better than road but it also had its disadvantages – from elephants on the tracks to sheer tedium. The size of India meant that it often took several days to get from one place to another. If the train crossed any of the dry regions, fine dust seeped in and covered everything – passengers, baggage, food – with a thick coating. The sweepers who came on every so often simply stirred up the dust a bit with their twig brushes. In the hot weather, in spite of the ceiling fans and the blocks of ice which were placed on the floor of the compartment every morning, passengers stewed as the sun beat down on the metal roofs.

European women were often appalled by the Indian stations with their noise and confusion and dirt. Indian families squatted patiently on the platforms waiting for their trains to come, unrolling their bedding, cooking their meals, washing and gargling with complete unconcern at the tap. Dogs, chickens, even cows wandered about scavenging for stray bits of food. Beggar children tapped at the windows, pointing to their mouths and using the only English word they knew: 'Mummy, Mummy.'

Some found the stations fascinating. There were stalls selling hot spicy snacks, piles of sweets, sherbet, oranges, bananas, figs, dates. Hawkers with trays on their heads ran alongside the train as it pulled in – men with green coconuts (opened for their juice), men selling mangoes, soda water, lemonade, and bright red raspberry-ade. Others held up jugs of cold water or giant kettles full of spicy, milky tea, which, curiously enough, was refreshing in the hot weather. There were vendors with magazines and books in a score of Indian languages and in English – even, as one lady traveller noticed, with the latest issues of journals from Home like the *Strand* and *Good Housekeeping*. British children loved best the things their mothers disapproved of: trays of gaudy glass bangles, or wooden and clay toys painted with bright flowers and birds.

Travel in India, as women were to learn, revealed a curious attitude in their own men, who were ambivalent towards the Indians in this as in so much else. While they harboured the deepest apprehensions for the safety of their women and children, they let them travel great distances on their own, with only Indian servants for company and protection. Emily Eden, in India with her brother Lord Auckland, when he was Governor-General from 1835 to 1842, came across a case where three small children were being sent to the Hills alone, without even their names written down; they were being passed from one set of bearers to another. When Henry and Honoria Lawrence were travelling together across the north Indian plain barely three weeks after she had given birth to their first child, he often rode miles ahead, leaving her to be carried in her litter. On one occasion, the baby was very sick and she feared that she herself was dying. She tried in vain to send a message ahead to her husband. When he finally came back to find her, she was clutching her baby by the roadside in despair. Yet in later years Honoria Lawrence with her small son covered hundreds of miles from Kurnaul, north of Delhi, to Gorakhpur over in the east without any trouble at all. As she wrote for the benefit of friends at Home, it was quite common-place for an Englishwoman to find herself 'travelling with twenty men or upwards at night through a country where for hours no habitation is seen, she very unlikely to speak a sentence of Hindustani intelligently ...' All this too 'on the very ground where *thugs* are slaying scores, hundreds of travellers, strangling a man for half a crown's worth of silver ornaments he may happen to have, or not unfrequently, without any purpose of plunder, merely to keep their hands in'.

When they finally reached their destination, the women found that their new homes also took some getting used to. Until the end of the nineteenth century, the most common form of housing for Europeans was the bungalow – a square mud-brick building with a thatched or tiled roof, and with large verandahs running around the outside. The walls were often over a foot thick, to keep out the heat. If the bungalows were part of a cantonment they were marshalled with military precision along the roads. In the north of India, they had only one storey; in the south they often had two. The rough walls were washed with colours which, according to the author of *Indian Outfits*, 'would make the aesthete shudder'. Often there was no garden but a patch of beaten earth and a few miserable shrubs. In the cities, the British, especially those who were not very rich, lived in boarding houses or flats. (After the First World War, 'mansions', as blocks of flats were grandly called in imitation of Home, became quite the fashionable thing.) The wives of the ordinary British soldiers stationed for a few years in India were, as usual, the worst off; until late in the nineteenth century their only accommodation was a screened-off corner in the barracks. By the twentieth century, they had their own houses, with government-issue furniture.

Inside, the bungalow was stark indeed to women raised in English coziness. The ceilings were high, with rough, uncovered beams: plaster ceilings only provided a home for rats and snakes. The walls were whitewashed, because wallpaper was merely a temptation to white ants. The windows were small because of the heat in the summer, and, because glass was expensive, they usually had shutters instead. Some old-fashioned bungalows had iron grilles that fitted into the window frames so that the shutters could be left open at night with safety. The floors were often beaten mud (since termites loved wood), covered with grass or bamboo matting. Lighting all this, at least until electricity spread in the twentieth century, were candles or paraffin and coconut-oil lamps. The general effect was of a gloomy austerity.

Something that most women found disconcerting at first was the lack of privacy. In most bungalows, there were no corridors: the rooms simply ran into each other and sometimes the only barrier between them was flimsy screens made of split bamboo. Even when there were folding doors they were often left open to catch the breeze. Servants usually did not bother to knock – what could they have knocked on, after all? 'It is nearly impossible', complained the Wallace-Dunlop girls, 'to escape for one moment from the prying black eyes and stealthy movements of these numerous attendants.' It did not take the women long to get used to it, although few perhaps went quite so far as the memsahib who used to sit naked in her chair as she gave the day's orders to her cook and bearer.

It was up to the women to try to create something that looked cosy and British. They discovered that it was not an easy task. Most bungalows were let unfurnished and the furniture that could be rented or bought in the local bazaars somehow always looked Indian. They could hide the beams and lower the ceilings by stretching white cloth across – as long as they did not mind the scratchings and scurryings of the insects and small animals with which India abounded. It was slightly alarming to wonder whether it was a cobra or a rat over one's head; it was also unpleasant if one of the larger inhabitants of the ceiling died. The floor could be covered with carpets – if a cloth soaked in corrosive sublimate was laid down first to kill the white ants. Just as British women in India wore British clothes, so they dressed their surroundings with as much as they could of Britain. They covered the Indian-made chairs and sofas with chintz and cretonne from Home; they hung curtains made of material from the bazaars or, better still, of sheeting from Home that could be dyed and redyed. The high bare walls might be broken up by a painted band around the base and patterns around the top. 'A very good way of producing a pretty effect', advised Steel and Gardiner, 'is to take out a paper frieze, mount it on coarsest muslin like a map, and tack it with brass nails to the wall.' The women put up pictures – reproductions, photographs of their families, their own watercolours. They allowed Indian touches – brass pots from Benares or, for the sporting household, tables whose legs were antelope horns. Isabel Savory said of the standard bungalow at the end of the nineteenth century: 'The rooms are invariably dark, and almost always bristle with a hundred terrible little Indian, Kashmir and Burmese tables, stools and screens.'

Whatever the embellishments, there were inescapable reminders that you were not at Home: the shape of the rooms, the presence of the Indian servants, and probably a *punkah* hanging from the ceiling. As Fanny Parks described it, the *punkah* was 'a monstrous fan, a wooden frame covered with cloth, some ten, twenty, thirty, or more feet (3–9 m) long'. That was the north Indian style; in Bombay and parts of Bengal *punkahs* were made of polished wood. Memsahibs tried to disguise them or at least make them prettier. Sometimes they decorated them with painted designs or covered the whitewashed frame with flowered calico and tacked on flounces. When *punkahs* first came into use in the late eighteenth century, the *punkah* coolie who kept them in motion squatted in a corner of the room; in the nineteenth century he was banished to the outside of the house. In the hot weather, he pulled on a long frayed rope which disappeared through a hole in the wall and the *punkah* swayed gently over the room, as bits of flaking whitewash drifted down. Until well into the twentieth century, when electric fans largely replaced them, *punkahs* were standard furnishings.

There were parts of the Indian house which would never look like anything at Home – verandahs, for example. Women often screened them in with bamboo trellises up which they grew creepers – bignonia (like the North American trumpet vine) with its masses of reddish-yellow flowers, passion flower with its white and purple blossoms, or ivies of various sorts. Inside was a cool green room which they furnished with grass matting and more plants – maidenhair ferns on tall stands, hanging baskets with pink creeping geraniums, achimenes with their showy red, white and purple flowers, flower boxes with more geraniums, or begonias or violets. Here the memsahib supervised the tailor who sat cross-legged in one corner or interviewed the servants or chatted with callers. Furniture on verandahs was not what one might find at Home. India, wrote Edith Cuthell, who lived in Lucknow before the First World War, 'is the land of loll. There are chairs for each sex and size – long bamboo couch chairs; small grass chairs, cretonne-clad, corresponding to wicker ones in England; heavy dark teak, or mahogany chairs, with wide cane seat and tall curling backs, monsters, with great flat wooden arms splayed out to receive the Sahib's extended legs.' And in the arms of the big wooden chairs were holes where a tumbler for long drinks could rest.

The other room in the typical British establishment which took some getting used to was the bathroom. Each bedroom had its own bathroom attached; indeed in the larger establishments there was often one each for the sahib and the memsahib (the former distinguished only by a piss-pot on a stand). At Home, during the nineteenth century, the upper and middle classes had become used to water closets and hot and cold running water. In India, the big cities were getting modern water and sewage systems by the end of the nineteenth century, but in the *mofussil* coolies continued to carry hot water from the kitchen and cold from the well. In one corner of the bathroom stood a tin bath and sometimes not even that. Ethel Savi's first house as a bride before the First World War had simply an earthenware pot two feet (60 cm) tall and a tin mug for the bather to pour water over himself. The water ran away into the garden through a hole in the floor – also unfortunately convenient for snakes to crawl up. The other piece of furniture in the bathroom was a stately wooden commode with arms – the 'thunderbox' to generations of British. (An invariable accompaniment was the black and yellow box of Bromo paper.) Under the seat was an enamel bowl. When it had been used, the sweeper, who usually waited patiently outside, entered with a basket or a cloth to cover the bowl, which was borne away for cleaning and, if the memsahib was strict, for disinfecting. Women fresh from Home found it all rather embarrassing.

Shopping, like clothes and houses, was the same mixture of what was familiar and what was not. In the eighteenth century, according to the author of *Hartley House*, Calcutta already had fifty shops where ladies could spend lavishly – some, it was said, up to 40,000 rupees in a morning. Their husbands may have objected but 'controul is not an article of matrimonial rule at Calcutta'. By the end of the nineteenth century, Calcutta boasted department stores – a branch of the Army and Navy, Hall and Anderson's, and Whiteaway and Laidlaw, which was said to be like a small Harrods. The upper management was invariably European, the clerks usually Eurasian. The big cities also had bazaars, which were more Indian. Along Calcutta's Bow Bazaar (infamous in the eighteenth century for throat-cutting at night) there was a cheerful, some said squalid, profusion of stalls. Parsees sold an extraordinary assortment of goods, from dried fish to Bibles to ice-skates. An energetic shopper might even find 'pathetic three-legged memorials of old Calcutta, springless oval-backed sofas that once upheld the ponderous dignity of the East India Company, tarnished mirrors which may have reflected the wanton charms of Madame le Grand'. (Madame le Grand, as a young and beautiful bride, gave Calcutta society much to gossip about in the 1780s; she ended her days as the Princess Talleyrand.) In part of Bow Bazaar, too, was the heart of Calcutta's Chinatown, where the Chinese merchants sold silks, carved ivory and painted porcelains; it was whispered that there was an opium den somewhere near as well.

As the British began to take the heavy responsibility of the Raj more seriously, they attempted to impose some order on the native shopping quarter and so they built covered markets – in Madras the Moore Market; in Bombay the Crawford Market, with reliefs by Kipling's father, Lockwood, over the front entrance and flagstones brought from Caithness in Scotland; in Calcutta the Hogg Market, where 'John Chinaman turned out marvellous imitations of British footwear' and the contents of the shops spilled out onto the pavement. Here the memsahibs could send their servants to buy the daily supplies and here they could venture forth themselves. They either took their own bearers with them or hired one of the porters who stood at the doors with large baskets. To pay, the memsahibs simply signed a 'chit' (apparently derived from the Hindustani word for letter), which was presented later. (The word of the ruling race was its bond, after all.)

Away from the big cities, the opportunities for shopping were much more limited. The local bazaar, if the area was sophisticated enough to have one, rarely stocked the sorts of goods Europeans required.

Sometimes the Club ran a small store. Women out in the *mofussil* also got accustomed to relying on mail order. The big shops put out catalogues, and the newspapers such as *The Pioneer* and the *Civil and Military Gazette* were full of advertisements. You sent off to Calcutta or Bombay, or perhaps even to Europe, and you paid through the post office when the goods arrived. Sometimes enterprising women ordered a box of clothes on speculation to sell to their friends. The system worked well on the whole, although occasionally things went astray: Julia Curtis once spent a hot weather in borrowed clothes because the garments she had so carefully ordered had been sent a thousand miles in the wrong direction.

Finally, women all over India bought from the travelling peddlers. Box-wallahs, as they were called, sold an astonishing variety of goods: the Wallace-Dunlop girls noticed 'pickles, sardines, perfumes, groceries, crockery-ware, millinery, dresses, shoes, hosiery and stationery', all in one load. Some called regularly to sell meat, or fish, or vegetables. Others, less frequent, sold frivolous but beguiling toys – ivory trinkets, painted balls, carved buffalo horns, papier-mâché boxes from Srinagar. And there were box-wallahs who specialized in silks, shawls from Kashmir, cottons from Bombay or even Lancashire. Rosamund Lawrence was enchanted by her first encounter with one who pulled layer after layer of silk from his box: 'It is as though a rainbow had penetrated into the dim verandah.' She tried to persuade him that he was wasting his time, that she intended to buy nothing. 'But Memsahib', he replied disarmingly, 'I do not wish to *sell*. If Memsahib only look at my beautiful sil-iks I go away happy.' In some parts there were wild-looking men who came from the jungles with ferns and orchids, even with young panthers.

Women in the *mofussil* also had to accustom themselves to the fact that they had to make do without the services of doctors or hairdressers or dentists. If they were lucky there might be a doctor only a few hours away; dentists were much rarer. They usually put up with toothache as long as they could. Monica Campbell-Martin once estimated that it would cost nearly a month of her husband's salary to have her tooth filled in Calcutta. Occasionally enterprising dentists arrived on tour with collapsible dental chairs.

The fundamental and inescapable fact of life in India was probably the climate. The exiles came to feel that it was typical of the country in its variety and in its immense scale – the oppressive heat, the torrential rains, the clouds of dust. Indian storms were characteristically sudden and violent, blowing off roofs and bowling over those unlucky enough to be caught outside. Guidebooks made much of the dangers: India's weather was an enemy to European complexions, European energies, European habits. The author of *Real Life in India*, published shortly before the Mutiny, described what could happen to a woman: 'she falls a victim to indolent habits and coarse indulgences – the sylph-like form and delicate features which distinguished the youth of her arrival are rapidly exchanged for an exterior of which obesity and swarthiness are prominent, and the bottle and *hookah* become frequent and offensive companions.'

The British divided the Indian year into three parts – the cold weather, the hot weather (they never called it 'summer', possibly to distinguish it from the civilized weather of Home), and the monsoon or 'the rains'. The contrast was greatest in the north (except in the northwest, which did not get the monsoon rains); the south never got quite so hot or so cool. The cold weather lasted from October to March, during which it was chilly enough at night, in the north, for woollens and fires. In the daytime the temperature might go up to 80°F (27°C or so; more than one new arrival mistook this for the real hot weather. During this season, ladies stayed on the Plains with their husbands. There were parties, sports, all sorts of amusements. Around March the air began to heat up, and by April the sun was scorching and baking the north.

Towards the east, in Bengal and Assam, and in the west, in Karachi for example, the climate was wet – temperatures in the summer months were between 90° and 100°F (32–38°C), but the humidity was often 100 per cent. Women usually had to change their clothes four times a day. 'I feel', said Rosamund Lawrence of her time in Karachi, 'like a lump of sugar slowly disintegrating in a tumbler of water.' Across the Plains and up in the northwest the heat was drier but also greater: 100°F, 110°, up and up the thermometer went. With their thick walls and high ceilings, the bungalows did not get quite as hot inside – a mere 95°. One day in Allahabad in June in the late nineteenth century, the ever-curious Mrs King took the temperature in the full sun; it was 169° (76°C). Not surprisingly, she reported, 'My head often feels as if it were fried.'

Early mornings were the only time when the heat relented slightly. By mid-morning it was almost painful to go out; the ground burnt underfoot, and anything metal, even in the shade, grew too hot to touch comfortably. 'You long to take off your skin and sit in your bones.' At night their beds burnt 'like bricks', said one woman, and when they woke from their fitful sleep, their sheets were soaked with sweat. When they bathed, the towels felt as if they were heated. 'Hour after hour,' *Indian Outfits* warned prospective memsahibs, 'the heat seems to increase; you get no rest at night, even though you may have your bed taken out into the compound and a sort of impromptu punkah rigged up over it; you wake up with a sense of suffocation.' Even the toughest found it hard at times. Fanny Parks gave way to an unusual fit of depression in the particularly bad summer of 1833: 'Nothing is going forward, stupid as possible, shut up all day, languid and weary; this India is a vile country.'

The unfortunate writhed with prickly heat rash and there were other irritations, bearable perhaps in cooler weather, intolerable in the heat. At night the Indian noises multiplied as the heat brought out new insects and other fauna. Cicadas kept up their ceaseless whirring, frogs croaked away in chorus, even the birds made a din. The most hated was the aptly named brain-fever bird; its scream went on and on and on through the days and late into the nights. '"Brain-fever, Brain-fever, BRAIN-FEVER!" he screams in an ever ascending scale till even I who never weary of the cawing of rooks, or the harsh cries of peacocks before rain, could wring his neck', wrote Rosamund Lawrence.

Before hill stations became fashionable in the mid-nineteenth century, British women had to endure the heat with their men. They took off their stockings and put away their corsets, if they had any, and wore loose white dresses. There were many ways of coping; some the British took from the Indians, some they discovered for themselves. They learnt to build their houses against the heat, and to screen them against the sun. They rolled up their carpets and put their draperies away. They hired *punkah* coolies. They also adopted the native practice of putting screens of roots of the fragrant vetiver grass in the openings of their doors and windows. The *khus-khus tatties*, as they were known, were kept wet by a servant, so that when the hot winds blew a refreshing breeze came through. They learnt to cool bottles of beer or water by wrapping them in wet *khus-khus* or lowering them into wells. They put clay jars of water inside larger vessels that were filled with water and saltpetre, which brought the temperature down. They dampened their pillows and moved their beds, as the Indians did, into the garden. They dined in the garden as well, sometimes with a block of ice under the table.

Around 1830, some ingenious exile had invented the 'thermantidote', which combined the principle of the *khus-khus tattie* with the paddle wheel. It was built into the wall or set in a door or window frame. A coolie turned the handle so that a constant breeze was sent through the dampened *tatties*. By the second half of the century, it was also possible to get ice. In the 1830s an enterprising American had sent a cargo of apples packed in ice to Calcutta; the apples survived, and, much to general amazement, so did a lot of the ice. Shipments of ice from Wenham Lake in the United States became a regular occurrence. The British also learnt how to make their own. On cold nights in the winter months in the north, coolies would put out shallow earthen saucers of water. In the early morning, before the sun was up, they gathered the ice that had formed and packed it in pits. In some areas, according to Mrs King, they harvested 50,000 to 60,000 lb (23,000–29,000 kg) a night. And in 1878 the first ice factory opened in Calcutta; by the twentieth century most stations where there were any number of Europeans had their own factories.

Women learnt to vary their daily routines to take advantage of cooler moments. They got up at 4 or 5 a.m., had some tea and toast, and went out for their daily exercise while the heat was still bearable. Some drove, some rode, and the more energetic had a game of tennis or golf. The author of *Indian Outfits* was quite lyrical about the early morning's possibilities: 'This is the time for exploring, for wandering through the fields, looking at the various crops, discovering the new roads and pretty little bits of rural life, making sketches of old mosques, tombs, and the like – possibly seeing the troops manoeuvre on the *maidan* [parade ground], or taking *chota hazari* with your friends at a little distance.'

Chota hazari or *hazri* – breakfast – was between 7 and 8. The old hands recommended that it be kept light, but it is doubtful whether they always took their own advice, since it often included egg dishes, fish, curries, and, in the hard-drinking pre-Mutiny days, a glass of claret. After breakfast, the lady was advised to do some gentle housekeeping, take a bath – but not in cold water – and perhaps read until lunch. After lunch, she was expected to retire to her bed for a sleep as fitful as the one the night before. As the sun went slowly down, she got up, bathed again, and, if she could face the evening heat, went out for a gentle drive. At all meals it was considered advisable to cut down on meat.

'*Don't give in to it, and it will give in to you*', Steel and Gardiner exhorted their readers. The women who lived in India in the heyday of the Raj could have endured the hot weather better if they had not been expected to continue to dress as though they were at Home. Even on the hottest days, they wore stockings and dresses, which fell, until after the First World War, in heavy folds to the ground; and, until standards were relaxed during the Second World War, they never went out with their arms bare. Underneath they wore petticoats and camisoles and, for much of the Raj, the inevitable stays – the iron frame for the memsahib just as the ICS was the iron frame for British India. Up to the 1920s, when they went out in the early morning to play tennis they wore petticoats under their long skirts. If they went riding, they wore light jackets. *The Complete Indian Housekeeper and Cook*, while firm on the ability of Englishwomen to survive the heat, listed a stifling amount of garments for the hot weather. First came a combination suit of silk or open-weave flannel, then corsets made of net, a petticoat buttoned to those, and a silk camisole to cover the corsets. Over that, it was suggested, a light woollen tea-gown would be suitable wear in the mornings. 'A lady will find', said the authors triumphantly, 'the discomforts of clothing in a temperature over 98° reduced to the minimum compatible with European ideas.' Many women also added cork spine-protectors and flannel cummerbunds. These last, said Mary Frances Billington in her book *Woman in India* (1895), should be worn day and night round the lower abdomen 'as it is of the first importance to women to avoid anything like cold in the organs peculiar to the sex'. Is it surprising that by the middle of the nineteenth century those who could afford it fled to the Hills with their children, their pets, and their favourite English plants?

The end of the hot weather throughout most of India came in June with the annual monsoon. The skies gradually grew paler with the dust. Then a small cloud would appear, and another and another. As the clouds piled up in a great heavy mass, the temperature climbed higher still. The sky would grow darker and a strange pewter-grey light would steal over the earth. Everyone waited breathlessly for the sudden wonderful moment when, if the monsoon was a good one, the thunder rumbled and the rains came crashing down. The Indians welcomed the monsoon, as they still do today, with prayers of gratitude and rejoicing, and even their reserved rulers permitted themselves a feeling of relief. Between rains the skies were blue again and there were glorious sunsets.

The monsoon brought its own problems. The rains were not gentle showers but solid downpours – as much as 15 inches (38 cm) in a day – and they lasted for three weeks in some parts, in others for a couple of months with only intermittent breaks. Rosamund Lawrence remembered her first monsoon: 'We are living as though under a waterfall. The air seems solid with water, and the lungs like saturated sponges unable to draw in more.' Most roofs developed leaks; at night the inhabitants slept under umbrellas. Pictures rotted if they were left on the walls. Hairpins grew rusty overnight. Bright green mould crept over shoes and books and furniture. Sheets and towels were always damp and beds smelled of mildew. Insects multiplied with abandon. 'Fishtail insects feed on the pictures, and white ants devour the bamboo matting on the floor', wrote one memsahib. Clothes left on chairs overnight were often riddled with holes by the morning. Women put their kid gloves in bottles with stoppers and their best dresses and rugs in tin-lined boxes.

The rains brought the insects out in greater quantities, but they were always a nuisance. At dinner parties moths and flies fluttered in through the unscreened windows, crashing into the diners' faces, flopping into their food. There were dung beetles, the size of small walnuts, and stink beetles, which gave off a foul smell if they were crushed. White ants, the bane of so many housekeepers, ate their way remorselessly through whatever took their fancy – books, laundry baskets, clothes; and then, in a sudden and equally unpleasant metamorphosis, took to the air and flew in clouds, dropping piles of gauzy wings as they went. There were caterpillars, some harmless but others which caused a painful rash at the merest touch. Centipedes appeared of appalling size: Mrs Clemons, in Madras in the early part of the nineteenth century, once saw a black-and-yellow-striped one almost a foot long which presented, she found, 'a most formidable appearance'. There was the 'eye-fly', which hovered just on one's eyelids. The gallant Lady Falkland, in Bombay just before the Mutiny, who never allowed discomfort to impede her powers of observation, managed to find beauty even in the insects: 'The long, graceful, green mantis ... moths with wings which seem made of delicate gold and silver tissue; some look inlaid with mother-of-pearl ... a long, dark yellow hornet-shaped insect, with no end of joints ... blister flies, with either ruby or emerald-coloured bodies.'

Some of the insects were dangerous. The scorpion's sting could kill. Fanny Parks, who was disconcerted by very little, noted cheerfully in her memoirs of life in north India: 'May eighteenth – killed a scorpion in my bathing-room, a good fat old fellow; prepared him with arsenical soap, and added him to the collection of curiosities in my museum.' Lady Dufferin encountered yet another danger in church during her stay in the 1880s. The clergyman had just started the service when the congregation saw carriages rushing off past the door, followed closely by the viceregal bodyguard. 'There was a great commotion outside', she reported, 'and all the men in the church got up and began to shut the doors and windows. I could not imagine what was the matter, but the word "bees" soon began to be whispered about.' Had the bees got into the church, the ladies would have had to protect themselves by pulling their dresses up over their heads.

Of all the insects the most hated was the mosquito. Its whine was maddening in the still of the night, its bite infuriating, and, as Sir Robert Ross discovered at the end of the nineteenth century, it also carried malaria. To keep what Lady Falkland called 'those greedy little mosquitoes' at bay, the beds were draped in great tents of fine muslin. In the nineteenth century, women often also wore anti-mosquito 'sleeping drawers'. In parts of the country where malaria was endemic, they wore long white canvas boots, even under their evening dresses, for protection.

The British also took copious doses of quinine as a specific against malaria. They swallowed it plain or in the more palatable shape of Indian tonic water, perhaps with gin added. Post offices in India generally sold quinine, and polite hostesses sometimes handed it round to their dinner guests. It was impossible, however, to avoid malaria entirely, especially if one lived in the malaria-infested parts. The unfortunate victims grew so used to repeated attacks that they usually did not bother to call in the doctor. Malaria struck suddenly, with little warning: Monica Lang was sitting quietly after dinner when 'Every bone in my body felt as if it was being relentlessly twisted by some unseen hand.' The only cure was more quinine and aspirin. With luck the fever broke as suddenly as it came, leaving the victim soaking wet and weak. While it lasted, though, the afflicted shook with cold even in the hottest weather. Rosamund

Lawrence, on her first encounter with malaria, lay surrounded by hot-water bottles under rugs, coats, blankets, eiderdowns, even cushions from the chairs – and still she shivered. Once she managed to get an attack of malaria and typhoid together. Her fever lasted for a month; she and her husband discussed what to do with their child if she died. When she finally pulled through, she was emaciated except for grotesquely swollen legs, which had to be put, according to the doctor in charge, into cylinders and steamed twice a day. This had no effect; her legs finally returned to normal when she recalled the treatment given horses at Home and asked to be carried into salt water.

In matters of health, it was generally agreed that women were especially at risk. 'It is rightly admitted', wrote an eminent doctor, Edward Tilt, in the 1870s, 'that women break down sooner than men.' He painted a grim picture of the fate of British women in India, prey to every disease and with chronic inflammation of their wombs. Women frequently married too young and failed to take care of themselves properly: 'The menstrual flow becomes too frequent or too abundant, or is too painful.' The memsahib foolishly tries to carry on her social round, 'but the effort induces abdominal pains, nervousness, depression of spirits, and perhaps hysteria'. Miscarriages follow and the women get up too soon, their wombs now 'permanently congested, irritated, if not ulcerated'. Sometimes they can be cured at Home but often it is too late. He urged the women to take care of themselves: to eat and drink in moderation, to exercise regularly, to avoid visiting, dancing, and riding when they were menstruating, and, best of all, 'to impart to the womb, by means of a vulcanized india-rubber syphon, a portion of that bracing influence so largely given to the skin by the daily use of cold water'. The British worried about longer-term effects. It was generally believed, until after the First World War, that India's heat affected reproduction; European children settled permanently in India would, as *The Pioneer* warned in 1888, 'die out about the fourth generation, degenerating steadily up to that point'.

Illness and the prospect of an early death were daily fears that the British had to live with in India. They would have faced some of the same diseases at Home – typhoid, for example, and tuberculosis were still killing the inhabitants of Britain as late as the twentieth century. India, however, seemed to have an excessive quantity and variety of diseases; people could be quite well one moment and dead within the same twenty-four hours. In 1880 the mortality rate among the wives and children of British soldiers stationed in India with their regiments (the only group for whom statistics were collected) was almost three times what it was in Britain. Cholera, which can kill in a few hours after the first signs appear, was eradicated in Britain by the beginning of the twentieth century, but it remained endemic in India until after the Second World War. In the *mofussil* many women had to cope with sudden, violent disease on their own. At the same time, they also learnt to ignore minor illnesses: 'It was such a constant struggle to keep going, and so boring being ill yet *again*, that one didn't give in till one collapsed.'

Part of the standard equipment for a memsahib was a medical reference book: favourites for generations of women were *Dr Moore's Book of Family Medicine* and *Birch's Management and Medical Treatment of Children in India*. They also kept basics like castor oil, quinine, iodine, and chlorodyne, a patent medicine whose ingredients included morphine, on hand. Fanny Parks swore by opium as a cure for dysentery. They learnt not to show despair even when a case looked hopeless. Ethel Savi was brought a baby by a desperate woman who had made a terrible journey across burning sands and the Ganges in full flood. The child had a fever of 105°F (40.5°C) and acute dysentery. She managed to save it with the help of home remedies and sheer good luck.

Memsahibs also tried to get used to the failures: family, friends, acquaintances who were alive and well one day and dead and buried the next. The experience of Mrs Herbert Reynolds, wife of an ICS officer in Bengal, was not uncommon: 'During the year 1863, we suffered terrible grief in the deaths of two of our dear children, and at Christmas my sister died also from a sudden attack of cholera.' The women acquired, perhaps, a touch of the fatalism that they ascribed to the Indians. They took risks; although many fled to the Hills with their children when there were epidemics, others sent their children off alone and stayed with their husbands, hoping that they would be lucky. Sometimes they were. Lillian Ashby, who, with both a father and a husband in the Indian Police, had spent much of her life in the *mofussil* at the end of the nineteenth century and the beginning of the twentieth, discovered, as her husband tried to cope with a cholera epidemic from his camp, that one of the servants was storing all their food in convenient wooden boxes he had found – the coffins that had been used to cart off the dead to their funeral pyres.

Women coped with India's other menaces. The north suffered from earthquakes when rivers were tossed out of their beds and great fissures opened in the ground. Monica Campbell-Martin lived through the enormous Bihar earthquake of 1934. Her first warning was a noise like an express train; the thick walls of her bungalow started to ripple as though they were made of cloth. She rushed into the garden: 'The hills, the mountains, the trees, all were dipping and swerving. A hill disappeared like a scenic backdrop as I looked at it. Hundreds of birds flew by, screeching their terror.' Mad dogs sometimes got into their gardens and houses; kites swooped down and stole the food at garden parties; impudent monkeys, like the three a memsahib found sitting on her bed eating her biscuits, rummaged through their possessions. Dangerous animals they accepted with resignation. Monica Lang, in her years on a tea garden in Assam, had leopards, tigers and bears prowling around her bungalow at night. Once, while she drove a pony cart, she was stalked for some miles by an especially bold tiger.

Snakes were a threat even in cities. Women covered their verandahs with rough carpets to deter them, had the door sills raised, put out broken glass and special tin barriers at night, fixed wire netting across the drains in the bathroom, and sprinkled carbolic powder everywhere. Still the snakes got in. They fell on one's head and they got underfoot. The most deadly were the kraits, small, dark and difficult to see in the gloom of most houses. Fortunately they were lazy and did not always strike out in time. Cobras looked much more frightening, especially when their hoods flared out, and they were quicker in their reactions. One of their favourite haunts was the bathroom; many memsahibs had the experience of sitting transfixed in their tin baths while a cobra slowly surveyed the scene. And there were dozens of other snakes, some dangerous, some harmless – always unnerving. Monica Lang stood on a log in the jungle which suddenly shifted and revealed itself to be an enormous python.

Such things were alarming, but in a way they were easier to deal with than the other great difficulty of Indian life – the boredom. Young Ellen Thornhill, who should have known what to expect because she had been born in India, sent a friend a long description of routine on a small station and ended, 'And this is what I do every day and I hope you are not as sick of it as I am.' In the 1860s Florence Marryat complained of exactly the same thing: 'each sun set as it rose, and left a feeling behind it of an utterly wasted day.' One lady with fever, who heard that she was despaired of, replied that her only feeling was one of 'extreme thankfulness'. It is scarcely surprising that some women became bores about housekeeping, boasting of their triumphs over box-wallahs, servants, white ants. Or they filled up their empty days with ridiculous quarrels; Anne Wilson knew of a small hill station in the 1890s, for example, where the only two women residents cut each other dead as a result of a dispute over the milk supply. Less energetic women lapsed into an almost permanent lethargy. Mrs Sherwood, herself busy with children, writing and good works, noted what she called 'a common problem' in the wife of the Collector in Mirzapur, whom she met in 1810: 'She had not the bodily strength of controlling either children or servants, she seemed to have lost all motive of action, all power of exertion.' Some took refuge in drink. Mrs Ashmore, in the 1840s, noticed ladies quietly downing glass after glass of champagne in an effort, she thought, 'to remove the extreme depression and lassitude which are superinduced by the climate'.

What is impressive is the number of women who rose to the challenges of life in India. They often managed with aplomb, pouring paraffin and boiling water daily down the cracks in their floors to kill the white ants, stepping on snakes, and shooting mad dogs. Isabel Gross, on the Northwest Frontier between the wars, had to keep her head down in the car for fear of snipers and lived in the bungalow where her husband's predecessor had been murdered: 'But no such horrors overtook us, & I was extremely happy up there, with that marvellous garden & a reasonable climate.' Some even loved the hot weather on the Plains. Frances Smyth, who lived in military cantonments all over the country, found that 'India heaved a deep sigh, when all the women and children left, and became herself. You really felt you were getting to know the real India, and not just the superficial British cantonment type of India.' Rosamund Lawrence spent much of her time in the country far from other Europeans. When her husband left her alone with the servants in the middle of a jungle while he carried out a tour of inspection, she found even the loneliness rewarding. 'How lovely these long and lonely days! Before I left England it had become the fashionable craze to take a week's starvation cure. Friends told me of the clearness of vision, of thought, of understanding, the rarefied feeling which possessed them after the first two days of discomfort. All clogging deposits of food gone. I too feel like that, freed from gossipy, inessential talk.'

6

WOMEN IN DANGER

Publicly the British expressed supreme confidence in their ability and indeed their duty to rule India. Privately they could not help but wonder uneasily what would happen if the millions of Indians they despised should decide to turn on them. An image that recurs in Anglo-Indian writing is of an India about to erupt. And the apprehension, at times the outright fear, that the British residents felt of India was most acute when women and children were threatened. Women were the soul of the race, children its future. They stood for innocence and purity; they were also dangerously vulnerable.

The one event above all others that symbolized British fears about India and their women was of course the Mutiny in 1857. In the eighteenth century, European women had been captured, sometimes even killed, by Indians. Mrs Fay, for example, ended her first voyage to India in 1779 as the prisoner of the Indian governor of Calicut. It was also widely believed that a Mrs Carey had been among those unfortunates who were imprisoned in the Black Hole of Calcutta. Nobody at the time made any particular fuss about them; their sex did not make their fate somehow more appalling. The Mutiny was on a larger scale, of course, but British outrage was also a result of changed social attitudes.

The Mutiny might never have happened if the British had not started taking their responsibilities seriously. India must be ruled efficiently and justly; it must have railways and telegraphs. And the hold of paganism must be challenged – or so thought the Evangelical Christians of the powerful new middle classes. Previously Indians had paid as little attention to the British as to any of their other rulers, but the new activism alarmed them. Peasants objected to paying higher taxes; princes who had been deposed longed for their former power and wealth; Muslims looked back nostalgically to the glories of Mughal rule; and Brahmins, the priests of Hinduism, feared for their caste and their religion.

The discontent was intensified when the energetic Marquess of Dalhousie was appointed Governor-General in 1848. In his eight years in office, he pushed through a series of measures which left bitter and resentful Indians in their wake. He greatly increased the size of the territory in India that was directly ruled by the British, using methods which were legally correct but morally wrong. Traditionally in India adopted sons were considered the equal of natural ones for the purposes of succession and inheritance; Dalhousie announced that the practice would no longer be accepted. States without proper heirs became part of the British territory. Shortly before he left India, Dalhousie seized the greatest plum of all – the fertile state of Oudh. The King of Oudh did have natural heirs, but conveniently the British discovered that the court at Lucknow was wasteful and frivolous, and the ruler himself corrupt and debauched. In February 1856 they took over Oudh. The resulting discontent was fanned by the deposed royal family, who had not been given pensions, and by the courtiers, the servants, and the purveyors of luxuries, who had lost their livelihoods. The British were good at making enemies in the years before 1857. Still another was the young Nana Sahib, who so charmed the British residents of Cawnpore with his elaborate parties; he had suddenly found that he would no longer have the title and pension that he had expected to inherit from his adoptive father, the Peshwa of Poona.

Appropriately, what set fire to large parts of India was a new cartridge for the native army. It was in fact a technological advance of which the British were proud: instead of the cumbersome process of loading a gun separately with shot, powder and then wadding to keep the first two in place, a soldier would be issued with a paper cartridge containing a shot and the right amount of powder. He would simply bite the top off and load his gun, pushing the paper, which had cleverly been greased, down the muzzle last. The grease, unfortunately, was rumoured to include both pig and cow fat – offensive to both Muslims and Hindus. There was trouble in regiment after regiment and the weather grew hotter. In May, the Mutiny started, first in Meerut just north of Delhi, then across northern India. The garrison at Delhi was overrun; Cawnpore, on the Ganges, fell; and at Agra and Lucknow desperate garrisons were besieged.

The mutineers, who seemed to have few coherent plans, massacred Europeans at random. The first 'martyrs', as the British called them, were at Meerut on Sunday, 10 May. The pregnant wife of a British officer was hacked to pieces by a Muslim butcher; a Mrs Dawson, who was in bed with smallpox, was burnt to death; and other women were cut down as they tried to flee. Mrs Muter, the wife of an officer who escaped, passed the body of an Englishwoman in a ditch 'so disfigured by wounds as to be with difficulty recognized'. In Delhi, in the following days, there were similar horrors. A missionary's daughter and her friend hid in a cupboard; they were dragged out to their deaths. The wife of the manager of the Delhi and London Bank killed two of her attackers with a boar spear before she was finally overwhelmed. The 'enormously stout' Mrs Foster, whom Emily Metcalfe had met in happier circumstances nine years earlier, was badly bruised in a fall from the wall of the Red Fort; her companions had to abandon her and she was never heard of again.

It was the women's misfortune that the spring of 1857 had been exceptionally cool. As a result many of them had delayed their departure for the Hills. By May it was too late. The Mutiny took hold of northern India like a brushfire, flaring up here and there. There was trouble in Indore, in Jhansi, and in a score of smaller stations. It never spread to the south, and the great cities of Calcutta and Bombay remained calm. But all through the north in those frantic weeks bewildered European men, women and children stumbled across the countryside in terror. The sun beat down on them as they looked desperately for food and shelter. Often they did not speak any Indian language, so that even well-disposed Indians (of whom there were many) appeared threatening.

Their stories survived to horrify successive generations. English-women who had shortly before been waited on hand and foot by their servants now had to beg for food and drink water from the ditches beside the roads. Mrs Wood fled from Delhi towards Kurnaul, about 50 miles (80 km) to the north, with her wounded husband and one other woman. They were stopped by thieves who stole their horses and their money, and so the two women walked on, dragging Dr Wood between them. Their shoes wore out and their feet were burnt by the hot sands and cut by thorns. Frequently women had bleeding hands and ear lobes: even if they escaped the mutineers, they were likely to fall into the hands of common thieves who ripped their jewelry from them. A party of thirteen men, women and children who had fled from Delhi were attacked by an armed band who stripped them of everything of value. The young Lieutenant Vibart saw with horror 'the unfortunate ladies in the grasp of these savages. One of them had her clothes literally torn

off her back, whilst the others were treated with similar barbarity.' Near
Aligarh, Lieutenant Cockburn came across a party of refugees, 'the poor
women, naked and bleeding, insulted and abused'. Madeline Jackson,
who was only seventeen in 1857, saw her host shot in front of her when
the Mutiny broke out in Sitapore, north of Lucknow. 'The poor baby
they took on a spear and threw into the river.' Madeline and her brother
escaped towards Lucknow; 'I remember thinking how lovely the jungle
was and said to my brother "I can't bear to be killed."' She was lucky;
although her brother was shot by mutineers, Madeline was merely held
prisoner for several months with two other women.

The fate of the women in Lucknow was to become part of British
legend. There, thanks to the foresight of Sir Henry Lawrence, the Chief
Commissioner, the Residency had been prepared for a siege. Those
Europeans who survived the initial massacres had a place of safety – of
sorts. Food ran short; disease increased daily; and the mutineers kept
up a steady bombardment. The Residency was not designed as a fortress
and there were few places in it that were secure. Lawrence himself
was killed in his bedroom. Miss Palmer, a colonel's daughter, had her
leg shot off. A mother who sat with her children saw her baby's head
blown off. Mrs Case, the wife of an officer, wrote in her journal that she
wondered 'what would be the feelings of any lady suddenly transported
from quiet peaceful England to this room, around which the bullets are
whizzing, the round shot falling, and now and then a loud explosion,
as if a mine were blowing up which I think is almost worse than all
the … fire of musketry. It is an awful time.… The nights are dreadful.
One looks forward so anxiously for the first ray of daylight.'

The women passed the long summer months trying to keep themselves and their children alive. Often they did not know what had
happened to their husbands. Some still had servants with them; others
did everything for themselves, fetching water, collecting sticks, cooking
their meagre rations. They made clothes out of old scraps of material;
even the Residency's billiard cloth was cut up. They helped to nurse the
sick and the wounded. 'Never', wrote Martin Gubbins, the Financial
Commissioner in Oudh, 'has the noble character of Englishwomen
shone with more real brightness than during this memorable siege.' They
watched helplessly as the children died from malnutrition and disease.
A young officer's wife, eighteen years old, lost her baby on 1 July; when

the tiny corpse was taken away, she wrote, 'with that form my heart seemed to leave my body'. On 8 August, Mrs Bartrum, the wife of an army doctor, wrote in her diary, 'Another has been taken away: poor Mrs K. has lost her child, such a sweet little thing that it was petted and loved by all in the room.' On the 17th, Mrs Brydon (wife of William Brydon, who was famous as the sole survivor of the British retreat from Kabul) recorded in her journal, 'Mrs Green … died last night and Mrs Levin's baby the night before. Major Bird's baby was buried this evening.'

They were tormented by the flies, which swarmed over their food, and the mosquitoes, which bred in the fetid pools of water around the Residency. Many women fell sick with dysentery or fever. The rats grew bolder; one lady recorded that a huge one 'ran up to me but my screaming frightened it away'. There was a much greater worry to torment them: what would happen to them if the rebels won? Some kept poison with them, others found reassurance in the promise of an officer to blow them all up so that the mutineers could not rape and torture them.

At least at Lucknow those who managed to hang on were finally rescued – seven months after the start of the Mutiny. The women and children at Cawnpore were not so lucky. There was no Sir Henry Lawrence to prepare a defensible position. When the Mutiny started on 2 June, the only refuge was some barracks surrounded by a trench and a low mud wall which offered little protection. Casualties mounted sharply. Mrs Williams, wife of an army officer, was shot in the face and took two days to die. Her daughter, who was caring for her, got a bullet in the shoulder. There was not enough food right from the beginning and the only well was dangerously exposed to the mutineers' fire. Some of the women were heroic. W. J. Shepherd, a clerk, who was one of the few to escape, described them: 'I have seen them patiently attending upon their wounded and suffering husbands and fathers unremittingly night and day, exposed to all sorts of dangers, themselves labouring under sickness, surrounded by young children whose cries and wants at any other time would be enough to send the best of mothers mad.' Others cracked; one ran out of the encampment with her two children, apparently seeking a quick death for them all.

Suddenly, when it appeared that the garrison could hold out no longer, a ray of hope appeared. The local rajah – the same Nana Sahib who had been treated shabbily by the British – wrote to the commander promising that, if the defenders laid down their arms, they would be given a safe passage down the Ganges to Allahabad. It has never been established whether Nana Sahib was sincere in his offer or whether he intended something else all along. On 27 June, the tattered remains of the garrison made their way to the river bank, where some wooden boats awaited them. No sooner were they on board, however, than the Indian troops who had been watching their departure opened fire. It was a massacre. As the British tried frantically to push the boats into the current, the mutineers waded out to finish the job. A Eurasian woman who survived described the scene later: 'Some were stabbed with bayonets; others cut down.... We saw it; we did; and tell you only what we saw.... Children were stabbed and thrown into the river. The schoolgirls were burnt to death. I saw their clothes and hair catch fire.' Only one boat managed to escape. While the mutineers slaughtered the rest of the men, about 125 women and children were hauled ashore by Nana Sahib's men. Miss Wheeler, daughter of the general commanding the defenders, was taken off by a sepoy. Her fate was to become one of the most popular of the legends of the Mutiny: she was said to have taken her abductor's sword while he slept, cut off his head and those of the rest of his family, and then thrown herself down a well. (Years after the Mutiny, however, a Roman Catholic priest spoke to an old lady as she lay dying in Cawnpore, who said that she was Miss Wheeler and that she had passed a happy life with her sepoy.)

The majority of the women and children were taken to a small house called the Bibighar (House of the Lady) after the mistress of a British officer who had once lived there. Nana Sahib sent enough food to keep them alive; his initial intention may have been to use them as bargaining counters should the British win back control. Ironically, it was the approach of a British relief column that persuaded him to get rid of them; he did not want witnesses to the attack on the boats. The Indian soldiers whom he ordered to shoot them refused. Eventually a motley crew, including a couple of butchers, rushed into the Bibighar with swords and knives. The testimony that the British later collected painted a terrible scene. After the executioners had left, groans were heard from the house during the night. In the morning, 'the bodies were dragged out, most of them by the hair of the head'. All (and some may have been still alive) were thrown down a well, which was to become one of the most important monuments of British India. A magistrate, J. W. Sherer, who arrived with the relief force, said, 'on looking down you could see only a tangled mass of human limbs entirely without clothing'. In the Bibighar, the floor, according to a witness, 'was littered with trampled, torn dresses of women and children, shoes, slippers and locks of long hair, many of which had been severed from the living scalps by sword-cuts'.

Young Lieutenant Nicholl, who was among the troops sent out from Britain to put down the Mutiny, wrote in his diary that he dreamt at night 'of women hanging by their hair, children with their throats cut and other horrors'. By the time his ship arrived at Calcutta, he had pledged himself to 'avenge the deaths of the poor women and children in Delhi'. Other men took similar vows. When William Howard Russell travelled up-country for *The Times*, the walls of the *dak* bungalows had been covered by soldiers with exhortations: 'Revenge your slaughtered countrywomen! To—with the bloody Sepoys!' Young Minnie Blane, who had been forced to flee from Jhelum to the uncertain safety of Lahore with her newborn baby, wrote to her mother in the most ferocious tones: 'Christmas is drawing near and I wish I could feel as charitable as you do. It sickens me to hear people talk of Merry Christmas and showing mercy towards wretches who have been guilty of every foul deed ... No punishment is too great for those inhuman monsters. When I think of the pretty elegant girls and their charming mothers, and the brave men I met in Cawnpore coming up here and their terrible fates, it makes me want to shoot every Indian I see.'

Wild rumours spread about the particular horrors suffered by women. They had been crucified, hung up by their hair, raped (or, as the language of the time had it, dishonoured). For years after there were also unsubstantiated reports of fair-skinned women kept prisoner in Indian households, or perhaps too ashamed to come back to their own people. Lady Canning, wife of the Viceroy at the time, wrote to Queen Victoria that 'there is not a particle of credible evidence of the poor women having been "ill-used" anywhere', and Sir John Lawrence, brother of the defender of the Residency at Lucknow, thought that, while some women had possibly been raped in Delhi, most had been killed at once. The Commissioner of Police in what was then known as the North-Western Provinces, where much of the Mutiny had taken place, later interviewed sixty-three witnesses and said 'the most searching and earnest inquiries totally disprove the unfounded assumption that at first was so frequently made and so currently believed, that personal indignity and dishonour were offered to our poor suffering countrywomen'. Yet all those stories of rape or kidnapping became part of the folklore of the Raj.

In putting down the Mutiny, some officers and men took savage reprisals, shooting Indian prisoners out of hand, blowing them to pieces at the mouths of cannon, hanging them as slowly as possible. The revelations of what had taken place at Cawnpore brought new heights of fury and further refinements of punishment. Indians suspected of having been involved in the massacre were forced to lick clean part of the bloodstained floor in the Bibighar. Then they were executed.

In time, the British calmed down. They realized that not all Indians were their mortal enemies. And as the power and magnificence of the Raj grew, they became confident again in their ability to manage India. Yet they never forgot entirely. Their children were told about that terrible time; Ethel Savi listened as a young girl to the stories of a neighbour in Calcutta who had lost her husband in the Mutiny at Agra and who herself had only escaped death by hiding in a large earthenware water jug. Memories were also kept alive by the books – diaries, histories, novels – that came out year after year to wring the hearts of their readers with the sad fate of people very like themselves.

There were physical reminders of the Mutiny dotted about India. The Residency in Lucknow was never rebuilt; what was left became a museum. On one of its ruined towers a Union Jack flew day and night until the British left, as a memorial to those who had died there. In Cawnpore, the infamous well was surrounded by a garden which contained a marble statue to the dead. In St John's Church in Delhi, the walls bore memorials to those 'cruelly dead' in the Mutiny. In Meerut, where it had started, the Mutiny was a vivid presence years later. Iris Portal lived there for a time between the two world wars: 'On the gates of the bungalows were plaques which said, "Here Mrs So and So and her three children were killed and thrown down a well", or "Here Captain and Mrs So and So were found hiding and killed" and so on. There was one bungalow near by where they had to take their beds out into the garden, not only for the heat but because things happened, like doors blowing open when there was no wind. Dogs would never stay in the house, and it was emphatically haunted. They all felt it and they all hated it, and that was one of the Mutiny bungalows with a plaque on it.'

Until the Second World War it was the rule for British troops all over India to carry rifles with live ammunition to church, so that they could never again be surprised as they had been in 1857. From that time on, too, the British looked for warnings of another Mutiny, often in the most unlikely places. In 1893 and 1894, for example, planters and officials in Assam grew alarmed at the appearance of pats of mud with hair stuck in them on the trunks of trees. The 'tree-daubing' spread into Bihar. What did it mean? The British could not help thinking of how the Mutiny had been preceded by the mysterious passing of *chapatis* (the unleavened Indian bread) from Indian to Indian. There were stories in the press about sinister holy men who were somehow involved (again there was an uncomfortable parallel with the Mutiny). There were rumours of plots to kill all European planters. A mark appeared on a statue of Queen Victoria in Madras, and in Bombay someone tarred the statue of a former governor. No uprising materialized and, as it turned out, the marks on the trees were probably caused by buffalo scratching themselves. In 1907, on the fiftieth anniversary of the Mutiny, there were proposals to gather all women and children into forts for safety. The Mutiny, the young ICS officer Malcolm Darling wrote in a letter home in 1906, was 'a kind of phantom standing behind official chairs'.

Even in everyday life, many people felt, India also posed a moral threat. Indians lacked a proper sense of decency: look (although the ladies tried not to) at the flimsy clothes they wore. Florence Marryat complained, 'There is something in the idea of gentlemen who never wear any clothes picking the fruit you eat which is not at all appetising.' In Calcutta in the 1880s Bengalis were not allowed near the bandstand in the Eden Gardens because their 'transparent clothes' might upset the British ladies who came there to take the evening air.

Indians seemed excessively interested in sex. The former editor of the *Civil and Military Gazette*, an important Anglo-Indian newspaper, wrote a book in the 1920s on India in which the first chapter is entitled simply 'The Land of Sex-Mad Millions'. In Hilda Swabey's novel *The Chief Commissioner* (1912), the full lips of the wicked Rajah are said to denote 'the sensuous disposition of his race'. Indians lacked self-control –

especially, the lady writers hinted delicately, in sexual matters. In *The Englishwoman in India* (1909), Maud Diver warns her readers that they must expect their Indian servants to have lots of children, 'for celibacy is an outcome of civilization'. A missionary echoed a common complaint when he referred to 'immoral practices of the grossest kind' which the Indians did not keep secret 'but performed in public'. The Hindus were particularly shocking because sex appeared to be thoroughly mixed up with their religion. Hindus worshipped such odd shapes: the *lingam*, which was quite defiantly phallic; the concave *yoni*, whose significance was also unmistakable. In their temples the dancing girls who served the gods were also prostitutes. Some temples had carvings that were obscene (or erotic, depending on your point of view). Memsahibs who went sightseeing were carefully steered away from them by their escorts; indeed, a popular nineteenth-century guidebook advised tipping local guides at a particularly notorious temple so that they would not call attention to shocking scenes. When Susan Daly wanted to see some of the beauties of Lucknow her husband put his foot down: 'Henry cannot bear me to go to any of the public places on account of the pictures and especially the Statues. There is a beautiful garden close to our Park Gates; it was a favourite place of resort to the late King and his women. I have often wished to see it but Henry insisted on making a voyage of discovery first and returned much scandalised at the statues. "What harm could it do me to see them" said I, "I would not have any of the young fellows suppose you had seen such things Susie, for the world. You must not go." So of course I have not gone there, but other ladies have I know.'

It was largely taken for granted that all Indian men lusted after European women. That was one of the lessons the Mutiny was presumed to have taught. Ever after, in moments of tension, rumours would circulate among the British that posters had gone up in the bazaars urging Indians to rape white women. The situation of the missionaries who went into Indian houses to teach Indian women caused some concern. In 1883, a 'District Judge' wrote to *The Friend of India*, another Anglo-Indian newspaper, to point out the terrible risk that they were taking. They had no protection from 'familiarity or insult from the male members of the household…. I cannot', he said discreetly, 'put matters as clearly as I should otherwise wish, because of the extreme delicacy of the subject, and the repugnance with which the mind dwells on such matters.' A memsahib described to J. R. Ackerley what had happened when a servant had tried to warn her that she was about to step on a particularly poisonous snake. She had been too sick to pay attention to what he was saying: 'Then the servant did a thing absolutely without precedent in India – he touched me – he put his hand on my shoulder and pulled me back.' Although she recognized that he had saved her life, she told Ackerley, 'I didn't like it all the same, and got rid of him soon after.'

A particularly awkward situation had arisen at the beginning of the twentieth century when qualified Indians began joining the Indian Medical Service. The British, whether civilian or military, had grown accustomed to using the government's medical staff for their needs and, in fact, on the smaller stations there were no other trained doctors. Given their assumptions about the intentions of Indian men, it is not surprising that many British women were alarmed at the prospect of going to an Indian doctor. In 1914 the main British political organization, the European Defence Association, warned the government of India that 'to force upon European ladies, more especially in maternity cases, practitioners of secondary qualifications, or as the case may be, practitioners of alien race and customs, is to create a position which no British Government should tolerate for one moment'. Of course, the Association was suspiciously eager to point out, the objection was not based on racial grounds but on the need to preserve the 'intimate relationship that must exist between doctor and patient'.

Sometimes, however, the British wondered whether their women – the weaker sex after all – would always behave as they should if they were tempted by the lascivious Indian. On one occasion, at the end of the nineteenth century, the government of Bengal asked a maharajah to stop his visits to the popular hill station of Darjeeling 'since he had contracted the unfortunate habit of presenting English ladies with bouquets that contained diamond ornaments'. The memsahibs of the Raj were, like their counterparts at Home, not supposed to enjoy sex much. What if India weakened their restraints? The British had only to look at Eurasian and lower-class European women in India to see the possibilities. Such women had a reputation for being hot-blooded, and, unfairly, British men found them very attractive. Radclyffe Sidebottom, who was in the Bengal Pilot Service before the Second World War, looked back on the summer months in Calcutta, when most of the respectable white women had gone to the Hills, with considerable nostalgia: 'The weather was hot and passions were high and you behaved in quite a different way. The girls that you couldn't be seen with during the cold weather, the Eurasians and the "poor whites" who were absolutely riddled with sex and very beautiful were comparatively fair game. You hadn't got to marry them and they courted you.' Evenings with them were sometimes known as 'B' parties. 'What happens?' asks the newly arrived Englishman in Rumer Godden's novel *The Lady and the Unicorn*. '"Usual thing," said William. "They behave very well and we behave very badly, and then they behave worse."' Perhaps the hot blood could be explained away as the result of some Indian ancestor or at the very least too long an exposure to India. Perhaps not.

Evidence that some Englishwomen might welcome advances from Indian men made their compatriots very uneasy. When the Maharajah of Patiala planned to marry Miss Florry Bryan, a music hall entertainer, in 1893, the government of India took steps to discourage him, not because she came from the wrong class but because she was the wrong race. The marriage, the government wrote to the Maharajah, 'will render your position both with Europeans and Indians most embarrassing'. (The Maharajah ignored the advice and married Miss Bryan.) In 1901 the Indian government was apprehensive about sending Indian troops to London for Queen Victoria's Diamond Jubilee. As the Viceroy, Lord Curzon, explained, 'The "woman" aspect of the question is rather a difficulty, since strange as it may seem English women of the housemaid class, and even higher, do offer themselves to these Indian soldiers, attracted by their uniform, enamoured of their physique, and with a sort of idea that the warrior is also an oriental prince.'

The sexual threat to British women was one that both attracted and repelled the Raj's writers. In Mrs G. H. Bell's *Sahib-log* (1910) a memsahib rages at the 'unworthiness of the native mind'; 'especially', she adds darkly, 'when one knows what would be the fate of white women in India, if the balance of power left the Englishman's hands even temporarily'. A favourite plot involved a villainous Indian (frequently a nationalist as well) scheming to get his hands on a pure English girl. Writers who were part of British society in India titillated themselves and their readers with the possibility, but they always drew back from portraying what they dreaded. It was left to two outsiders, both men, to treat the subject more seriously.

E. M. Forster visited India first in 1912–13, when he travelled extensively. Although he had introductions to the highest levels of British society, he also, unusually, spent a good deal of time with Indians, especially Muslims. In 1921–22, when he worked as personal secretary to the Maharajah of Dewas Senior (to distinguish him from the junior branch of the family, which also had its maharajah), he saw very little of Europeans. His temperament and his liberal philosophy did not predispose him to like British society in India, and his experiences there confirmed him in the view that most sahibs and memsahibs were smug, shallow, and philistine. After the publication of *A Passage to India* in 1924, Forster asserted that he had tried to be fair 'to the poor Club'. Its members can perhaps be excused for feeling that he did not try very hard.

The only sympathetic Europeans in *A Passage to India* are outsiders: the schoolmaster, Fielding, whose opinions reflect many of Forster's own, and the visitors from England, Mrs Moore and her young friend Adela Quested. It is never clear what Forster thinks of these last two: Adela Quested is brave but a prig; Mrs Moore, apparently a kind and gentle old lady, becomes bad-tempered and indifferent to the sufferings of Adela and her son after her experience in the Marabar caves. 'She seemed to say: "Am I to be bothered for ever?" Her Christian tenderness had gone, or had developed into a hardness, a just irritation against the human race.'

Forster also hints at the old accusation that British women were responsible for the gulf between the races. Adela and Mrs Moore are not memsahibs, but, for all their good intentions, they bring grief to Indians and almost destroy the friendship between Fielding and the young Muslim Dr Aziz. When the expedition to the Marabar caves begins to go wrong, Fielding thinks with hostility, 'I knew these women would make trouble.' Later, after the disaster of Aziz's arrest and abortive trial on the charge of attempting to rape Adela Quested, Fielding tells her that her whole endeavour to see 'the real India' was doomed: 'The first time I saw you, you were wanting to see India, not Indians, and it occurred to me: Ah, that won't take us far. Indians know whether they are liked or not – they cannot be fooled here.'

When it was first published *A Passage to India* infuriated the British in India. Not only did Forster introduce the unthinkable, but he made it clear that he did not think it important in itself. He deliberately left unanswered the question of what actually happened to Adela Quested in the Marabar caves; as he explained in a letter written to William Plomer in 1934, 'I tried to show that India is an unexplainable muddle by introducing an unexplained muddle.' What difference did it make if something – or nothing – had taken place? To the exiles in their Clubs it did matter. While they made much of Forster's errors (he slipped up in his description of legal procedures, for example), the one thing they did not dispute was the way in which the community closed ranks to protect its women. But what was to them a matter of pride was to Forster yet another count against them. He mocked their noblest sentiments; his fictional memsahibs and sahibs had never liked or accepted Adela Quested, yet they found it convenient to use her alleged assault as a symbol of the martyrdom of all white women in India.

Indians had long complained that they were reduced to stereotypes in British writing about India; now Forster gave his compatriots the same treatment. The men he portrays are pompous bullies, the women desiccated shrews. E. A. Home, who had served in the Indian Educational Service, expressed the reaction of his more moderate fellows in a long letter that was published in the *New Statesman* on 16 August 1924. He praised Forster's depiction of his Indian characters, but of the British in India, he asked in bewilderment: 'Where have they come from? What planet do they inhabit?' As for the memsahibs, Home could only say, 'I think they are scarcely worth discussing, so inhuman are they without exception.'

Paul Scott knew India when the Raj was dying, and was never part of it himself. He was there, intermittently, with the British Army between 1943 and 1946. Perhaps because their time was running out, Scott found the British in India fascinating. His four novels known as *The Raj Quartet* – *The Jewel in the Crown*, *The Day of the Scorpion*, *The Towers of Silence* and *A Division of the Spoils* – started appearing twenty years after he had left India, but are set in the 1940s. They resemble *A Passage to India* in using assaults on Englishwomen as central incidents. Edwina Crane, an elderly missionary, is threatened with rape by a band of drunken hooligans, who finally content themselves with beating her up and killing her Indian colleague. Daphne Manners, the niece of a governor, is actually raped. Scott handled the second incident, in particular, in a way that would have been inconceivable in a novel written at the time by a member of the Raj. Before she is raped by a gang of Indians, Daphne Manners has been making love with a young Indian. When Hari Kumar, her lover, and other young men are wrongly arrested for the crime, she does her best to provide evidence that will prove them innocent. Finally, and this could never have happened in one of the novels written by, say, Maud Diver or Ethel Savi, the British authorities themselves are shown as unjust, dilatory, or, in the case of the sinister policeman Ronald Merrick, plainly dishonest.

There is an echo, too, of *A Passage to India* in Scott's description of the reaction of the British community. The commander of the local infantry brigade congratulates Merrick on his prompt arrests: 'once the story got round that an English girl had been outraged there wasn't a white man or woman in the country who wouldn't rejoice that the suspects were already apprehended.' And when Daphne Manners refuses to testify, the community turn on her much as Forster's sahibs and memsahibs did on Adela Quested when she changed her testimony about what had happened to her in the Marabar caves.

In *The Raj Quartet*, however, there are British characters who remain aloof from the community reaction. Daphne's aunt, Lady Manners, for all that she is part of the establishment, stands by her when she decides to have the child which may be Hari's or that of one of the anonymous Indians who raped her. Sarah Layton, the colonel's daughter, never meets Daphne but she is attracted by what she learns about her. Sarah herself forms a close friendship with a young Indian, which might, but does not, develop into a romance.

By the time Scott wrote his four novels, there was no Raj left, no sahibs and memsahibs to send furious letters of protest from their Clubs. Some old India hands said privately that he had got them wrong, that it had not been like that at all in India, but who cared to listen to them? The Raj had been an embarrassing joke in post-war Britain; by the 1960s it was about to become an object of amused nostalgia. And, as had happened with *A Passage to India*, even those who did not like aspects of the writing did not deny that the British community in India would have reacted with fury and alarm to attacks on their women.

It would be wrong to leave the impression that the British in India passed their days in a state of constant anxiety or indignation. Ethel Savi was never frightened in the twelve years of living in the wilds of Bihar. 'The confidence the natives had in Johnnie, and their genuine respect and affection made it a matter of honour that, in his absence from home, we, his wife and his children, should be as safe in that isolated spot, surrounded as we were by hosts of Indians, as in an English village.' The Raj was, as George Orwell once said, a giant confidence trick, but the British in India themselves fell for it most of the time.

7

COURTSHIP AND MARRIAGE

The British in India found talk of sacred bonds and indissoluble unions extravagant. Marriage was necessary, even if it was not made in heaven; it was useful to a man and, practically, the only career for a woman. Just as the same Anglo-Indian families over the generations sent their young men to work in India, they raised their daughters to become memsahibs. Like generations of women in her family before her Iris Macfarlane felt she had little choice but to obey her mother and return from Britain to India to find a husband. Looking back at her great-grandmother, who had a reputation for being very difficult, Iris was forgiving: 'She was trapped like all the women of her time, and sprung the same traps for her daughters, who in turn arranged cages around theirs. This, her great-granddaughter, was the last to beat her head against the bars.'

Bringing out wives from their own country was a sign, too, that the British were serious about India. By the 1850s, the government of India was actively discouraging its officials from marrying native women. The only men who still took Indian mistresses were the planters, and it was understood that when they did take proper, European wives, they would pension off the other woman. The subject was known about but not usually discussed – 'too indelicate a matter', according to one planter's wife. One young bride, fresh from Home, killed herself when she discovered her husband's past. Another left as soon as she discovered that her new husband had six children by a local woman.

Girls, whether they were brought up in India or at Home, were given an education intended to equip them with the accomplishments that would make them desirable on the marriage market. Ethel Savi, who grew up in Calcutta just after the Mutiny, recalled that 'a girl had to play the piano or be considered quite ineligible for matrimony and a social life'. In the twentieth century, sports like golf and tennis supplanted the piano. Ethel Savi's own daughter, Dora, was much sought after because 'she rode well, entered for all the ladies' events, played a good game of tennis, and was a useful fourth at bridge'. Sewing was an asset, as was a suitable hobby, such as sketching. Girls born in India also learnt how to run a household by helping their mothers give out stores and supervise the servants. What was not wanted was an over-educated woman. When, in the 1920s, Jon and Rumer Godden's aunt suggested that they might study algebra, geometry and Latin, their father's reaction was swift: 'Nonsense ... Girls don't need to learn such things.' Iris Macfarlane was sent to seven different schools in England for no apparent reason other than her mother's whims. When a headmistress at one suggested that Iris could get a scholarship to Oxford her mother did not entertain the idea for a moment.

The result of such limited educations, wrote one disenchanted observer, was a girl whose ambition 'is now to be a skilful lawn-tennis player, a good dancer, a brilliant fabricator of chaff – chaff being the staple commodity of Indian conversation'. Victor Jacquemont, a critical young Frenchman who toured India in the 1830s, prayed 'God preserve me from ever having an English wife!'

Equally important was what girls did not, indeed must not, learn about and that was anything to do with sex. Perhaps that was why most British parents in India had such a strong prejudice against their daughters' studying Indian languages; who knew what undesirable knowledge the girls might also pick up? Innocence, as the British described it, was much prized, to a later date than it was at Home. Ethel Savi's mother, who married at the age of fifteen in 1855, had been carefully brought up 'pure and unsullied'. The grateful groom sent his mother-in-law a warm letter of thanks, 'assuring her of his immense reverence for his bride's child-like innocence'.

A girl's reputation for chastity was vital and must be defended. In the 1880s, the highest levels of the government of India became involved in a lovers' tiff in Fategarh in the United Provinces. Surgeon-Major Reid had become disillusioned with a Miss Tytler and had sent her an angry and hurt letter in which he accused her, among other things, of being the cast-off mistress of a junior officer. 'You have cured me', he wrote bitterly, 'and saved me from anyone being able to say that I had married a sub's old slippers.' He went on to describe her as 'one that had thrown herself at the head of everyone in turn with effect'. His final example of her depravity was that 'losing her colour [she] rouged herself up to the eyes for a lawn tennis party'. The unfortunate Miss Tytler made plans to go to the hill station of Naini Tal to escape the summer heat and, no doubt,

Surgeon-Major Reid as well. He threatened to follow her: 'I will be able to enjoy tit bits of scandal, of which I expect there will be lots.' She tried to reason with him; in response he promised to send her another rude letter, this time written on postcards. By this stage of the affair, the young lady's brother, seriously alarmed about his sister's reputation, appealed to Reid's superior officer, Surgeon-General Sir A. Christison. An unofficial warning to stay away from Naini Tal was sent to Reid. It provoked yet another of his furious letters. He told Christison that his intervention was 'the tactics of a Jew'. The resulting reprimand for insubordination had no effect at all; indeed he accused his superior of being 'spoony on the girl'.

A comic enough little melodrama, but the important point is how seriously the authorities took the threat to an unmarried girl's name. The Commander-in-Chief of the Indian Army recommended that Reid be compulsorily retired. His recommendation was finally overruled by the Secretary of State for India in London, who pointed out, reasonably enough it seems today, that the private correspondence and conduct of the officer had nothing to do with the performance of his duties.

Accomplished yet innocent, educated but not over-educated, the young girls were ready to meet their husbands. In many cases, the courtship took place at Home before the bride-to-be had seen India at all. Others came out with the 'fishing fleet'; others still were courted and married without ever leaving India. Sometimes the couple never met at all until they were engaged; an exchange of letters and photographs was enough. While there were variations in style, courtships followed the same businesslike lines. The man needed a wife, the young woman a husband. Interested friends and relatives created opportunities for them to meet. India offered gymkhanas, balls, moonlight picnics. Until the First World War, unmarried girls were chaperoned but the rules in India were looser than at Home. At balls, for example, there were secluded spots – *kala juggas*, or 'dark places' – with massed flowers and ferns and sofas where a couple could sit out a dance. Courting in India sometimes had other features unknown at Home. One young couple who were living in a wild part of India were accompanied everywhere by a Gurkha bodyguard; when they begged him to leave them alone for a few minutes, he simply grinned and sat down firmly with his knitting.

Girls took a risk if they got engaged at Home before they had seen India. They shrugged off the warnings about the heat, the insects, the diseases, the boredom of life in small stations. At a distance India was glamorous: the rajahs in jewelled turbans, the elephants in harness trimmed with gold and silver, the spacious bungalows, all those servants. In 1856, Minnie Blane was only twenty when she met her handsome captain from the East India Company's army. They married on short acquaintance and went to India soon after. She rapidly became disillusioned both with her husband and with life in India. By 1860, having survived two difficult pregnancies and the Mutiny as well, she was writing sadly to her mother: 'Had I but a faint idea of Indian life with a penniless and helpless officer, nothing would have induced me to marry and come out here, and now we are without hope of getting home until we are old and worn out.'

Sometimes engagements took place years before the wedding. The men returned to India to establish themselves in their careers while their brides-to-be waited – and waited. Not surprisingly, there were couples who did not recognize each other when they finally met again. Or perhaps they found that the reality was not quite so attractive as the memory. One young man who had been living for a long time in the *mofussil* was so horrified by the latest in European fashions proudly worn by his unfortunate fiancée that he told her it was all off. 'He could not possibly marry a girl who made such a guy of herself.' A small man was suddenly confronted with a girl who had grown enormously stout in the years since he had last seen her: 'Good heavens! … am I expected to marry *all that*?' Sometimes the young man was told at the dockside that the engagement was over – usually because the girl had met another man on the voyage.

Most of the unattached girls who ventured out in the fishing fleet found that their trouble was repaid. The lucky or the cunning got themselves engaged before they landed. In 1922 Kathleen Wilkes was travelling to India to take up a post as a governess. She met a man and 'in a few days under a full moon on the Red Sea we became engaged, much to the delight and interest of many people on board ship.' Not everyone was delighted. 'In my cabin there was rather a senior lady who, rather looking down upon me as a governess, said, "Oh, I hear you've got engaged to young Griffiths. You've done well for yourself, haven't you. Don't you know? He's one of the heaven-born – the Indian Civil Service!"' (The ICS were often compared to Brahmins, the 'heaven-born' at the summit of the caste system.)

Boredom could be as all-enveloping as the heat, and as destructive
to the spirits. This couple in the Punjab have their cat and dog
for distraction, but for the moment, at least, not much else (16).

17

18

Wife and mother was the role assigned to the women of the Raj. Some married in India, like Esme Hamilton, whose wedding to Captain MacRae of the 45th Rattray's Sikhs took place at Dera Ismail Khan in 1914 (17).

The author's grandmother, Olwen Carey Evans, came to India in 1921 with her husband, who was physician to the Viceroy, Lord Reading (18); she remembered being bored and homesick at times.

Ayahs, or maids, looked after the children and were loved in return (see pp. 163–64). In the Impeys' Calcutta house *c.* 1782 (19) a boy runs to his *ayah* while a wet nurse tends his young sibling. (The bed is a reminder of the children's vulnerability – protected by curtains, a netting cage, and dishes of water under the feet to discourage climbing insects.) In the 1940s in Bihar, Deputy Commissioner W. G. Archer and his wife, Mildred, had only one *ayah*, Mariam (20), for their two children (see also Ill. 50).

19

20

While the children were small they were made much of in India. The author's mother (21), protected by a topi as she pushed her doll's pram in the 1920s, looked like a proper member of the Raj. Grooms held their ponies when they rode (the girls demurely side-saddle, 22). The playhouse of the Archer children c. 1945 (23) was made for them by their parents' chief *chuprassi* (see Ill. 33), a Santal tribesman, and took the form of a Santal house.

Older children are missing from almost all the pictures; both the boys on these pages were soon sent away to school. Photographs survived as reminders – here in the Residency at Srinagar in 1895 (24).

21

22

23

24

25

26

Shopping took many forms. In Calcutta in the 1820s you could go to Taylor's Emporium (25) for elegant china, pictures, and chandeliers and sconces – of that distinctive Anglo-Indian form, with chimneys to protect the flames from the draft of the *punkah* (see Ill. 26). Except for the scantily clad Bengalis, the scene might be in Regency England.

The box-wallah (26) brought his wares to your house (see p. 105). This scene sketched by Mrs Belnos *c.* 1830 would not have changed much by 1947.

27

28

LADIES' AND GENTLEMEN'S HELMETS.

Callers at the Army and Navy Stores in Calcutta a hundred years later (27) could choose hats that nodded to both fashion and the climate, and dresses whose loose shapes and thinner materials at last did the same. Outside the metropolises, what the box-wallah could not provide was selected from the Army and Navy's mail-order catalogues (28), here of 1935–36 (for the hats, see pp. 92–93).

29

30

The Mutiny of 1857 was still, fifty years later, 'a kind of phantom standing behind official chairs'. At Cawnpore (29) would-be rescuers found pathetic hats, shoes, books, and bloody handprints. (Young Lieutenant Crump, who made this sketch on the spot, was killed shortly after at the relief of Lucknow.) The women's and children's bodies had been thrown into a well. The memorial erected to mark the site became a place of pilgrimage; this photograph (30) was taken in 1899.

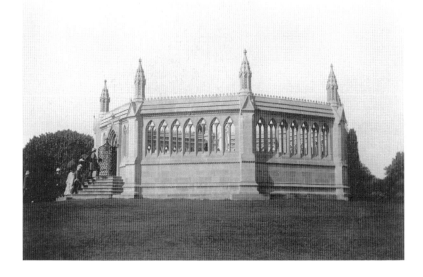

What was left of the fishing fleet sailed on to wreak havoc among the ranks of unmarried officials and officers, planters and businessmen. Cold weather in the Plains (preferably near a military cantonment), a hot season in a hill station: that was generally enough to get a girl married off. With such a surplus of unmarried men, she had to be very ugly or very difficult to please not to find a husband. In the eighteenth century, when few women had braved the long voyage to India, anxious bachelors scarcely waited for the formality of an introduction before proposing to eligible ladies. Sophia Goldborne, heroine of *Hartley House*, described to a friend in England the curious customs at church: '*all* ladies are approached by sanction of ancient custom, by *all* gentlemen indiscriminately, known or unknown, with offers of their hands to conduct them to their seat.' It was a delightful experience to be in such demand: 'the attention and court paid to me was astonishing; my smile was meaning and my articulation melody: in a word, mirrors are useless things in Calcutta, and self-adoration idle, for your looks are reflected in the pleasure of your beholder, and your claims to first rate distinction are confessed by all who approach you.'

Given such attention, it is not surprising that many of the girls became accomplished flirts. Sometimes they overdid it. The 'Spin' was the girl who went just a little bit too far. In Iltudus Prichard's *Chronicles of Budgepore*, about a fictional station in the late nineteenth century, the delightful Miss Sophy Wilkins turns its small society upside down as she works her way through the local bachelors in ascending order of importance. She first gets engaged to a young lieutenant, then to a more senior officer. She next turns to the 'civilians'; her third engagement is to a young assistant civilian (one of the lower appointments in the ICS) but he does not last long. Her final conquest is the Collector, a very powerful figure. The rejected suitors salvage at least their purses by selling the furnishings intended for their bride to the next lucky man: 'They used to say in Budgepore that it was quite a common thing to see the carts laden with the furniture going from house to house, indicating the direction in which Sophy's affections had been transferred.'

As long as the girl made a suitable marriage in the end, flirting was regarded with amused tolerance. One, even two, attachments to young but penniless men were allowable but she must not forget that the rest of her life depended on her making a good match. The young French traveller Captain Edouard de Warren in the mid-nineteenth century found the calculations involved sordid. He describes the fate of a young girl just arrived in India: 'Her aunt tells her, day and night, that she should not lower herself by dancing with anyone below a very senior civilian or a military officer holding a staff appointment and in a position to give her the three things considered in India to be the first essentials of conjugal felicity: a massive silver teapot, a palanquin and a set of bearers to use by day, and a carriage in which to drive in the evening. She is thus impelled by an outrageous ambition to refuse in the course of a few months some really eligible wooers of whom she would not have dreamt in England, while she dances till she is out of breath and her hair gets dishevelled in order to draw into her curls some old nabob with spindle legs, in whose mummy there is not a spark of heat, whose soul for the past twenty years has been concentrated on rupees.'

Yet girls had to be at least a bit calculating when they chose a husband. It was not pleasant to be shipped Home as a 'returned empty', in the rather curious phrase used. The *Lays of Ind*, a collection of comic verse popular in the nineteenth century, makes gentle fun of the serious purpose that lay behind the flirtation. 'Arabella Green or The Mercenary Spin' gives a young girl's creed:

I do believe in dress and ease,
And fashionable dash.
I do believe in bright rupees,
And truly worship cash.

I do believe in marriage quite,
But don't believe in gents,
Unless you bind them pretty tight
By way of settlements.

I do believe entirely in
The Civil Service ranks:
The best are worth a deal of tin,
And none exactly blanks.

This attitude was the same at all social levels. In fact, for poor women, marriage quite literally meant survival. Mrs King was amused to find that the wives of British soldiers who had gone off to the Second Afghan War in 1878 had got themselves engaged – sometimes three times over – just in case their husbands never came back. Hard-hearted perhaps, but there were no widows' pensions in those days.

Men usually asked only for women who were available and who would fit into their hearty world. A girl could, however, be too high-spirited: in Meerut in 1880, for example, an engagement was broken off when the girl appeared as Ariel over her fiancé's objections at a fancy dress ball. (The story ended more or less happily: she raffled off her wedding cake; it was won by her former lover; and all got together to eat it at a picnic.) Few men were as earnest as William Wilson Hunter of the ICS, who wrote in the 1860s to his intended that she must not, as many wives did, expect 'conversation or backgammon all the evening .... It is a dreadful fate – that of a woman who takes away her husband's chance of greatness.'

It was important, if not essential, that the future bride be of the 'right' class. In 1882, when the Church Missionary Society was worried about the increasingly eccentric behaviour of 'our brother at Aligarh' (who was preaching long and incomprehensible sermons), the solution was simple: he must marry 'one who is a thorough lady'. A common figure in the literature of British India is the raw young man who falls into the clutches of the wrong sort of woman – by the latter part of the nineteenth century that often meant someone with a suspicion of Indian blood. In Kipling's story 'Kidnapped' the victim is 'the estimable, virtuous, economical, quiet, hard-working, young Peythroppe'. He falls in love with Miss Castries: 'She was good and very lovely – possessed of what innocent people at Home call a "Spanish" complexion, with thick blue-black hair growing low down on the forehead, into a "widow's peak," and big violet eyes under eyebrows as black and as straight as the borders of a *Gazette Extraordinary* when a big man dies.' She was, alas, 'impossible' – 'The little opal-tinted onyx at the base of her finger-nails said this as plainly as print.' (Although this was a myth, young men surreptitiously went on inspecting the fingernails of girls of doubtful ancestry.) Peythroppe's friends save him by kidnapping him until the wedding date has passed. Poor Miss Castries takes the blow quietly:

'She said that, if she was not a lady, she was refined enough to know that ladies kept their broken hearts to themselves.' As so often with Kipling's stories, the message is ambiguous. Was British society right to break the hearts of young people? On the other hand, is it right or even safe to ignore convention?

Courtships tended to be brisk affairs. Mrs Helen Mackenzie, in India just before the Mutiny, wrote of one couple's romance, 'It is quite à l'Indienne for they only met three times before they engaged themselves.' The men could not take a chance, given the imbalance of the sexes, of waiting too long. (They had already waited until they were well established in their careers – with the result that husbands in India were often a good deal older than their wives.) If they went hunting wives at Home, as many did, they had the deadline of their return passage. Since leaves long enough to go Home only came every five or six years, they had to use their time efficiently. Military men, it was said, worked with particular precision. If they were making no progress with a girl after one or, at the most, two weeks, they cut their losses and moved on. Up to the middle of the nineteenth century, some men opted for arranged marriages (just the sort of thing that was said to be an indication of the Indians' backward state). The Kidderpore Orphanage in Calcutta – mainly for the daughters of British officers and Indian mothers – held monthly balls until well into the nineteenth century where bachelors from the *mofussil* could find wives. At a similar institution in Byculla, in Bombay City, it was one of the responsibilities of the headmistress to marry off her charges. A bachelor applied to her and, after she had vetted him, a suitable girl was chosen to have tea with him. The proposal was expected the day after the tea party and the orphan, unless she was very strong-minded, did not refuse. When all was settled, the school provided a trousseau. The practice died out as communications between India and Europe improved and prejudice grew against the Domiciled Europeans and the Eurasians.

The proposal of marriage was equally brisk and unsentimental. Sahibs were supposed to be strong and silent. Julia Curtis, who had come out in the 1890s to visit her brother, a planter in the south, had no idea that she was being courted by one of his neighbours. While it was true that her future husband called at the bungalow frequently, he spent all his time talking to her brother about tea planting and sport. It was only when he built himself a new bungalow and told the unsuspecting Julia that it was waiting for a mistress that she suddenly realized his intentions.

Some men were a little more romantic. General Sir Ian Hamilton, who started his career in the Indian Army in the 1870s, was proud of having outsmarted both his superior officer – who did not want him married – and other more eligible suitors to win his bride. 'The immortal hour struck' for him in Simla, 'during a cotillion at a Viceregal Lodge Ball, whereat, in one of the figures, the men had to jump through paper hoops and choose their ladies out of the group who stood at the far end of the room. My hoop was of pink paper and suddenly something quite unpremeditated – my good genius it must have been – spurred me on to take a real flying leap and catch Jean. The band was playing a Mazurka, I shot through the hoop like an arrow and the next second Jean and I were gallivanting in the Mazurka. Being the first couple to pass the Viceregal platform we were given a round of applause and our destiny was writ upon the stars.'

When it came to the wedding, few were unconventional enough to get married, as Henry and Annette Beveridge did in the 1870s, in a Registry Office by a native official. 'We are in a Bengali country', Henry argued, 'and must try to school ourselves into seeing Bengalis in office and yielding to them the submission due to their office.' Most couples got married in a church as a matter of course. Everything was done to make the wedding as much like one at Home as possible. Family and friends rallied around to help with the church and the wedding breakfast. Only a year after the Mutiny, Minnie Blane was writing proudly to her mother about her role in Miss Charlotte Smith's wedding: 'I went up and helped her and her sister with things, and decorated the Cake Favour Baskets and the table. In fact I flatter myself that everything would have been vile without me!'

For the more elaborate weddings, invitations, in silver or perhaps white with a silver border, were sent out months before. The champagne was ordered from France, oysters from Bombay, tinned *pâté de foie gras* from a branch of the Army and Navy Stores. The bride wore clouds of white tulle, and a veil with a circlet of myrtle or orange blossom. If her family could afford it, the dress came from Home or from one of the big shops in Calcutta or Bombay; otherwise the invaluable *durzi* came up with something. There would be a white cake on a stand and a display of the presents – photograph albums, vases, clocks, cruets, silver salvers – with which the young couple were going to start their housekeeping.

Honeymoons were often as brief as the courtship. If the couple had been married at Home, they were at least able to enjoy the long voyage out together. In India, they usually went to a hill station if the husband had time. (Ian Hamilton broke with convention by taking his mother-in-law along on his honeymoon; she had come out from England to see her daughter married and it seemed a pity that the two women should not have some time together.) Some stations also had 'honeymoon bungalows' for those couples who did not have the time or the money to go away.

In many cases, husbands had to hurry back to their jobs soon after the wedding and wives found themselves trying to make sense of the role of wife of the District Commissioner, perhaps, or colonel's lady, sometimes in a remote part of India, miles from their fellow Europeans. In 1914 the newly-wed Rosamund Lawrence received an elaborate welcome in Belgaum, her husband's district some 300 miles (500 km) south of Bombay. When their train pulled into the station, 'the platform itself was packed with representatives of the Indian gentry who had come in from many miles around'. She never forgot the moment: 'the crowds, the dark faces, the turbans pink, green, white, gold and deep rose, the sunshine, the dust, the heat – and now the door was open, and what I after learned to be pattawallas in stiff white, with scarlet belts and turbans, were salaaming deeply to Henry and myself as we climbed down onto a red carpet.' As the band played, the Lawrences were festooned with garlands of roses and Rosamund Lawrence shook hands with everyone in sight, including, to local amusement and perhaps slight consternation, the servants.

Though Ethel Savi had grown up in India, her Calcutta girlhood had not prepared her for the reception she got at her planter husband's estate. The household was waiting for them as they reached the river landing: 'The entire area from the water's edge to the front verandah was fluttering with pennants in various hues, and red bunting carpeted the clay of the bank in a strip for my honourable feet to tread. "WELCUM" was painted on a sheet of foolscap by one of the servants.'

Not only were their surroundings often strange and far from home and family, but the brides also found themselves with a husband they barely knew and whose sexual demands could be frightening. Many, like their contemporaries at Home, had only the sketchiest idea of the physical side of marriage. Margaret Smith was a naive nineteen-year-old when she married a tea planter from Assam before the First World War. She was appalled at her first encounter with sex: 'It is for *this* that girls are given wedding presents and congratulations, actually congratulations!' Her husband made matters worse by telling her that other women submitted willingly to their husbands' demands: 'Apparently, this thing, which I loathed and dreaded, was appreciated by some women, and necessary to all men.' Flora Annie Steel was more resilient. Although she had an 'inborn dislike to the sensual side of life', she was carried through her honeymoon by sheer curiosity: 'I simply stared.' Monica Lang had a happier experience. She had approached her wedding night in terror thanks to lurid tales from a housemaid, but the next morning she awoke to 'the glorious realization that I was in India, I was married, I was deliriously happy, and I had come to the conclusion that poor Emily, after all, must have been completely out of her mind'.

Adjusting could be far from easy. Margaret Smith on a particularly remote tea garden had no one to advise her, and in her misery she suggested to her husband that she help pay for a mistress for him. Another man, perhaps, might have reacted with understanding, but her husband was furious. The marriage never really went well from that point. She had no one to talk to except her husband, nowhere to go but the end of the drive in front of her bungalow: 'Except for the buzzing of mosquitoes, the sound of native tom toms in an adjoining village, or my husband's voice, talking Hindustani, the silence, as I retraced my steps to the hot verandah, was like that which a prisoner must feel immured in solitary confinement.'

Women longed for simple things they had always taken for granted – a visit to the shops, a chat with friends, the sound of a doorbell ringing. Some could not endure the loneliness: they had hysterics (like the bride in Assam who took to her bed and wept for days on end), threatened to kill themselves, or, occasionally, simply gave up and went Home.

Almost invariably there was also trouble with servants, who were used to the carefree ways of a bachelor. When Julia Curtis first arrived in her new bungalow all the servants promptly gave notice. Husbands who might have made the adjustment easier were busy with their work.

Fortunately, or not, there were usually older women in the neighbourhood to dispense advice, even on the most intimate details of married life. As she struggled to cope, the bride was urged to take her new responsibilities seriously. One of the first of these was to provide a place for her empire-builder to rest and refresh himself. As Rosamund Lawrence saw herself, 'It is important that I should keep Henry well, and able to carry on his exacting work, that I should be there as a buffer between him and annoyance, exude oil when things go wrong.'

Did wives ever get tired of the part of selfless helpmate? It cannot always have been its own reward to tend the daily needs of their husbands and children. Some women resented the work that kept their husbands from their sides. Even the most loyal and industrious occasionally showed a rebellious twinge. Anne Wilson, whose husband was an important official in the Punjab, poked gentle fun at the endless files that he and his colleagues found so important. It reminded her, she said, 'of a man I once met, who was so accustomed to writing historical leaders for a well-known newspaper, that if you made a trivial remark about the last outrage in Ireland, he instantly harked back to the death of Abel, and traced outrages through every successive century, till he reached the occasion of Pat hitting his landlord on the head and announced his opinion of how he should deal with the fact!' She added with mock contrition that it was 'dreadfully disrespectful and preposterous of me to presume to criticise a civilian's handling of files'.

A difficulty that most faced was that, especially on the smaller stations, there was little else for them to do. (Flora Annie Steel held that fact responsible for half the matrimonial troubles in India.) At Home, said a correspondent of *The Pioneer* in 1881, there were all sorts of opportunities for women to be useful: 'ambulance classes, hearing lectures, visiting the hospital with flowers and other helpful contributions to the great campaign always in progress against the want, and disease, and aridity of the everyday life of the many.' Why, he demanded (more in sorrow than in anger), 'should the bright, noble girl of India be debarred from all these good things and sink into a selfish, gossip-stuffed creature?'

Sometimes it was the husbands themselves who discouraged their wives from making themselves useful. Susan Daly, who was with her officer husband in 1855 in what was then the small station of Karachi, complained to her mother: 'This place is very dull in spite of an endless round of gaiety, never satisfying, though one enters into it I scarcely know why. Life passes in a profitless kind of way and I see no way of improving it. I did think together with Mrs Dansey and one or two other ladies of entering into some plan of visiting among the soldiers' wives and children and trying to improve them, but our husbands strongly objected to this, there is no actual want among them, but a great deal of immorality and bad conduct I fear. Henry says I should do no good, and he does not like me to go amongst them, saying "the respectable ones are all well off and want no assistance, and you will not benefit the others and may expose yourself to much that is unpleasant". I am not sure whether this is right, but we shall probably so soon leave, that I could not hope to do much good.' The Mutiny, which was shortly to come, reinforced the reluctance of the British to do anything that might look like interference with Indian customs and so set off another wave of rebellions.

The other memsahibs, too, were generally suspicious of earnest-ness. When Iris Portal went to do volunteer work at a Salvation Army hospital, the reaction of her friends was to ask when she was going to start banging her tambourine. She also discovered that the strict rules of hierarchy in British society in India meant that younger women dared not initiate any charitable projects: 'If one happened to be beneath the sway of a burra memsahib who was not interested in social service, there was nothing one could do about it!' Only the wives of army officers had an approved outlet, in the shape of the families of the ordinary soldiers, for whatever charitable instincts they might have possessed. Even then, in the case of wives in Indian regiments, they were restricted by a nervous government as to what they could do. They were forbidden to give information about birth control to Indian women unless they had the husbands' permission.

While there was probably no greater proportion of ill-assorted couples among the expatriates, the strains on a marriage were greater than they might have been at Home. British families in India were expected to mirror the virtues of the Raj and a wife was expected to stand loyally by her husband and whatever institution he worked for. The newly married Iris Macfarlane did her best to be a good wife of the regiment. She sat through boring mess dinners listening to the colonel repeat his stories. Pregnant with her first child she sat through a hot afternoon as the troops sacrificed goats and bullocks as part of a festival. When she felt overcome with nausea and tried to leave, the colonel waved her back. The next day his wife, the *burra memsahib*, called to reprimand her.

At Home at least, the family and friends could act as a buffer or as a solace. In India, the frequent moves and the distances made it difficult to cultivate strong ties of friendship. Ethel Savi, shortly after her own wedding, made the acquaintance of an unhappy woman, wife of the manager of a nearby estate, who was childless and virtually friendless. Her husband was repeatedly unfaithful. The wretched woman could not get evidence for a divorce on the grounds of adultery or desertion or physical cruelty. (In the last case, she would have had to provide two impartial European witnesses.) When a young and handsome bachelor was sent as the local magistrate, it was almost inevitable that she should fall in love with him. He apparently reciprocated, but with more common sense than romance applied for a transfer out of the district. She continued to endure life with her husband, but some years later Ethel Savi learnt that she had killed herself after another affair had ended unhappily.

Yet another burden was imposed by the practice of sending children Home to be educated. Wives had to choose between staying with their husbands and accompanying their children. Husbands were sometimes left alone for several years at a time. Some men found consolation with other women, but most filled up the days alone with work, sport and the Club; they were bachelors again without a bachelor's freedom from responsibilities. They toiled away, sending pathetic letters Home to remind their families that they still existed. As an observer at the beginning of the twentieth century put it, 'An Englishman's life in India has been described as that of a man who worked hard to maintain a wife and children who he seldom sees.' Many marriages were never the same after these long separations. The wife got used to being self-reliant and independent in England; when she did rejoin her husband, they found it difficult to re-establish the former intimacy.

Money was also a frequent source of trouble in a marriage. In spite of the common impression, not all the British in India lived in princely opulence. Few had private means, and salaries, even in the ICS, were stretched thin to cover expenses like schools for the children at Home and the fares back and forth. In addition, those in government service were expected to entertain at a certain standard. Champagne was the only acceptable drink at dinner parties, even for junior officers. Rosamund Lawrence was one of a number of strong-minded ladies who tried to set a good example by not serving it at their tables; none of them had the slightest effect on the community. Non-officials, too, entertained lavishly. The planter in particular, as the humorist George Aberigh-Mackay wrote in the 1880s, 'lives in a grand wholesale manner; he lives in round numbers, he lives like a hero'. And it was easy, as the inexperienced found to their cost, to run up enormous bills without noticing, because merchants in India gave credit freely.

Minnie Blane's marriage probably would have gone sour even with lots of money available, but a habitual shortage of cash and the appearance of one baby after another made her life a misery. Her letters to her mother are filled with financial worries. A year after her wedding, when she was recovering from the birth of her first child during the Mutiny, she found a letter from a creditor which showed that her husband had considerable debts from the period before his marriage. 'In fact on top of the mutiny and its horrors, it is almost the last straw that could break me.' Minnie struggled to cope with the loss of most of their possessions, but 'now all our movements are all unsettled, and everything is so expensive. Even our food is rising, and I am sometimes quite done for and have a good cry, which sometimes does one good.' Her husband was no help at all: 'He has for so many years been accustomed to his Mess, and to spend *double* what he has, that I really wish I had never been married.' In April 1860 she sent a particularly sad letter to her mother to explain that, yet again, their debts had forced them to postpone a trip Home. 'Yes, Mamma,' she wrote, 'as you say I am much changed, and feel sometimes that it would be a relief to die and so have no more troubles.' (She was only twenty-five at the time.) Later still, she wrote: 'Bills flood in, he has not the money to pay, the trades people are abused, and it all ends up in the Civil Courts. We can hardly keep a servant, and there is constant bickering and fighting in our home.' Only the news of someone else's troubles distracts her briefly from her own: 'So Napoleon has had an attempt made to assassinate him! Those French are always up to something.'

Minnie eventually divorced her unsatisfactory husband (both married again and both returned to live happily in India); but that solution was not available to all unhappily married women.

Divorce had a certain stigma, particularly for the one who had been the 'guilty' party. (According to the law the injured party had to sue the other for divorce; adultery was the ground commonly given.) Men in government service were reluctant to be gentlemanly and let their wives sue them, in case their chances for promotion were jeopardized. On the other hand, for wives to accept the role of the guilty party meant that they were damaging their good name, often their only asset.

The further down the social scale one went, the less seriously either marriage or divorce was taken. That was especially true of the British soldiers serving in India. As only a minority were given permission to marry, many simply contracted various forms of liaison with local women, usually Domiciled European or Eurasian. The women, in their ignorance of British law, assumed that they were properly married, and the truth came out only when a regiment was called back Home. One officer, who was responsible for organizing the passage of wives and children just before the First World War, found the experience harrowing. He announced that the women should come to his office with marriage certificates and the registration record of their children's births so that he could draw up a proper list. 'The storm that burst around me was such as I never want to experience again.' He was besieged by frightened and angry women, their crying children with them. Very few had the proper documents: 'The most extraordinary pieces of paper were placed before me which quickly showed up the whole tragic affair. For every genuine legal document there were a dozen which were just scraps of paper of no value whatsoever.' The soldiers, ever resourceful, had made their own documents, 'on coloured or printed paper such as beer-bottle labels or labels from tinned food.' (It is said that the colonel of one regiment avoided such scenes simply by locking up the locally acquired wives and children in a big shed until the ship had sailed.)

The soldiers themselves regarded such 'marriages' as temporary. Indeed, even when they were legally married, they sometimes tried to use their posting back to Britain to cut distasteful ties in India. The unfortunate Mrs Hooper in Lahore got a letter in 1921 from Private Hooper of the 5th Devons to tell her that he loved another woman. His wife could follow him to Britain but, as he assured her, 'misery would be our outlook, wouldn't it? ... I hope', he added heartlessly, 'this will find the children and yourself in the best of health for I am in the Pink at present.'

In the majority of cases, couples learnt to cope with each other. The husbands expected to be obeyed; the women learnt how to get their own way. Some women indeed became a tremendous help to their husbands; they went on tour with them, learnt about their work, and wrote up their notes for them. Mrs Mackenzie argued that life in India in fact produced some exceptionally happy couples: 'they become knit much more closely than when each has a thousand distractions, and separate ways of spending the day.'

Certain spectacularly successful marriages, like that of Henry and Honoria Lawrence, were held up to successive generations as shining examples. He was one of the great administrators of the nineteenth century; she was fascinated by India, fascinated by his work. She followed him from one difficult post to another with scarcely a murmur. When she died in childbirth after seventeen years of happy marriage, he seemed to his family to be simply waiting to join her. Three years later, in 1857, he got his wish in the Residency at Lucknow.

Yet there were the repeated rumours about the sahibs' mores; while that had not bothered the free spirits of the eighteenth century, it did bother their descendants. It is impossible to determine how much truth there is in the accusation that the British in India committed adultery with scarcely a second thought. Certainly conventions, at least for married women, were looser than in middle-class circles in Britain. Husbands and wives often spent long periods of time apart from each other and they were not expected to live monastic lives. Flirting was a normal part of life in India; strings of young admirers collected around married women (in spite of the grumblings of older men about 'poodle-faking'). How far did they go?

In 1882, The Pioneer devoted a long and serious article to the question. Yes, it said, society was more open in India and men and women were thrown together more often than in Britain. Flirtation, as a consequence, had become 'a game admirably adapted to Indian habits.' Generally the game was a harmless one, but 'of course occasions will occur where the woman is a fool and the man a knave, and evil results ensue'. And it is striking in the records of the Punjab High Court, for example, how often adultery took place in small stations or in closely knit communities such as colonies of railway workers or soldiers. (One regiment notorious for its enthusiastic adultery was popularly known as the 'Fornicating Fifth'.) Hill stations, too, offered plenty of temptations. Even in the nineteenth century, Ethel Savi recalled, 'women were ready to make merry in the mountains while their husbands toiled on the plains'. There were unattached men and plenty of opportunities for lonely wives to meet them. Maud Diver, writing in the twentieth century, said severely that the great dangers were 'amateur theatricals and military men on leave. It is hardly too much to say that one or other of these dominant factors in Hill station life is accountable for half the domestic tragedies of India.' And Frank Richards, who served as an ordinary soldier in India before the First World War, felt that it was almost impossible for the young and pretty wife of a soldier to remain faithful to her husband if she were sent to the Hills on her own. The NCOs stationed there would invite her to all sorts of parties and 'she would have to be very level-headed and virtuous to resist all the temptations that came her way.'

Hints of scandal were plentiful. Malicious tongues gave cruel nicknames to pretty and indiscreet women – the Treacle Tart or Betty-Bed-and-Breakfast. There was said to be a hotel in Simla – or was it in Naini Tal? or Darjeeling? – where the manager rang a bell early in the morning to warn his guests to get back to their own beds. The reported remark of a Calcutta prostitute was passed on with great relish by old soldiers like Sir Bindon Blood: when asked why she and her colleagues did not go to Simla, she replied, 'We should have no chance with the amateurs.' The British themselves blamed some of the rumours on their way of life. It was easy to be discreet at Home, but in India they lived openly, surrounded by servants who noticed their every move. One lady said, rather proudly, 'at least it is open and above-board. You see and know the worst.' The experienced said that the only way in India to keep adultery a secret was to commit it on the night mail train. In any case, according to the code, affairs did not hurt the authority of the Raj in the way that taking a bribe from an Indian would have done.

8

CHILDREN: OUTPOSTS
OF EMPIRE

Minnie Blane's sister-in-law, who also lived in India, had thirteen children in fifteen years. She was only doing – a little excessively perhaps – what was expected of British women everywhere. The assumption that women existed to marry and bear children was so widely held that it was hardly ever discussed at all. Wives of childless marriages were unfortunate; the rare women who preferred a career to marriage were regarded as so exceptional that they scarcely counted as women at all. 'Affectionate wife', 'tender mother' – those were the qualities thought worth commemorating on women's tombstones.

Children were a sign that the British were established in India, that the community was 'sound'. And the presence of white children showed that British men had firmly abjured the bad old practice of keeping Indian mistresses. The consciousness of the British that they were the ruling caste, that the Raj was going to endure, was somehow demonstrated by the fact that they were propagating themselves. Evelyn Bell, who lived with her husband in Poona in the early part of the twentieth century, called British children 'outposts of Empire'. They had to be protected and they had to be trained to shoulder their share of the burden of the Raj.

It was no easy matter bearing and raising children in India. In the years before modern medicine had started to deal with the diseases that were endemic there, mothers faced an unending struggle to keep their children alive. A tombstone in the cemetery at Benares shows that a couple known only as John and Elizabeth lost six children in infancy between 1834 and 1842. Sometimes the stones carry sad little verses, like the one to Sarah, who died, together with her infant, in the hot weather of 1820:

Just fifteen years she was a maid
And scarce eleven months a wife

Four days and nights in labour laid
Brought forth and then gave up her life.

Partly because children were so vulnerable, women bore a great many. In any case, until the twentieth century, there was not much they could do in the way of contraception. Often they did not even know what was available (male doctors were reluctant to tell them). Margaret Smith, who had four difficult pregnancies in rapid succession, experienced a feeling of 'almost incredulous joy and relief' when she finally found out that birth control existed. The more usual alternative for women who did not want to produce one child after another was to try to bring on a miscarriage. Hot gin and quinine, violent exercise, and crawling upstairs backwards were all said to work. Veronica Bamfield, who spent much of her life in India in the twentieth century, first as the daughter of an army officer and then as the wife of one, knew of a woman who had gone to the Indian bazaars six times for abortions.

Pregnant women received lots of advice, some clearly local, such as the injunction that they should stay away from hot, spicy dishes which might harm the unborn child. (It was also the custom to stop the *punkah* at the moment of birth, no matter how hot it was, presumably to protect the infant from drafts.) Expectant mothers should be especially careful of themselves in India, said one authority; they could take moderate exercise but must avoid the excitements of riding, dancing, lawn tennis or badminton. *Birch's Management and Medical Treatment of Children in India* also urged them to remain 'placid and equable in temper, happy and good-natured' as they waited for the child to arrive. They must live quietly but in bright and cheerful surroundings. 'The dismal in thought and action must at all times be banned.'

Childbirth itself was bound to be a frightening experience for these women, not least because it was difficult to obtain proper medical care. Women in the bigger cities had access to doctors, nurses and hospitals, but those in the smaller stations had to take whatever was available, and that usually meant military doctors. Until the end of the nineteenth century those doctors had the reputation, in part deserved, of being drunken sawbones. Nor were they sympathetic to the women's sufferings: even after the use of chloroform was accepted in Europe, doctors in India continued to think it an unnecessary luxury.

(Nurses were not necessarily any kinder; when Monica Lang begged for something to deaden the pain, she was told, 'you got yourself into this and you have to get yourself out of it.')

Indian midwives were used as a last resort, but European ones had little or no formal training either. Often they were simply the wives of ordinary British soldiers stationed in India who wanted to make a bit of money. Their quality was as variable as that of the doctors. When Minnie Blane was expecting her first child, she wrote reassuringly to her mother in England that she had at last found a good midwife: 'Our great comfort is that she drinks neither wine, beer nor spirits of any kind. So many of these women do so to excess.' On 1 March 1857, she still sounds quite cheerful: she is seven months pregnant and busy moving into her new house in the military station of Jhelum. In her next letters, she is having problems with her Indian servants and the weather is becoming oppressively hot. She has met the station doctor but does not much like him: 'the sort of man who takes no interest whatsoever in his patients'. When her child, a son, arrives in the middle of May, the doctor's behaviour justifies her apprehensions: 'He is so rough in his treatment, indeed he hurt me much more in "taking pains" than in all my labour.'

Poor Minnie Blane; she did not have time to recover before the Indian Mutiny broke out. In June, for safety, she was sent off to Rawalpindi, some 75 miles (120 km) away. The journey, in 120°F (49°C) heat, turned out to be futile; after three days in Rawalpindi, she was summoned back to Jhelum, the European officers in command of the native troops having decided that they were loyal after all. Their faith was misplaced, and on 7 July the Mutiny broke out in Jhelum. Minnie and her son barely escaped with their lives.

The injuries she had suffered giving birth did not have a chance to heal; indeed they became infected. At times, she was not able to walk at all. In September 1857 she informed her mother, 'I have endured agony every day for months.' She was treated with caustic and finally operated on by a new, more competent doctor. At the birth of her second son, a year and a half after the first, she was again to suffer, this time with what she described as 'inward piles'. The treatment ranged from leeches to hot fomentations on her stomach, from enemas of opium to 'the Galvanic Battery'.

Bearing children was only one part of the obstacle course; keeping them alive was the next. It was considered desirable for mothers to nurse their own infants, but if they would or could not it was usually possible to hire an Indian woman as wet nurse. The guidebooks give advice on their selection, care and feeding. In *The Complete Indian Housekeeper and Cook*, Steel and Gardiner reminded their readers that the wet nurse 'should not be treated as if she were merely an animated bottle'. Some memsahibs discovered to their horror that their wet nurse might slowly starve her own child so that theirs could be kept alive.

Children could die with appalling suddenness. Steel and Gardiner offer a chilling list of what they describe as common ailments – abscesses, bites of wasps, of scorpions, of mad dogs and of snakes, colds, cholera, colic, dysentery, fever, indigestion, itch, piles, sunstroke. They might have added malaria, typhoid and smallpox for good measure. To make things worse, the methods of dealing with most of these diseases were not really understood until the end of the nineteenth century. In November 1857, Major-General T. W. Mercer's son, Franky, had a sore throat which did not at first seem serious. 'On the 30th November we observed a great difficulty in his breathing'; the doctor was summoned but did not come right away. 'The next morning', wrote the father in his diary, 'he came and to his infinite horror and surprise found the disease had taken another form. Laryngitis or inflammation of the throat had set in. Our dear child was in imminent danger. Every remedy was resorted to but alas! it was too late – in 36 hours we were bereft of our child – perhaps the most promising of our flock.' Harriet Tytler, who was later to be the only woman at the Siege of Delhi during the Mutiny, lost her second child in 1850 to lockjaw; the doctor confirmed his death with a 'Thank God I have no wife or children to bother me. Good night.'

Mothers took what measures they could to keep their children healthy. By the twentieth century, if they were conscientious, they made sure that all the water and milk was boiled. Indeed, they often sent their children off to parties with their own little jugs of milk. They wrapped tiny cholera belts around the children's stomachs. They poured castor oil down their throats since it was believed that the Indian climate caused an unhealthy sluggishness in the infant bowels. They put mosquito netting over them at night or, in the case of small children, little gauze-covered cages. All the authorities insisted that children be kept away from spicy Indian dishes. *Birch's Management* warned mothers that the heat in India created 'a morbid appetite for a class of food which may sooner or later prove injurious'.

Books written specifically for mothers in India urged the same attention as at Home to breaking bad habits. If children sucked their thumbs, one writer suggested that they should be broken of the habit by having a folded newspaper bandaged to their elbows so they could not bend their arms. If they wet their beds, the cure, according to *Birch's Management*, was to wake them regularly during the night and to tie a cotton reel or a cork around their waists so that they would not be able to lie on their backs in their sleep. And they must at all costs be prevented from masturbating, 'a dangerous habit', warned a guide written in the 1920s, 'which may affect the after life of the child'.

Almost all British mothers, even the poorer ones, had either nannies or *ayahs* to help look after their children. (The difference between the two servants was indicated by their dress: nannies, even Indian ones, wore European clothes, *ayahs* saris.) Well-to-do households often had one *ayah* per child as well as a man whose sole job was to wheel the infant sahib or memsahib about in its pram. Upper-class families sometimes imported European nannies and governesses, but they were expensive and apt to get homesick. And how did one treat them? They could not be expected to mix with the native servants – but, at least in the case of nannies, they could scarcely be on the same footing as their employers. Europeans born in India or Eurasians were cheaper, but they tended to be touchy about status. Besides, they spoke with that unfortunate 'chee-chee' accent which no British mother of any pretensions wanted her child to learn. Among *ayahs*, some memsahibs swore that hill girls were the best; others preferred Christian converts from Madras. From the children's point of view, *ayahs* were gentler than most nannies. In adulthood, men and women still kept the memory of a much-loved *ayah*, usually a small, plump woman with gleaming, oiled hair, dressed in a white sari, who had sung to them, comforted them, and told them wonderful Indian stories. Nancy Vernede, as a child in Lucknow, always went to sleep with reassuring noises of her *ayah*'s soft singing and the faint clash of her bangles outside the door.

There were potential dangers, of course, in leaving children to the care of Indian servants. According to *Birch's Management*, children could not possibly learn the necessary virtues of obedience, self-control and hard work from them. Stories also circulated about *ayahs* who wiped their charges' eyes on the edges of their saris and thus gave them ophthalmia; or those who gave children opium to keep them quiet; or who fondled the penises of little boys in their care. And Indians spoiled children; they cuddled them more than the parents thought necessary and picked up their toys after them. Lillian Ashby, who was brought up in Bihar, described her childhood, rather coyly, as the 'Land of Spoildom'. British children in India grew up accustomed to having their whims obeyed. As Steel and Gardiner put it, the young British were 'proverbially captious, disobedient, and easily thrown out of gear'.

That was worrying, not just for the sake of the children themselves but for the Raj as well. Even children had their part to play, no matter how small, in the upholding of British prestige. And they must learn to deal bravely with being sent away to British schools where they could learn to be good members of the Raj. A distant aunt of Iris Macfarlane who was sent to a boarding school in Simla in the 1860s got a brisk letter from her mother reprimanding her for constantly crying and saying she was homesick: 'and for this reason I cannot write to you any more my dearest child, until you have conquered your homesickness and settled down'. Children must be trained, as the Viceroy Lord Lytton told the boys of Bishop Cotton's School in Simla in 1880, 'to show themselves worthy of the position they hold by the uprightness of their lives'. They must remember 'that there is nothing so dangerous to our position as that the lives of Europeans should be disgracefully and dishonourably spent'.

Although very young children of both sexes wore little gowns and petticoats, by the time they were walking they were dressed more like adults, girls in dresses and boys in little suits. As girls grew older they gradually went into longer skirts, and, until after the First World War, they were expected to put on the all-important stays when they reached puberty. Like their parents, British children dressed more formally towards the end of the day, even in the hottest weather. Girls wore several layers, all starched and edged with lace, from pants and vests next to the skin, to petticoats and frilly dresses, even in the inter-war years. Little boys wore slightly fewer clothes, sailor suits perhaps or miniature versions of their fathers' uniforms for special occasions.

It was the mothers, too, who organized the elaborate children's parties (so like the adult ones). There were children's balls and children's fancy dress parties where miniature cupids, butterflies, elves, columbines, Mary Stuarts amused themselves under the anxious eyes of parents, nurses and *ayahs*. For her son's first birthday party during the First World War, Rosamund Lawrence transformed her dining room into an underwater grotto; giant paper fish hung from the ceiling and there were mother-of-pearl shells instead of plates. Her son was dressed as a water-baby in green chiffon festooned with pink shells and seaweed. There were usually special entertainments for the tiny guests: Indian jugglers and conjurors, or the weaver-bird man who had trained his birds to do all sorts of tricks, including firing off a miniature cannon. Viceregal children's parties were the grandest of all; Lady Dufferin gave one in Simla in the 1880s where the entertainment included two elephants for the guests to ride.

The great question troubling the mothers was whether their children, in spite of all these efforts, would stand comparison with their contemporaries at Home. Nineteenth-century speculations about the effect of climate and environment on racial character made a profound impression on the British in India. Mothers made their children wear topis lest the Indian sun burn its way into their brains. Many had a deep aversion to using Indian wet nurses: who knew what the children might imbibe along with Indian milk?

The Indian climate, it was widely agreed, would damage children permanently if they were exposed to it for too long. A child kept in India, warned an eminent physician in 1872, 'will grow up slight, weedy, and delicate, over-precocious it may be, and with a general feebleness'. To begin with, food grown in India did not have the same nutritional value as food grown at Home. Moreover, excessive heat did dreadful things to the system. *Birch's Management* assured its readers (and over the years they were numerous) that 'the higher the external temperature, the more susceptible is the system to nervous influences'. The blood grows thinner and the circulation slower, and that in turn leads to weakened muscles and congestion of the liver, spleen and bowels. The child, the authors added, had a lowered resistance to germs; it would probably also have loose joints and curvature of the spine. Empirical evidence seemed to bear out the experts. The soldier Frank Richards recalled that 'Children born in Barracks were referred to as "barrack-rats": it was always a wonder to me how the poor kids survived the heat, and they were washed out little things.'

Physical damage was just the beginning; worse still were the moral dangers that India posed. Since most of the children spoke Indian languages before they spoke English, there was a serious danger that they would pick up native ways of thought. You must not expect, said the novelist Maud Diver, to keep young minds untainted 'in an atmosphere of petty thefts and lies.' And they might hear too much: Kate Platt, a doctor who wrote a guide to health in India in 1923, explained, 'The Indians themselves live very near to nature, and the events of birth, marriage, and death, as well as the primitive emotions, are discussed openly and without reticence. Children see and hear things which perhaps at the time may make little or no impression, but may have a far-reaching influence on character and temperament.'

By the end of the eighteenth century, some wealthy families had started to educate their children at Home. In the nineteenth century, as communications improved, the practice grew. Any parents who could possibly manage it sent their children away to boarding schools by the time they were seven years old, partly after the example of the middle classes at Home, but also because the fears about the effects of India on children took ever more elaborate forms. Children brought up in India were felt, even in the twentieth century, to be somehow of inferior quality, a belief which affected the marriage prospects of girls and the careers of boys. Until the very end of the Raj, both government and many businesses reserved higher posts for those educated in Britain. (If parents could not educate all their children away, boys got preference.)

The lower levels of British society in India – the smaller merchants and planters, perhaps, or subordinate civil servants – could not afford the luxury of sending their children Home. Instead they sent them to the Hills, to schools like St Paul's in Darjeeling or Bishop Cotton's in Simla, with solidly British curricula. (In 1901 there were 5,000 such pupils.) And their mothers faced the same sort of choice as upper-class mothers did. Should they go to the Hills with their children or stay in the Plains with their husbands? At least the periods involved were not so long. There was one school term – from March to November. When the cold weather came, children were sent home for their holidays.

Further still down the social scale, there were the children of railway workers, of ordinary soldiers, of vagrants perhaps (like Kipling's Kim), who were a constant worry to the government. If they lived where there were no European schools, they remained unschooled; their parents clung desperately to what remained of their status by refusing to allow their children to go to school with 'natives'. In the larger centres, there were special day schools for European children, which were educating about 24,000 by the beginning of the twentieth century. By then, the government of India had also set up Summer Homes for Soldiers' Children in the Hills to give some of those condemned to India at least a break from the heat.

Children who went Home were a minority but an elite one; if they returned to India, they would take their places in the upper levels of the Raj. Whenever possible, their mothers went Home with them; otherwise they were consigned to relatives or foster parents. This was typical of the general impermanence of much British life in India. Neither children nor parents could develop a web of family relationships such as their contemporaries in Britain enjoyed. And this left the children, as they grew up, poised uneasily between India and Britain and belonging to neither.

Except for those wives who took the opportunity to escape from their husbands and from India, the separation was hard on everyone emotionally. For the children, being sent away was the greatest shock of their early lives. It was one from which some of them never really recovered; is it surprising that they found it difficult to trust anyone ever again? They went from a world that was rich in colour and emotions to one that was cold and cramped. In India, they were spoiled and made much of; in Victorian and Edwardian England, they were thrust into a society where children were seen and not heard. They went to schools where India was to be driven out of their systems and Britain drummed in. Unless their mothers stayed to supervise the process, it was hard for the children not to feel abandoned. Sometimes they reacted by hating their parents, sometimes India; to this day, there are men and women who blame that country for separating them from their parents.

Jon and Rumer Godden were left by their parents in London when they were five and six-and-a-half years old. The grandmother and the aunts who took charge of them were kind, but the girls felt themselves exiled from all that was warm in their lives: 'The aunts were so truly good, so noble and so dedicated, but never, in all that tall dark house, was there a gleam of laughter or enterprise or fun, and slowly, slowly our lives began to loosen from their roots – far away now; Mam, Fa, Nancy, Rose seemed like little figures in a frieze looked at long ago and were slowly being covered over in the quiet gloom of the succeeding London days. That is perhaps the secret agony of children separated from their family – the agony that slowly, inexorably, they must forget.'

There were other agonies. The classic account of what a child might suffer is Kipling's 'Baa Baa, Black Sheep'. The story was so close to Kipling's own experience as a child that he actually kept the names of the couple who took charge of him and his sister. In the story, Punch, aged five, and Judy, aged three, are left with Uncle Harry and Aunty Rosa. The little girl adjusts quickly and becomes the pet of the household. The boy does not. He is spoiled and undisciplined by English standards. 'As the unquestioned despot of the house at Bombay, Punch could not quite understand how he came to be of no account in this his new life.' He becomes the Black Sheep of the house, guilty of sin whatever he does. The story ends, as it did in reality, on a note of qualified happiness. The boy is restored to the healing love of his family – but things will never be quite the same again. 'Not altogether, O Punch, for when young lips have drunk deep of the bitter waters of Hate, Suspicion, and Despair, all the Love in the world will not wholly take away that knowledge.'

British mothers in India knew what their children might suffer if they left them at Home, and were faced with an impossible choice: to abandon their husbands or their children. Maud Diver advised them to vow never to desert either for more than four years at a stretch – scarcely a satisfactory solution. If they defied convention to keep the family together in India, as some did, they were accused of sacrificing their children's happiness to their own. 'It is for their welfare,' said Julia Curtis, the wife of a planter, firmly, 'and sentiment must be pocketed.' The two great duties of memsahibs were marriage and motherhood, and they knew that they would have to fail at one or the other.

The tie between parents and children was difficult to maintain under such constraints. There were children who saw their mothers or their fathers only once every three or four years. 'I can never see the little first tottering steps, or hear the first attempts at words', wrote Nora Scott to her mother, who was looking after her first child in England.

Often, when these children and parents finally met again, they did not recognize each other; the children had grown, the parents were only dimly remembered. A girl whose mother did not recognize her when she finally came to visit her at her English boarding school felt that 'something snapped in her heart'.

During the First World War, when German cruisers made the journey Home as risky as it had been in the old days, the British kept their children in India well beyond the age considered safe – and the children survived. As soon as peace came, though, the practice was resumed. The government of India began to help with the expense of the passage, at least for its employees, and, by the end of the 1920s, the first experimental air service between Europe and India promised to shorten the journey still further.

Motherhood in India was ultimately unsatisfactory for many memsahibs. They had been told that they must bring up their children to be a credit to the Empire – but that usually meant letting others bring them up. The mother who stayed with her husband while her children were at Home or up in the Hills had the comfort of knowing that she had done her duty. She had her memories, as Julia Curtis said sadly, 'of a few short but exquisitely happy years when she had her babies all to herself'. She had the brief, dutiful letters written by her children at school. She had their pictures: 'I could not help noticing', wrote Monica Campbell-Martin in the 1930s, 'how one thing was common to all of us .... It travelled with us everywhere. Whatever homely things were left behind, one was always unpacked at each halt and put on the table in the tent, or above the fireplace in the rest house. It was the photograph of the child, or children at school in England.'

9

HOUSEKEEPING

'An Indian household can no more be governed peacefully, without dignity and prestige, than an Indian Empire', wrote Flora Annie Steel and Grace Gardiner. The management of her house was one of the greatest tests faced by the memsahib. 'The end and object is not merely personal comfort but the formation of a home – that unit of civilization where father and children, master and servant, employer and employed, can learn their several duties. When all is said and done also herein lies the natural outlet for most of the talent peculiar to women.' And, in her miniature empire, the woman of the Raj had many of the same problems as the men on their larger stage. How was she to rule her subjects? How was she to keep India under control? Success was measured by the way in which she dealt with her domain. 'Chota Mem' ('Junior Memsahib'), author of the guide *The English Bride*, published in 1908, declared, 'In calling on a new acquaintance, I have invariably been able to judge a woman's character by her drawing-room and servant.'

Women new to the country had to cope with their strange houses and alien servants. Even those who had grown up in India had sometimes picked up little from their mothers. New brides had to muddle through, learning the unfamiliar procedures, finding out what sort of supplies they needed to keep on hand, working out, often through painful trial and error, how much money they could spend. (Rosamund Lawrence remembered of those first days that she was near to tears in her ignorance and perplexity.)

There were dreadful meals, sometimes cooked by the inexperienced memsahib herself, sometimes produced by the cook she did not know how to talk to. Enormous bills for supplies appeared, run up by servants who assured her that all was in order. Awkward scenes took place when she ordered a servant to perform a task which he could not possibly do because of his caste. Minnie Blane complained uncomprehendingly to her mother: 'Actually the other day I desired my table servant to bring me the drawing-room lamp to clean, as I take charge of them.

He refused, saying that he would lose caste to touch it. Fool! I got so angry, and after a hard battle got my way, but really they are enough to drive one mad!' And some mistakes were simply embarrassing. There was the lady in Assam who ordered a servant to bring her an umbrella (*chatta* in the local dialect); unfortunately she used the word *chatti*, which means breast. Monica Campbell-Martin, in her first months in India, reduced a servant to helpless giggles when she asked him about his cold. She pronounced the word incorrectly so that it appeared as though she were asking him if he were married. When the servant answered yes, she went into considerable detail about a cure for his condition, from purgatives to a good rest in bed.

Slowly they learnt. They picked up enough vernacular to issue simple orders. They learnt not to ask a Muslim cook to handle pork or a Hindu one beef. They learnt that certain tasks could be done only by the sweeper. They discovered that even sweepers had their limits: they would not touch dead animals. For that, a still lower grade of Untouchable had to be employed.

They also learnt the importance of a routine. All the guidebooks for prospective memsahibs stressed this. A routine was a sign that the British housekeeper had not allowed India to make her lethargic and sloppy. It was also a way of ensuring that the dirt and disorder of the country were daily kept away from herself and her family. And Indians too would benefit – or so the optimists of the nineteenth century believed – through training in virtues such as punctuality, cleanliness and honesty. 'A few generations of training', Steel and Gardiner informed their readers, 'shall have started the Indian servant on a new inheritance of habit.'

Ironically, although few memsahibs ever knew it, Indian women in return thought them shockingly lax, for buying their flour and their spices ready-ground, whereas the good Indian housekeeper always cleaned and ground her own; and also for hiring men of low caste to cook for them.

While the memsahib was not actually expected to do anything around the house herself – indeed the servants were embarrassed and annoyed if she did – she was expected to keep an eye on everything. Some authorities argued that she should not try to keep too close a watch. 'Natives' ways in cooking', warned *Indian Outfits*, 'are not by any means nice, in fact, very often extremely nasty; therefore do not seek to know too much.' Generations of women horrified each other with stories of socks used for straining soup and fish patties shaped in the cook's armpits or rissoles held in his toes.

The memsahib usually started on her rounds after breakfast; otherwise, *The English Bride* told her, 'you might see or hear many little things to upset your appetite in the early morning.' She went out to do battle: the guides to housekeeping sound at times like military manuals. As a symbol of her heavy responsibilities she carried the household keys; only the most trusted of Indian deputies was allowed to take charge of them. First she interviewed her chief of staff, the head servant who might be called the bearer, the butler, the boy or the *khansama* (literally, 'master of the household gear'). In a well-run household, the cook appeared every morning, in a clean uniform, with his accounts for the previous day. The memsahib ran through them, occasionally pausing to question the consumption of eggs or possibly flour just to let the cook know that she was keeping an eye on him, and then together they planned the day's meals. The menu chosen, she visited the storeroom and issued supplies for the day, weighing food out on her scales. Sometimes, if she was very conscientious, she had a little book by her side to record every handful of rice or dollop of cooking oil. The cook then carried away the necessary supplies from the storeroom on a series of plates.

The mistress of the house also checked that the rooms were swept and dusted and that the kitchen was clean. If, after all this, she felt like it, she arranged the flowers that had been brought in by the gardener. She did not win all her battles; Mrs Fay in the eighteenth century was the forerunner of a long line of housekeepers who tried, unsuccessfully, to fight against their servants' custom of taking commission on the marketing. (Indian servants could bargain for better prices than any European could ever get; in turn they felt it only reasonable to charge a small fee.)

Indians, the memsahibs' creed ran, were also difficult to train because they were so deeply conservative. As late as the 1920s, a guide to housekeeping in India was warning its readers that 'Too much must not be expected from them; they find it very difficult to change their ways of doing things, and innovations must be very cautiously introduced.' The author of *The English Bride* went so far as to argue that 'Their brains are not properly developed and they cannot always see things in the same light as we do.' Yet in their attitude to their servants women not uncommonly sounded much worse than they really were. They condemned the whole race but they also made exceptions for their own servants. And there could even be real affection and trust between mistress and servant.

Not surprisingly, memsahibs were expected to take pains over the hiring of their servants. On some stations, the local Club kept a registry of reliable, or at least not especially unreliable, servants. Over the years certain guidelines developed. Servants who spoke English were not considered desirable, because they could learn the family secrets. Testimonials, purportedly written by former employers, should always be treated with suspicion; they had probably been bought in the bazaar or borrowed from another servant. Jokes circulated about servants being sent away with damning testimonials which they could not read. 'This man served in my employ for one month as cook; that was a month too long.' Or 'To Whom It May Concern: Mitto Ram the bearer of this letter has worked for me for three months. His bazaar bills are double those of any servant I have ever employed. He is the biggest liar I have ever met and he has lost most of my shirts.'

In hiring servants, memsahibs had to choose from a wide range of castes and religions. Muslims were preferred for bearers, perhaps a consequence of the British view, widespread after the Mutiny, that Muslims were more loyal than Hindus – and more straightforward, a quality which was often attributed to the fact that they worshipped only one god and were 'people of the book' just like Christians. In the north, in any case, servants were more likely to be Muslims because there were more of them around. Hindu servants could come from almost any caste. The sweepers, by nature of their profession, were bound to be Untouchables. Brahmins generally did not act as cooks because so much European food would have been polluting to them. On the other hand, poorer Brahmins, of whom there were many, frequently worked as gardeners. Christian Indians, for all the supposed civilizing influence of the masters' religion, were often disliked on the grounds that they were insincere in their conversion. They were believed to make dishonest servants.

Servants were to be treated with firmness and constant vigilance. A good memsahib would have good servants because she would keep them under her eye and, equally important, because she would set them a good example. 'An untidy mistress', said *The Complete Indian Housekeeper and Cook*, 'invariably has *untidy*, a weak one, *idle* servants.'

If a memsahib lost control of her household, it was for the same reasons that the British might one day lose control of India. If servants misbehaved, they must be disciplined at once. Many memsahibs kept their servants' pay in arrears, partly to prevent them from running away and partly so that they could dock small amounts in fines for various transgressions. It was a mistake, however, to be too severe. After all, Indians often sinned because they did not know better. 'Be patient with your servants', advised *The English Bride*, 'and treat them more or less like children, remembering that they love praise, and don't treat them as if they were machines.' The women – and they were not all that rare – who shouted at their servants and beat them were generally felt to be harming the prestige and dignity of the ruling race.

At the upper end of the social scale, the wives of viceroys and governors had armies of servants. When Lady Lytton arrived at Government House in Calcutta in the late 1870s, she discovered that she had a staff of some 300 Indian servants, including 100 cooks, which, she said, 'drove the Frenchman we took out nearly mad'. At the lowest levels of society, even the wives of ordinary soldiers or the men who worked on the railways had a servant or two. (This sometimes disturbed their social superiors: as one memsahib said of the soldiers' wives, 'they are more or less a poor feckless folk, their English physique enfeebled by the climate, and their moral fibre enervated by the unwonted possession of a servant or two.')

Ordinary middle-class women had a complement of servants that seems enormous today. Fanny Parks, that tireless traveller and observer, had fifty-seven in Allahabad before the Mutiny. Ten was generally considered the barest minimum. This was partly because until well into the twentieth century there were no labour-saving devices in household work. Moreover, the restrictions of caste meant that it was impossible to find a single servant who could do a great variety of household tasks. Besides, servants were fairly cheap. In the 1890s even the most expensive, a butler for example, cost only 20 rupees a month and a sweeper half that. Annette Beveridge had thirty-nine servants at a total cost of 250 rupees a month – not a great burden on her husband's salary of some 1,800 rupees a month. The employer had to provide housing (in the servants' quarters in grounds attached to the bungalow, known as the compound) but the servants looked after their own food.

Finally, servants were necessary for the prestige of the Raj: among other things that the British had picked up from India was that the number of servants was a measure of status. (Since the servants thought so too, employers were under considerable pressure to hire more every time the sahib got a promotion.)

The head servant was the key to good housekeeping. A dignified figure, usually in dazzling white and often with a many-layered turban, he took charge of the shopping, the general running of the household, and frequently – in spite of what the memsahibs said about Indian dishonesty – the household accounts. In some households he also acted as a valet for the sahib. He normally saw his mistress every morning after breakfast to report on the condition of her empire. Together they went to the storeroom for the ritual distribution of supplies. (In larger households yet another servant looked after the shopping and the storeroom.)

The storeroom was plain and functional. Its shelves held rows of earthenware pots and sometimes leftover paraffin (kerosene) tins, all with lids to protect their contents from black ants and other insects. If there were tables, their legs stood in small saucers filled with water or paraffin as a precaution against insects. Running an efficient storeroom was another of the signs of a good memsahib. *The Complete Indian Housekeeper and Cook* devoted considerable space to the subject because 'the want of method and comfortable arrangement is acquiesced in so calmly in India'. In the first place, the memsahib had to make sure that there were always adequate supplies on hand, from the basics of British cooking (sago, semolina, dried fruits, treacle, gelatin, flour) to the flourishes (chutneys, anchovies, sardines, and, for very special occasions, tinned truffles and caviar), as well as essentials such as candles, soap and matches. On the other hand, she must not stock too much because, in common with most memsahibs, she might have to move hurriedly. Keeping minimum stocks was easy enough in the big cities, where nearly everything could be bought locally; not so easy in the *mofussil*, where many things had to be ordered from miles away. There was an art in knowing how to order so that supplies ran out simultaneously; shipping costs were expensive and it made sense to order everything at once. Even with the mail-order catalogues, it was difficult for a young bride to foresee everything from vinegar to razor blades that might be needed over several months.

She had also to watch that the servants did not siphon off too much. If she was careless about this, they considered her fair game and increased their depredations. Staples such as sugar or rice had a way of dwindling at an astonishing rate. One article which seems to have caused constant guerrilla warfare between mistress and servants was the humble duster. The *jharan*, as it was called, was constantly disappearing, to reappear as a baby's shirt or an *ayah*'s scarf. Many memsahibs had a daily ceremony in which they received piles of dirty *jharans* and carefully doled out clean ones in exchange.

Except in the very remote areas, food and certain other necessities could be bought in the local bazaar. The usual meat was chicken or goat; if there were local Muslims it was usually possible to buy beef or a passable substitute in the form of water buffalo. In the days before refrigeration meat usually had to be eaten soon after the animal had been slaughtered. In the hot weather, Susan Daly told her mouher, she hung joints of meat in her sitting room since it was the coolest place in the house. 'Fancy a Butcher's shop in the drawing room!' On smaller stations, the British often joined forces in a mutton club (for obvious reasons the ideal number of households was four): a communal sheep would be raised and killed and the meat shared out. Vegetables were sometimes a problem if the families did not grow their own, for local supplies might consist of nothing but potatoes and some type of marrow or squash. There was fresh fruit the year round, at least papayas or bananas, which were easy to grow. Although Steel and Gardiner were rude about tinned food – 'at best the means of evading starvation' – housekeepers in the *mofussil* welcomed its advent. They could at least get a change and a taste of Home with tinned asparagus or salmon, even tinned haggis for the homesick Scots.

Getting water could also be a problem. There was no piped water outside the big cities before the twentieth century. Most bungalows had their own wells, but water sometimes had to be carried from the nearest river. When Annette Beveridge lived in the small Bengal town of Faridpur she described the procedure to her children who were at school in England: 'Every few days a bullock cart goes down to the big river and on it are fastened two immense black jugs and these are brought back full of water from the river. Then this is boiled and filtered before we drink it!'

31

Social life was both eased and made more elaborate by the numerous servants. For tea on the lawn in Calcutta in 1890, Mr and Mrs Thoby Prinsep and Lady Florence Streatfeild are attended by two table servants (in white) and two *chuprassis*, whose role was to announce new arrivals and add prestige (31).

32

Some of the staff retained by the Impeys in Calcutta *c.* 1782 are supervised by Lady Impey in her boudoir (32), shutters closed against the morning heat. Behind her stand the *munshi*, or interpreter, and a boy with a fan; she is receiving a new hat from the tailor. The other figures, reading anticlockwise from the tailor, are the Impeys' European butler; the steward with a list of purchases; a doorkeeper and silver-stick-bearer or usher (both standing); two thread-twisters (one using his toes); a *durzi* or tailor; the *mali*, bringing produce from the garden; two more tailors; an office messenger; another doorkeeper and stick-bearer; and, finally, two embroiderers. Lady Impey also, very unusually,

33

employed three Indian artists to record the local flora and fauna.

34

To attend the memsahib herself there were one or two *ayahs*;
William Tayler's illustration of 1842 shows them helping with her
toilette, under a large *punkah* (34).

Deputy Commissioner W. G. Archer and his wife, in Bihar near
the end of the Raj, had a relatively small staff (33). In the front row,
left to right, are the bearer, his son, the Archer children, the chief
chuprassi (a great friend to the children: see Ill. 23), the *ayah*'s
son with the family cat, the sweeper, and the *paniwallah* (water-carrier);
in the back row, a messenger, two office stenographers, the driver,
his son, the cook, and two *chuprassis* with distinctive sash and badge.
Absent are the *khitmutgar* (table steward) and *ayah* (see Ill. 20).

35 Breakfast was substantial, even in hot weather, and due decorum
was observed, although the neatly corseted memsahib portrayed
by Tayler in 1842 (35) is slipping a scrap to her spaniel. Behind her
is a boy with a fly-whisk (another fly-whisk hangs on the wall).
All the lights are protected by chimneys; a carpet covers matting
on the floor; there are flowers and English china on the table.

36

37

Preceding page. Behind the scenes things were not necessarily serene. The memsahib kept an eye on the store cupboard and on the weighing of supplies (36; see pp. 172 and 174–75) – sometimes, as the author of these sketches, Captain Atkinson, wrote *c.* 1860, 'personally supervising with a detective's skill the operations of the kitchen'. Other women thought the kitchen (37) best avoided if you wanted to keep your appetite (see pp. 171–72 and 185). Pots bubbled on an open charcoal range; chickens were killed and plucked; and spices were ground on the curry-stone. Kitchens like this were still common in the *mofussil* in the 1940s.

Fun and games ensured health as well as amusement. One of the favourite pastimes of the British was the gymkhana with serious and not-so-serious competitions, such as this one in southern India, *c.* 1900 (38).

Picnics were always popular. Hostesses providing refreshments for tennis (40) were advised to 'avoid stickiness and surprises'. At a more intimate picnic on a hike in the Simla hills in 1920 (39), as Loulette and Herbert Douglas investigate the hamper, surprise seems to be part of the fun.

38

39

40

41

42

Meeting Indian women presented problems
– the physical barrier of *purdah*, and language
and cultural differences (intensified as the
British became 'the ruling race'). Perhaps
the most accessible were the Parsees, of
the region around Bombay, who were more
Westernized and more often spoke English.
This party for ladies (41) is in the Bombay
house of a wealthy Parsee early in the
twentieth century.

By the 1930s, personal friendships were
slightly more common. Iris Portal and her
friend Mrs Moos (42), photographed with
their children at Mahableshwar in 1937,
were exceptional in doing welfare work
(see p. 153). (Mrs Moos, wife of a Parsee
doctor, did not usually wear Western dress.)

The other great field of battle for the memsahib was the kitchen. Here she waged a constant struggle to make sure that the servants kept it clean and that the cook produced British meals and did not cheat her too much. A good housekeeper inspected the pots and pans daily, both for grease and to see if they needed re-tinning. (Some women made the mistake of buying pots with handles; the Indian cooks did not like them and usually managed to hammer them off.) At first the kitchen itself came as a shock. Anne Wilson, in the Punjab at the end of the nineteenth century, found 'a little darkroom, with a board on the mud floor to hold the meat, two tumble-down brick "ranges" in one corner, a stone receptacle in another into which the water is thrown, to run out through its hole in the wall into a sunk tub'. The kitchen was often separate from the bungalow, possibly with a covered walkway leading to it. It had no running water and the stove was simply a rectangle made of bricks with a draft in one side and a hole in the top. The oven was usually a tin box placed over the hole.

The cook himself was a very important part of the household, and there were the usual sorts of rules about hiring one. Goanese from the west coast were said to be good, but then they were usually Christian, which roused suspicion; on the other hand they did not have any tiresome food prohibitions. Other memsahibs swore by the Mughs from the Burmese border, who were said to be the French chefs of India. It was difficult to entice reliable cooks to the remoter stations; one unfortunate memsahib who was living in Jacobabad (distinguished only by having the highest temperatures in the subcontinent) discovered that her cook had been running a brothel out of her servants' quarters and that he was probably riddled with syphilis as well. Many cooks drank, which caused difficulties when there was a dinner party. Poor Julia Curtis had a most unfortunate Christmas her first year in India: to begin with, her turkey was eaten by a jackal so that an old tough goose had to be hastily killed instead, and then, two hours before dinner was to be served, her cook was discovered dead drunk on the kitchen floor. Even worse was the discovery of a memsahib on the northeast frontier that her cook had not only been running a brothel out of her kitchen but had also installed a young male lover. When she cried, 'How could he do it?' another servant answered, 'Vaseline, mem.'

If you had a good and reliable cook, *The Complete Indian Housekeeper and Cook* advised, 'do anything to keep him – short of letting him know that you are anxious to do so'. When they were good, Indian cooks were very good indeed, capable of turning out excellent meals on their primitive equipment. What is more, they did not make difficulties if their employers suddenly brought extra guests for a meal. 'For half the trouble,' Ethel Savi remembered with nostalgia, 'an English cook would have given notice on the spot.' If there was not enough food on hand, not enough plates or knives and forks, the cook would simply borrow from his fellow cooks working for other Europeans.

To help out the cook, there was a subordinate servant known simply as the cook's boy or, in Bengal, the *musolchi* (after the servant who used to carry torches in the eighteenth century). To wait on tables there was an imposing figure known variously as the *khitmutgar* (in the north), the *masaul* (in Bombay), or the *matey* (in the south). Grand households had numbers of waiters. They worked out of a small pantry attached to the dining room, sometimes called the *bottle-khana* or the *dispence-khana*. Here they kept the food from the kitchen hot over burning charcoal in special receptacles, and here they washed the dirty plates. They were also usually responsible for the lamps. *The Complete Indian Housekeeper and Cook* warned that they were capable of a slovenliness 'simply inconceivable to the new-comer to India'.

In addition to the bearer, the cook, the cook's boy, the waiter, and the sweeper (who swept, dusted, emptied the thunderbox and carried out the rubbish), most households employed a *bheesti*, whose sole job was to carry water for the bathrooms, the kitchen and the garden; messengers or *chuprassis* to carry all those endless 'chits' about the station; and watchmen or *chaukidars* (who in some areas were sensibly recruited from tribes of hereditary thieves). In the hot weather, it was usually necessary to hire *punkah* coolies. If the establishment ran to horses, then there was a groom – known in the north as a *syce* – and grass cutters to provide feed. If there were cows, a cowman was necessary as well. Households in the remoter parts of India would also have post coolies who went to fetch the letters and parcels and sometimes supplies, such as fresh meat. (They carried a little bell to warn off wild animals.) And we must not forget the washerman – the *dhobi* – subject of so many complaints and jokes. He took quite reasonable garments and linen and reduced them to unrecognizable tatters. He gave you something called 'dhobi itch'. If you made the mistake of giving him clothes over the weekend, he was quite likely to rent them out to soldiers' wives or Eurasian girls. The humorist who wrote sketches for the *Times of India* in the 1880s described this servant: 'Day after day he has stood before that great black stone and wreaked his rage upon shirt and trouser and coat, and coat and trouser and shirt. Then he has wrung them as if he were wringing the necks of poultry, and fixed them on his drying line with thorns and spikes, and finally he has taken the battered garments to his torture chamber and ploughed them with his iron, longwise and crosswise and slantwise, and dropped glowing cinders on their tenderest places. Son has succeeded father through countless generations in cultivating his passion for destruction, until it has become the monstrous growth we see and shudder at in the *Dhobie*.'

A servant who was of particular importance to the memsahib was the *ayah*, who in addition to looking after children acted as a lady's maid. Well-to-do women usually hired extra *ayahs* as they needed them. Even those who had not had their own maids at Home soon got used to the idea of having someone dress them and brush their hair. *Ayahs* waited up patiently at night to take care of their mistresses when they came home from parties. A good *ayah* became a friend to her mistress and often helped her through difficult times. The author of *Indian Outfits* had nothing but praise for hers: 'She was most tender and careful in sickness, nursing me through several severe illnesses; never took the value of a pin's head from me, and would, were I to return to India tomorrow, come back to me, if she were alive, and serve me as faithfully.'

Women also relied on their tailors – the *durzis* – who sat cross-legged on the verandah stitching away, their toes holding the material straight and their turbans stuck through with their needles and pins. *Durzis* usually moved from household to household according to demand, although a grand memsahib might have her own private one. They were often extraordinarily skilled and quick and could produce impeccable copies of garments. They could also, however, be unfortunately literal: Anglo-Indian folklore contains many stories of memsahibs who found that a favourite dress had been copied right down to the mends and patches. It was said that *durzis* had to be watched carefully because they might try to do other people's work.

British women in India tended to take the supervision of their establishments very seriously. (If they did not, their servants despised them for being lazy.) Some memsahibs learnt to speak one, two, or even several Indian languages so that they could communicate with their employees. They insisted that the cowmen milk their cows in front of them so that they could not water down the milk. (Some cowmen became very skilful indeed, with rubber tubes up their sleeves, so that they could add the water as they milked.) By the twentieth century, when Louis Pasteur had discovered how tuberculosis was transmitted, the memsahibs also made sure that the milk was boiled and kept clean in jugs with net covers weighted with beads. They checked daily that the drinking water was being boiled or filtered. They had their fresh fruits and lettuces washed in a solution of permanganate of potash, which, said Steel and Gardiner optimistically, 'destroys most bacilli'. If there were dogs – and what true British household did not have them? – the memsahibs watched while they were fed to ensure that their food had not been adulterated.

A thorough memsahib inspected the family quarters of her servants regularly. The mistress, according to Steel and Gardiner, was 'responsible for the decency and health of all persons living in her service or compound'. She cared for her servants and their families when they were sick. That sometimes caused difficulties because a high-caste Indian could not accept food or drink from the hands of an Untouchable European; the women got around it by handing over bottles of medicine with tongs or, if their servants were willing to stretch a point, feeding them when no one else was looking.

While servants certainly caused problems for the memsahibs, it cannot have been easy for the servants either, faced with a mistress who issued incomprehensible orders and then shouted at them for failing to understand, or who expected them to carry out tasks which would pollute them. What from one side looked like obstruction appeared from the other as a perfectly reasonable refusal. In spite of the obstacles, many women did manage to establish a close and even affectionate relationship with their servants. When Annette Beveridge had a child, the first person to hold it after its father was the bearer. The relationship appeared feudal on the surface, but in reality, over the years, trusted servants often exerted a good deal of influence over the household.

In Veronica Bamfield's family (her father was an army officer), the bearer took charge of all the money; if the family needed anything he doled it out to them.

There was often strong loyalty on both sides. Many of the British helped their servants out if they got into debt, or provided dowries for their daughters. And the servants reciprocated. One woman remembered her husband's bearer coming to announce the birth of a son with the words, 'The little sahib's bearer is born!' When Veronica Bamfield's father went off to war in 1941, the bearer, in order to save money, lowered himself to do the housework, and refused to take holidays until his sahib returned. Some servants broke their caste to look after their employers in times of sickness. During the Mutiny, many lost their lives trying to protect the families they worked for. In the Second World War for several anxious months it looked as though the Japanese were about to invade India; the gardener of one memsahib offered her shelter in his village. When their families left India, the servants wept; they waited for them at the dockside if they came back. One family left India for good in 1947; their *ayah* accompanied them to Bombay and when she was paid off at the quay, she threw the money into the water and covered her head and wept. Barbara Donaldson, daughter of a judge in the United Provinces and wife of a member of the ICS, who finally left India at Independence, had an old cook who was so worried about the family in post-war Britain that he sent them food parcels.

Sadly, many memsahibs did not realize the advantages of Indian servants – their patience and their loyalty – until they went Home. Where could you find an English nanny who would care for her charges with such devotion? Or a servant who would produce breakfast even though he had been up all night travelling? Indian servants were extraordinary for making the best of difficulties. In the great Bihar earthquake of 1934, one lady was sitting in a daze on her lawn outside her house, which had been reduced to rubble; her water carrier appeared, salaamed, and asked, 'Mem-sahib, what time do you wish to take your bath?'

One household duty which was a source of great pleasure to many memsahibs was caring for the garden, even though the British moved so often that planting a garden was an act of faith, which often went unrewarded. And even if the memsahib stayed in the same spot, every year she faced the hot weather which swept down on her tender plants

and withered them overnight. Some left it all to the gardener – the *mali*
– who was a standard part of the typical establishment. He watered and
weeded and planted, and as long as there were a few bright flowers in pots
along the verandah, the lady of the house need not worry herself further.
The *mali* was also supposed to supply her daily with cut flowers for arranging; the sensible memsahib did not inquire too closely about where the
copious armloads of blooms came from (perhaps a neighbour's garden?).

More ambitious women took charge themselves, which sometimes
meant that they got their own hands dirty; more usually, they told the
mali where to plant and weed and cut. (When Fanny Parks went out
to do her daily gardening in Allahabad before the Mutiny, she was also
followed everywhere by a bearer carrying an enormous umbrella.)
In their gardening, as in so much else that they did in India, British
women tended to make things more difficult for themselves by trying to
produce as English a garden as possible. The standard compound around
a bungalow had beaten earth. With a type of creeping grass called *doob*
and hours of the *mali's* time and gallons of water, this could be made
into a lawn of sorts. And they grew English flowers from seeds sent out
from Home or from those grown in India in public gardens. (The locally
produced seeds, it was felt, were never quite as good as the true British
ones.) Petunias, pansies, larkspur, sweet peas, phlox, snapdragons, all
filled out the Anglo-Indian flowerbed. Skilful gardeners might even
grow violets: 'dear little English flower!' as one lady exclaimed. It was
a challenge to raise a particularly delicate plant under the hot Indian
sun. Edith Cuthell, the author of several short stories about India, who
gardened in Lucknow before the First World War, was especially proud
of her bed of watercress: 'how, out here, one prizes the common things
of everyday "home" life!'

Gardening enthusiasts pored over the catalogues that were sent
from firms in Calcutta, or Poona, or, best of all, from Home. They grew
boxes of seedlings and took hundreds of cuttings. They drove for miles
if they heard that a fellow-gardener had a plant they wanted. On the
larger stations they showed their results at the annual flower show.
'We are told', Mrs King reported sadly in the late nineteenth century, 'that
the envy, hatred and malice caused by the judges' award is very great.'

By and large, however, these gardens were never quite like Home:
flowers bloomed together – a rose next to a chrysanthemum – that

never did in Britain, and they lacked scent. (It was a standard joke that everything smelled in India except the flowers.) Indigenous Indian plants could never be kept out entirely. Bougainvillaea, hibiscus, hedges of plumbago, were allowed in on sufferance. It was felt by some experts that they produced too exuberant an effect; Mrs Temple-Wright, author of a popular gardening book, advised, 'let the beauty of the garden harmonise with the dainty taste of the drawing room.'

Over the years quite a few women learnt to disregard conventional views on the proper garden and to appreciate the advantages of gardening in India. Mrs King noticed that 'roses never grow in England in the joyous lavish way they do here.' Monica Campbell-Martin was enchanted by the speed with which things grew: 'In India the gardener has very little waiting to do. In the monsoon, shrubberies newly planted will flower in two months' time. Creepers gallop over archways and pillars at such a pace they over-reach themselves, and then they wave their arms about in myriads of curling feelers, stretching for somewhere farther to climb.'

With gardening, keeping the accounts, supervising the household's daily routine, doling out the stores, many memsahibs found an outlet for their energies. One guide warned its readers: 'Do make it a strict rule not to talk of servants and housekeeping when you go out in the afternoon. One so often sees groups of women at the club comparing notes about how much firewood costs, and what their cook's daily bills amount to, etc.' Such advice usually went unheeded. Since the women of the Raj were kept at arm's length from most of what was going on in India – only partly by their own choice – they created their own small worlds and entered into them wholeheartedly.

SOCIAL LIFE
AND AMUSEMENTS

Social life was a curious mixture. Most women seem to have accepted the formality easily: 'One could look on it all as taking part in a play', said one. Calling cards, dance programmes, long white gloves lingered on in India well after they had disappeared at Home. The presence of lots of servants made it easy to be formal; the need to uphold the dignity of the Raj made it desirable. Yet new arrivals were also struck by the determined enthusiasm with which the sahibs and memsahibs pursued their amusements. 'Jolly' was the word most frequently used. 'No one is old in Calcutta', Anne Wilson noticed on her first visit in the 1890s. 'Everybody is of the same age, and that is about twenty-five, and one is entertained by young creatures playing practical jokes on their friends (whose hair, purely by accident, is white).'

What the casual visitor failed to notice at first was the desperation which so often lay beneath the bustle and the jollity. Except in the big cities, there were no theatres, no concert halls. There were few lending libraries, and English books and journals were difficult to get and expensive as well. Entertaining – with the planning beforehand and the gossiping afterwards – expanded to fill the long days which stretched before the women. The more they kept busy, the less time they had to think of their children and families so far away.

It is true that there were some functions reserved for men – Masonic dinners, mess nights – but generally men and women shared the same social life, indeed more, perhaps, than their contemporaries at Home. Over the years, the women came to see their social role not just as a pastime but as a duty. Even in the remotest parts of the Raj, they carried it out with determination. A civil servant who went to Nepal in the 1890s, then a journey that involved trekking through wild country, was amazed at the sight that greeted him in Kathmandu – 'the English Political Agent's wife holding an "At Home", the band playing, and tennis, badminton, and afternoon tea in full swing'. The older ladies drummed into the younger ones that it was their duty to be sociable for the sake of their husbands' careers. Lady Birdwood, who was the sixth generation in her family to live in India, said of her marriage to a soldier in 1931: 'The army wife was not expected to do anything or be anything except a decorative chattel or appendage of her husband ... It didn't even matter if she wasn't beautiful, so long as she looked reasonable and dressed reasonably and didn't let her husband down by making outrageous remarks at the dinner table.' If they grumbled privately, most women accepted their responsibility. Lord Curzon's American wife, Mary, wrote to her father from Simla in 1902: 'George never does any social functions of any sort and they all devolve on me. I do them all. He has not gone out once since he came back, so I go through all the endlessly long list, bravely making his excuses and telling no one how he suffers and works. Duty is a wonderful incentive, and I have inherited my devotion to it from you, and I know it is a great help to G. to make the effort for him. So I go out to races, parties, concerts, weddings, prize-givings, polo matches and the Lord knows what. It is all work and very little pleasure.'

The first step in launching oneself in local society was the ritual of the call. Until that had been done, the newcomer did not exist socially. (Some memsahibs methodically kept an account book with the names of their callers, the dates of the calls, and the dates of their own return calls.) Calling was by no means a simple operation. As C. C. Dyson, who travelled extensively in India before the First World War, complained, 'The rules vary in different Presidencies, and contain many mysteries which are pitfalls to the new-comer.' The great question was who called upon whom. Ladies, of course, never called upon bachelors. In parts of western India, all new arrivals waited for the opening moves from the local residents. Throughout most of the country, however, the newcomer made the opening moves – except for brides, who always had to wait demurely to be called upon. (The wives of officers in British Army regiments stationed temporarily in India – in a breach of the rules that was much resented – did not as a rule call on their counterparts in Indian Army regiments.)

Dressed with proper formality and armed with a sheaf of visiting cards, the caller went from bungalow to bungalow. Bachelors might go by themselves but unmarried women were escorted by their hostess. The lady of the house was traditionally 'not at home'. A servant solemnly took the card (or cards, if there were several ladies in the household) and the caller left secure in the knowledge that the harvest for such labour would eventually come in the form of invitations to dinner or tea. A bride usually left it to her husband to make the first return calls; his calls were then returned by husbands and wives together; and finally the lady whose husband had initiated the whole mating dance was allowed to accompany him to return those calls. In the hill stations where the paths up to bungalows were often steep, the occupants thoughtfully nailed up boards with their names and underneath a small tin box with the message 'Not At Home' for cards. In the planting districts, where the distances to be covered were great, the rules were relaxed and the caller was received on the first call. When Julia Curtis, as an unmarried girl, was staying with her brother in south India in the 1890s, she sent a coolie ahead with her dress to a friendly bungalow while she rode over; the lady she called on would then take her around the neighbourhood to make as many calls as possible.

Certain days might be favoured for calling. In Calcutta a round of calls was customarily made after Sunday-morning service. All over India, however, the correct time for men was the same: at the height of the midday sun. The complaint of the Madras correspondent of *The Pioneer* in 1882 was to be echoed through the years: 'We are behind hand, conservative and punctilious in all matters of *etiquette*, but I doubt whether any one particular society here is more tenacious of its ancient privilege of causing the maximum of discomfort to a large class of well-intentioned bipeds than in its scrupulous adherence to the rule that all male callers shall introduce themselves between the hours of eleven and two.' Appeals of this sort had little effect on the women who regulated such things. In 1883 the ladies of Madras prevailed upon the *Madras Mail* to print the rules for callers, as approved by themselves, so that there should be no doubt about the correct procedure. It was only in the years between the world wars that calling began to die out; on the bigger stations most newcomers simply wrote their name in the visitors' book at the local Residence.

The ritual of the call helped to make new arrivals aware of one of the contradictions in the society they were entering. It was genial and fun-loving; it was also highly structured. Beyond certain broad divisions – between officials and non-officials, between Europeans and Eurasians – lay more and finer distinctions. The anxious hostess could consult the listings in the Warrant of Precedence; but as the wife of a member of the Educational Department remembered, 'it was like walking over broken glass barefoot to steer one's way socially when I first went out to Poona'. Women got even more annoyed than men about mistakes and there were unfortunate scenes over who should go in to dinner first. Rosamund Lawrence witnessed a clash between two ladies whose husbands worked for the railway: the one who thought that she should have had precedence over the other hissed menacingly, 'Your husband began as a station master and … *not on the main line.*'

It was, of course, much easier to classify people in India than at Home. India was like a gigantic company town: one employer – the government – overshadowed all others. 'Everybody', wrote that acute observer Anne Wilson, 'apparently knows everybody else's post and pay, and frank allusions are made to both upon all occasions; rather a novelty, as so many people at home have the same kind of scruple about summing up your income for you as they would have about decrying your pedigree.' Pedigree in India, except for the unfortunate Eurasians, counted for much less than position. Since almost all British men were in the country to work, there was a feeling, widely shared by both sexes, that what they had been at Home was not nearly so significant as who they were in India. 'Scorpion' wrote to *The Pioneer* in 1881 to say: 'Were all the Europeans in India put into a list showing actually what their real social precedence was, I think the eyes of many people in highly paid appointments would be opened, and they would be unpleasantly reminded of the fact that Indian officials out of India are nobodies.'

There was a tendency to react with dismay and even anger when the rules of precedence were flouted. Ethel Savi recalled in her autobiography the irritation that she and her husband caused in local society in northwest Bengal before the First World War when, although mere indigo planters, they had put up high officials on tour with whom they happened to be acquainted. The Kipling family caused even more ripples. Lockwood Kipling was a member of the Educational Service, which ranked low in the Warrant of Precedence; and what is more, both he and his wife, Alice, were intellectuals who wrote and sketched more seriously than was considered necessary. Yet they and their children, Trix and Rudyard, were taken up by Lord Dufferin, the Viceroy between 1884 and 1888, because they were 'interesting'.

In their love of rank and complicated social rules, the British were also influenced by their surroundings. The Indian love of ritual, the whole elaborate structure of caste with its rules that governed how you ate, how you married, even how you dressed, seeped into their collective outlook. Margaret Harkness, herself a memsahib in the years before the First World War, saw this: 'Many English people – most, nearly all, in fact – are caught in the mesh of Oriental pageantry that for one hundred and fifty years has been considered by England to be a necessary part of her rule in India.'

Caste rules are restricting but they also give shape to the daily round. The memsahibs gradually established a routine, with its daily duties and its daily diversions, that was to remain remarkably consistent until the Raj finally disappeared. There were changes over time, of course. In the eighteenth century, women were usually carried to social engagements in a palanquin; in the nineteenth, they were more likely to use a horse and carriage; and by the twentieth, they might use a car or, if very energetic, a bicycle.

The morning, the coolest part of the day, was usually kept for house-keeping and sitting on the verandah, perhaps with a few close friends, sewing and gossiping and drinking endless sodas and limes (after the First World War, there was less sewing and more bridge and gimlets, with gin added to the lime juice). What Julia Maitland noticed during her stay in south India in the early nineteenth century had scarcely changed a century later: 'A thorough Madras lady ... receives a number of morning visitors; takes up a little worsted work; goes to tiffin with Mrs C., unless Mrs D. comes to tiffin with her; and writes some dozen of "*chits*".' Later in the afternoon, the same women met each other again for tea or for a children's party.

Even in the twentieth century, memsahibs relied on the chit to arrange their day's activities. Chits kept social life flowing smoothly. Did a memsahib need to borrow a tinned ham, a servant, a dress pattern? Was she having a tennis afternoon, a children's tea party, a dinner party?

A messenger was sent out with piles of little notes and bore different little notes with answers back again. Some ladies made them into a work of art: in Bombay in the 1840s a French traveller, M. Stocqueler, noticed chits 'cunningly implicated into cocked hats, twists and other sacred involutions'.

Not surprisingly, some women grew bored with seeing the same faces day after day and listening to the same gossip about children and servants. 'Their minds', said Julia Maitland unkindly of her acquaintances, 'seem to evaporate under this Indian sun, never to be condensed or concentrated again.' There were exceptions – women who preferred to pass their days in other ways. They sketched, often quite well. They experimented with watercolours and, in the twentieth century, with photography. They made collections – of insects, of butterflies, of dried flowers. Few, perhaps, were as ambitious as the energetic Fanny Parks, who spent her days immersed in painting, sketching, silver and brass work, archery and chemical experiments.

The day was also the time for the sports so loved by the British in India. In both men and women, a love of sport was believed to show a 'sound' outlook. It was also considered good for the health, a way of sweating out the pernicious moral and physical influences of India. Women engaged in the same sports as men, except for those, like tent-pegging or polo, which were considered too dangerous for them. They shot, they rode to hounds (India did not run to foxes but it could provide jackals), they played tennis and golf. They competed against each other, in a spirit of friendly rivalry, in ladies' gymkhanas. And ladies' cricket matches pitted them against male teams, the men handicapped by playing left-handed with brooms instead of bats.

Horses were fairly cheap in India, and most women rode as a matter of course. The usual time for riding was before breakfast – in the hot weather, as early as four in the morning. Riding gave women exercise; it also gave them, temporarily, a feeling of freedom. It gave them a chance, too, to see an India outside the confines of their own milieu. Nancy Foster, sister of Jon and Rumer Godden, said of her morning ride: 'It took you where you'd never get in any other way. You always rode early before breakfast, riding for miles across country, riding out into the paddy-fields. You went through miles of mustard fields or beans with the most wonderful scent. You'd meet peacocks strutting about, you'd go through the villages and all the people were very friendly; they'd offer you a glass of milk or some fruit and they'd chat. I usually rode completely alone and never at any time, even at the difficult times, did I meet any unpleasantness or rudeness.' Riding was also useful socially. It provided wonderful opportunities for flirting, out of range of the ubiquitous chaperones. 'Doe-hacking' was the contemptuous term the old hands used for young men who went out riding with their girlfriends. On the remoter stations, before cars, riding was the easiest way for women to visit their neighbours. Julia Curtis thought nothing of going many miles just for an afternoon of tennis and gossip. The journey home, even though she was tired, also had its compensations: 'There were wonderful moonlight nights when we rode through endless mazes of coffee, across the open spaces of paddy fields, and through patches of bamboo jungle; and pitchdark nights when the going was slow, and the syce, bearing a hurricane lantern, had to light us on our way.'

Target shooting was another popular amusement. Regiments held competitions for their wives and daughters; by the twentieth century there was an all-India shooting competition for women. It was thought of as a skill that might come in useful one day – for shooting at more than just targets. Men of the Raj were conscious that their women might have to defend themselves. Monica Campbell-Martin, whose husband was working at the time as a mine manager in Bihar, was motivated purely by boredom; she tried shooting on a whim, found she was good at it, and eventually became a very competent hunter. The eccentric and dashing Lady Hailey was a famous shot. When her husband was Lieutenant-Governor of the United Provinces of Agra and Oudh at the end of the 1920s, she would ask her guests in Government House if she might pick them some canna lilies. If they said yes, she took up her .22 and cut a swath neatly across a flower bed.

There were slightly tamer sports – cycling, perhaps, which, according to Lillian Ashby, the policeman's daughter from Bihar, was considered 'daring and fashionable' in the 1890s. Archery was extremely popular in the second half of the nineteenth century. Kipling wrote in his story 'Cupid's Arrows' that it was 'as great a pest as lawn-tennis is now. People talked learnedly about "holding" and "loosing", "steles", "reflexed bows", "56-pound bows", "backed" or "self-yew bows"'. The heroine of his story – Miss Beighton, the 'Diana of Tara-Devi' – is being courted by a handsome but poor subaltern and a hideous but rich Commissioner. Her mother is determined that she shall marry for money. Barr-Saggott – 'the ugliest man in Asia, with two exceptions' – gives a diamond bracelet as the prize in a ladies' archery contest to be held on the Simla sporting ground of Annandale. Miss Beighton is favoured to win the contest and Barr-Saggott is favoured to win her hand. Her shooting is spectacular; with great deliberation and skill she throws both the contest and her chances at a good match. 'It was wonderful archery; but seeing that her business was to make "golds" and win the bracelet, Barr-Saggott turned a delicate green like young water-grass ... a chilly hush fell over the company, and Mrs Beighton took out her handkerchief.'

By the end of the nineteenth century, archery and croquet, another popular sport, were being supplanted by tennis and golf. Even in the smaller stations it was easy enough to make a tennis court, preferably on grass or failing that on beaten earth, and to lay out a rough nine-hole golf course (even if the greens were really brown mud). Labour was cheap and the government of India often donated the land. India added its own touches: crows that swooped down and picked off golf balls or, as Monica Campbell-Martin once noticed, leopard tracks that crossed the fairway where she had just been playing.

When Nancy Vernede was a young girl between the wars in Allahabad, where her father was a High Court judge, her parents often gave tennis parties. Between sets, the players ate the tea – 'sponge cake with rum butter, chocolate cake with walnuts, scones, sandwiches and curry puffs' – set up under the trees by the servants. Tennis parties were always popular; the guests amused themselves and the hostess simply had to provide enough food and drink. In selecting cakes, *The Complete Indian Housekeeper and Cook* warned its readers, the rule was 'to avoid stickiness and surprises'. Drinks should range from tea to claret or hock cup, and 'if a novelty be desired, it will be found that in the hot weather *granitos* and *sorbets* will be much liked'. The table should be prettily decorated with flowers and 'little daintinesses in the shape of embroidered cloths'.

Garden parties were usually more formal. Women wore their most attractive afternoon dresses and huge hats, sometimes lined with paper against the sun's rays. There was generally some sort of entertainment, a military band perhaps to play selections from Gilbert and Sullivan softly in the background. Garden party food was fairly predictable: in Lahore, for example, it was 'lettuce and tomato sandwiches, curry puffs, little iced cakes and Nedou's toffees'. Viceroys' and governors' garden parties could be very grand. A newspaper account of one at Viceregal Lodge in Simla in 1902 strikes the proper awed note: 'A curious hush came over the assemblage, and all eyes were turned in one direction. Then the band struck up God Save the King, and up walked Lord Curzon in frock-coat and top-hat, preceded by a single aide-de-camp in uniform. The men bared their heads in the sun and made an avenue, through which the Viceroy, leaning unwontedly on a stout stick, but otherwise looking well and active, walked to a large shamiana [marquee] and sat down with Lady Rivaz. Then the band returned to its ordinary promenade music, the people resumed their walking and talking, the refreshment tents regained their crowds, cheerful conversation resumed its buzz, and presently Lady Curzon moved out to converse pleasantly with friends. When the sun had sunk low in the clear heavens, the Viceroy and Lady Curzon left the grounds together, and thereafter the festive crowd dispersed.'

If there was nothing much else planned for the afternoon, there was always the Club. In spite of the objections of the diehards, women and children were allowed to use most Clubs by the end of the nineteenth century. Generally the bar was out of bounds to them: signs warned severely, 'Women not admitted beyond this point.' In compensation the women were given their own area, often nicknamed the *moorghi-khana* (the 'hen-house'); it was usually rather dark and unattractively furnished. They could, however, use the tennis courts and the swimming pools, and borrow books and magazines from the library. They could study the notice boards, where 'prams, ponies, sewing machines, hats, dresses, layettes, hens, goats, decanters, oil stoves, donkeys, rabbits, bicycles, mowing machines, gramophones, mattresses, cars, cradles, saucepans, and saddlery' were advertised for sale. As the Indian twilight gathered, and the men drifted into the Club from their offices, they could sit in sociable groups on the lawn or on the long verandah and have the first drink of the day. The preferred drink of the eighteenth century had been the 'brandy-pawnee' (brandy and water), but later sahibs and memsahibs drank gimlets, gin with Indian tonic, or whisky with soda, which came in thick green bottles. (The 'peg', as it was known, got its name, according to British humorists, because each was a peg in your coffin.)

The alternative to the early evening at the Club was a simple one: a drive or a walk to a fashionable gathering spot where the inhabitants could gossip again and flirt. On small stations, this was often nothing more than a dusty piece of earth with the imposing title of the Maidan. On a military station, there might be the added attraction of a small band-shell where the regimental bands took turns; when they played 'God Save the Queen' (or King) everyone knew that it was time for dinner. In the cities, the evening outing offered more variety. In Calcutta the fashionable strolled in the Eden Gardens or took a turn along the Strand beside the Hooghly River while the bands played. Until the middle of the nineteenth century ladies were often carried out in palanquins to take the evening air. Mrs Fay, in the late eighteenth century, had been much struck by the practice in Madras: the palanquins, she found, 'are often very beautifully ornamented, and appear in character with the country, and with the languid air of those who use them, which, though very different from anything I have been accustomed to admire in a woman, as you well know, yet is not unpleasing in a country the charms of which are heightened by exhibiting a view of society entirely new to me'.

The evening dinner party was not popular until the nineteenth century. In the eighteenth, most of the eating and drinking was done in the middle of the day. And what eating and drinking it was! A quite ordinary midday dinner for Mrs Fay was 'a soup, a roast fowl, curry and rice, a mutton pie, a forequarter of lamb, a rice pudding, tarts, very good cheese, fresh churned butter, fine bread'. The food was washed down with copious amounts of wine. 'It is customary', she added, 'to sit a long while at table.' Not surprisingly, the guests generally took to their beds afterwards until the cool of the evening revived them. Then they went out to pay visits or to parties, and ate a further, lighter meal at about ten.

In the more temperate nineteenth century, the main meal of the day was moved back until seven or eight in the evening, and by the time of the Mutiny, the old extravagance was beginning to die out. Colonel Kenney-Herbert, whose *Wyvern's Indian Cookery Book* was the best ever written on British cuisine in India, was quite proud of the change: 'Our dining of today would indeed astonish our British forefathers. With a taste for light wines, and a far more moderate indulgence in stimulating drinks, has been germinated a desire for delicate and artistic cookery. Quality has superseded quantity, and the peppery curries and spicy oriental compositions of the olden times have been gradually banished from our dinner tables.' Yet meals in India still struck visitors from Home as excessive. *The Complete Indian Housekeeper and Cook* urged its readers to struggle against 'the ludicrously heavy style of the ordinary luncheon', but with little success. Lunch – or tiffin – customarily ran to several courses: one suggested lunch in a cookbook published just before the First World War is gravy soup, followed by lobster mayonnaise, kidneys 'German fashion', cold game pie, salad, plantain fritters, cheese and toast, and fruit to finish up with. (The same book has a section entitled 'Dinner Menus for Dyspeptics'.) Afternoon tea, even without guests, offered a choice of sandwiches, cakes and perhaps sweets. For a simple family dinner another cookbook of the 1910s suggests 'Pea soup. Roast Chicken and tongue. Bread sauce. Potatoes, vegetables. Cheese, macaroni. Lemon pudding.'

By the second half of the nineteenth century, the British were trying to distance themselves from India even in their food. When tinned food came in, it was considered a compliment to guests to give them Home-grown delicacies out of tins; one naive lady, who had never been out of India, was overheard to say, 'doubtless nothing else was ever used at her Majesty's table'. Generations of Indian cooks learnt to make the right sort of dishes: the soups, the puddings, the savouries on toast, the cakes for tea. But Anglo-Indian cooking, like the British themselves, did not entirely escape from the influence of India. They still used more spices than people at Home would have done and they had their special dishes: the peppery mulligatawny soup, which was a regular feature of Sunday lunch, the hybrid dishes that they called curry and kedgeree.

Taking its cue from upper-class behaviour at Home, etiquette in India forbade the discussion of food. It was impolite to compliment the hostess on the cooking; it suggested that she had actually done the work herself. Perhaps it was just as well, for often there was not much to praise. Although menu cards were written out in French, there was nothing French about the food itself. Nor were other European cuisines much in evidence. Pasta, for example, appeared in Anglo-Indian cookery only as macaroni, 'either swimming in a tasteless white sauce round a boiled fowl or turkey', complained Colonel Kenney-Herbert, 'or baked with cheese in a pie-dish'. Excellent fresh and saltwater fish were available in most parts of India, but the fish course at a British dinner party was generally a piece of boiled pomfret (which would have tasted like a delicate version of turbot if it had not invariably been overcooked) or *seer* (which might have tasted something like salmon if it had been treated properly) or something out of a tin. The fish, to quote Colonel Kenney-Herbert again, was unfortunately 'not always at its best' and it was usually served with a sauce flavoured by 'Messrs. Somebody's Essence'.

Often hostesses did not take sufficient advantage of the variety of foods available in India. By the end of the nineteenth century, it was possible to get or grow almost all the familiar English fruits and vegetables in most parts of the country – potatoes, green peas, cauliflower, cabbages, spinach, artichokes, green beans, broad beans, carrots, parsnips, turnips, celery, even the tasteless giant marrow squashes so incomprehensibly loved by the British, and apples, pears, strawberries, peaches – as well as all the things not found at Home – okra (*bhindi* in Hindi), aubergine or eggplant (*brinjal*), sweet corn, yams, all sorts of herbs, mangoes, lychees. Colonel Kenney-Herbert was stern indeed about the lady of the house who spent tens of rupees on tins while begrudging her cook the basic fresh ingredients of good cooking.

Dinner was an occasion even for those who lived alone, miles from the nearest European society. The British really did dress for dinner in the jungle. The Wallace-Dunlop sisters, camping off the beaten track in mountains near Mussoorie in 1856, dressed in black silk dresses and twined wild clematis in their hair to visit a neighbouring encampment where they dined on wild goat steaks and partridges. To Jon and Rumer Godden as children in the small Bengal town of Narayanganj, the clothes their mother and aunt changed into every evening were the height of glamour: 'Mam had an evening dress of grey and cherry-coloured chiffon, another that was pink with beads, while Aunt Mary wore tunics and skirts of different colours – a russet tunic with a yellow silk skirt, a pale blue with plum colour.'

It was by her dinner parties that a woman was judged a social success or failure. The novelist Maud Diver asserted in *The Englishwoman in India* (1909): 'India is the land of dinners, as England is the land of five o'clock teas. From the Colonels' and Commissioners' wives who conscientiously "dine the station" every cold weather, to the wives of subalterns and junior civilians – whose cheery informal little parties of six or eight are by no means to be despised by lovers of good company and simple fare

– all Anglo-India is in a chronic state of giving and receiving this – the most delightful or the most excruciating form of hospitality. And who but the hostess is responsible for the destined adjective?'

All over India, from Madras to the Northwest Frontier, hostesses gave the same dinner party. After a drink in the drawing room, the party would be summoned to the dining room by the bearer. They went, except on informal occasions, in strict order of precedence. The dining rooms were usually gloomy; the furniture was heavy and dark, the lighting candles or, by the late nineteenth century, paraffin lamps, which left pools of shadow. (An enterprising hostess might use rose-coloured shades to give a becoming glow to the scene.) Overhead, on hot nights, a *punkah* or a revolving fan moved slowly above the diners' heads. At their feet there might be a small lamp to lure insects away from their ankles and, on very hot nights, a tub of ice. At the grander dinners a servant waited behind every chair; the hostess borrowed extra ones for her guests, as indeed she borrowed cutlery and cooks.

The table was almost always covered with a heavy white cloth and carefully decorated. Ropes of ivy twined with flowers and ferns snaked artfully across the cloth, and in the centre of the table there might be a silver bowl (no doubt a wedding present) filled with roses. Sometimes scattered about the table were small silver dishes filled with chocolates, pralines, crystallized fruit, stuffed dates or pickled ginger. Every place had its array of cutlery and its champagne glass. (In the early nineteenth century these were often provided with silver covers to keep insects from falling into the drink, but the custom gradually died out.) There were finger bowls on small embroidered doilies with a sweet-scented flower such as jasmine floating in them. At large dinner parties, each place also had a card with a guest's name and a menu in a silver holder. On the sideboard, proudly displayed, was the rest of the household silver – salvers, toast racks, the cups won in some sporting contest.

Seating had to be planned with care. The most senior lady went to the right of the host; the most senior gentleman on the hostess's right; and the other guests were carefully distributed in descending order of importance. Anne Wilson described in a letter the unfortunate novice hostess who seated an army officer in the wrong place at dinner. He informed her that he was a *full* colonel, only to get the cheerful reply: 'Are you really? Well, I hope that when dinner is over you will be still fuller!' Even with the help of the Warrant of Precedence, there were some who were difficult to place. What about the 'military civilian' (an officer seconded to the government) and his wife? Were they to go by his army or his civil service ranking? What about non-officials? or visitors from Home? In 1881, there was a lively correspondence in *The Pioneer* about the whole matter. 'Mohawk' started it off with an irascible letter to the editor which said, in part: 'As if the hostess in India did not have sufficient wearisome and irritating toil in the management of her household, without having to pander to the snobbishness of her guests, who are impressed with the importance of the seniority of their official positions.' Few of the letters that followed agreed with his assertion that his compatriots in India were snobbish. In any case, said the defenders, they were much less snobbish than they had once been. And 'Red Tape', true to his pseudonym, argued that the rules of precedence were in fact useful 'as a protection against the snobbishness of human nature'.

All dinner menus followed the same pattern – soups, fish, joints, puddings, savouries. *Indian Outfits*, in 1882, set out the following sample menu to guide the novice hostess:

POTAGES

Almond Soup   Clear gravy Soup

POISSONS

Pomplet [pomfret]   Tinned Salmon

ENTRÉES

*Croquettes of sweetbreads   Beef Olives with Tomatoes
Quenelles of partridge*

RELEVÉS

Boiled Turkey   Haunch of mutton

Rôts

Teal   Quails

Entremets

Maraschino jelly   Burnt cream
Meringuées [sic] filled with mango cream

Cheese

Fresh   Stilton

Ices

Lemon ice cream   Coffee ice cream

Dessert

Fruits in season   Cakes, biscuits, etc.

Indian cooks loved to play with mashed potatoes, colouring them red or green and shaping them into pears – with a clove for the stalk – or birds. For the sweets they produced wonderful baskets made of toffee filled with fruit salad and cream or castles made of ice cream.

At the end of the meal, the ladies stayed briefly while the port and madeira were brought out; and then they withdrew to powder their noses and arrange their hair in the hostess's bedroom. (Such was the respect for rank that the ladies solemnly used the commode in order of seniority – yet another reason why it was unpleasant to be a junior memsahib.) The men did not usually linger long over their port before joining the ladies in the drawing room. One of the guests might be persuaded to sing a popular sentimental ballad, perhaps from the 'Indian Love Lyrics', written by a wildly romantic memsahib called Adela Florence Cory (see p. 244) – which included the famous 'Kashmiri Song' with its cry for 'Pale hands I loved beside the Shalimar'. Or they might make up teams and play games such as Dumb Crambo, in which one team had to guess a word being acted out by the other. Favourite card games were whist or pontoon and, by the twentieth century, bridge. On less formal occasions, the games were sillier: the party might amuse themselves by sitting on the floor and blowing a feather across a tablecloth.

About an hour after dinner, the bearer appeared with a tray of whisky and soda, and the evening ended soon after. When the most senior lady got to her feet to take her leave, the other guests were bound by etiquette to follow her example without much delay. If any guests did have to leave earlier, as 'An English Lady' who wrote to *The Pioneer* in the 1880s discovered in amazement, they customarily got permission from the senior lady rather than from their hostess: 'Hearing this my brain reeled; I felt myself unequal to the task; I knew that nothing but a severe course of study on Indian etiquette would enable me to grasp the relative positions of hostess and guests as understood here.'

While the dinner party was the mainstay of British entertaining, evening brought other sorts of parties. In eighteenth-century Calcutta, card parties were popular, sometimes with music, as well, 'to fill up the space', as Mrs Fay put it: viceroys and governors held receptions of great formality. At the turn of the nineteenth century, Lord Curzon had 'Levées' (for gentlemen only), which were attended by almost two thousand, and 'Drawing Rooms' for the ladies, with four hundred at a time. Young Nancy Vernede and her friends in Allahabad had a simpler sort of party one evening on a barge. While their craft drifted slowly down the Ganges, they listened to the gramophone and ate a picnic, and, at a convenient sandbank, got out to play games.

And of course the dances! These ranged from formal balls right down to impromptu dancing after a dinner party. Often bands provided music, but sometimes the amateurs had to make their own; when Julia Curtis first went to dances at the Planters' Club the ladies took turns playing tunes such as 'Love's Golden Dream' and 'El Dorado' on the tinny piano. In the eighteenth century the sahibs and memsahibs danced minuets, cotillions, various country dances; in the nineteenth it was reels, mazurkas, waltzes, polkas, gallops and something called the Washington Post; and in the twentieth the two-step and the fox-trot made the long journey out from Home. New dances caused great excitement. Mrs Ashmore described a ball at Government House in the 1840s at which a few daring couples did the waltz for the first time: 'a dense ring was formed around them and the greatest anxiety was evinced to behold the unusual sight'. (Some ladies even scrambled up on chairs.)

All levels of society held dances, from the Viceroy down to the noncommissioned officers in the British regiments stationed there. (With gracious affability, officers and their wives and girlfriends dropped in on the men's dances but, as one middle-class girl reported to her family in England, 'except for a Paul Jones, where one got some very amusing partners, we danced among ourselves.') There were regimental balls, bachelors' balls, Club dances. In Calcutta in the nineteenth century, the Saturday Club came into existence for the sole purpose of allowing 'ladies and gentlemen' to meet every week for amateur theatricals and dancing. By the twentieth century many of the hotels and larger Clubs had started holding tea dances (sometimes known as 'flannel-dances' to distinguish them from more formal affairs) to fill up the interval between tea and the evening's entertainment.

At the grand official balls the ladies wore white gloves and worried about their curtsies. When Curzon was Viceroy, he customarily gave a state ball during the winter season in Calcutta, several smaller balls with around five hundred guests, and weekly dances as well. All over India, on stations where there were enough British, the senior official held a ball on the monarch's birthday. (Invitations to it were one of the great dividing lines between those who were socially acceptable and those who were not.) The larger Residences all had ballrooms as a matter of course. In Madras in the nineteenth century the floor in Government House was polished by fifteen Indians using coconut halves. When Lord Auckland was Governor-General in the 1830s, according to Lord Curzon's account, it was the custom to draw on the floor in coloured chalks 'either the arms of the illustrious individual whom it was desired to honour, or the arms of the Queen, the Governor General, and the Company .... Presumably', added Curzon with his customary thoroughness, 'the pictures were soon effaced by the assiduous soles of the dancers.'

Probably the favourite of all, from the nineteenth century right up to 1947, was the fancy dress ball. There would be the conventional Pierrots and Pierrettes, the Gypsy Queens and the Pirate Kings, and the figures in sheets supposed to be either Ghosts or Arabs – but many people put a good deal of work into their costumes. The *durzi* was called on to concoct something to dazzle the rest of society; women who were rich enough might even send away to Europe for their costumes. In the first half of the 1880s, Grant Duff, the Governor of Madras, and his wife were famous for their fancy dress balls. One required everyone to come in costumes made of Indian materials; another, in costumes based on the theme of the court of Louis XIII. (One young woman interpreted this rather loosely to come as The Cloud with the Silver Lining.) Lord Curzon gave a fancy dress ball to mark one that had been given a hundred years previously by Richard Wellesley, then Earl of Mornington; the guests and the viceregal court dressed in the costumes of their predecessors.

Women usually had a marvellous time because there were almost always more men than women at dances. Minnie Blane wrote to her mother from Rawalpindi in 1860: 'I went to a Ball on the 31st December given by the officers of the 4th Punjab Infantry. Very jolly, but myself and two other ladies *only* danced Waltzes and Polkas, etc. There were ten ladies present and thirty gentlemen. This is often the case of Indian parties. It is very tiring work as when a lady dances she is expected to dance *everything*, and the consequence was I went through nineteen dances and only stopped because my shoe cut me so much.' As with so much else in the life of the Raj, dances adhered to strict rules. At the official balls the aides-de-camp made sure that everything was in order, that the Viceroy or the Governor danced with the most senior rather than the merely pretty ladies. There were dance cards with little pink and blue pencils tied on with silk cords in order to avoid confusion about who was dancing with whom. The best way to get time with a favourite was to book the supper dance. The senior ladies might make sure that unmarried girls did not dance too often with unsuitable men. Sir Ian Hamilton remembered Mrs Parker, the senior memsahib of his regiment, giving him and his fellow subalterns their orders before a dance: 'The girls should dance with the Majors and Captains or the very charming Deputy Commissioner Monti Lang, because they might marry them, whereas they were strictly forbidden to marry subalterns, at least in the 92nd.'

The memsahibs also kept an eye out for incorrect behaviour. After the eighteenth century, for example, it was most certainly not correct for men to get drunk. Gentlemen were expected to behave as such when ladies were present. Sir Ian Hamilton recounted with admiration the perfect manners of a fellow officer in an awkward situation. A buxom lady in an exceedingly lowcut dress had a sudden accident: her breasts popped loose. Fortunately Swinburne, paymaster of the regiment, knew what to do: 'What a subaltern would have done heaven knows; in fact, I never heard of such a thing taking place at a ball; but religion, duty, and the habit of a lifetime came to the rescue of Swinburne and, bowing, he took the precious articles as if they were bags of rupees and with the words, "Pardon me, Madam," shovelled them back.'

Flirting was considered part of the evening's entertainment. It was held to be a mistake, however, for a woman to book too many dances in her programme with the same man; more than three dances in a row and the gossip started. If she was unmarried, rumour had her engaged, and if she was married, suspicion ran wild. The further down the social scale the stricter the rules governing behaviour: Dennis Kincaid talks of Sergeants' Dances in the inter-war years 'at which the etiquette was of terrifying strictness and a girl's reputation was gone if she were not returned to her parents by her partner as soon as each dance was over'.

India was capable of disrupting dances with unpleasant surprises. Emma Roberts, touring the country before the Mutiny, described the way in which a ball at Barrackpore (the summer residence of the Governor-General outside Calcutta) was ruined by a sudden storm: 'A very large proportion of the guests determined to go up by water, anticipating a delightful excursion by starlight; but the horrors of the storm burst upon them ere they could reach their destination; the Hughli ran mountains high, washing over the decks of the frail little summer-vessels and driving many on shore, to the consternation of their passengers and the utter ruin of their ball-dresses. The travellers by land were not better off; the horses took fright at the lightning; the road was rendered impassable by trees torn up by the roots; ladies terrified out of their senses, made an attempt to walk, and the party, when collected at last, presented a most lugubrious spectacle, a concourse of wet, weary, miserable guests, eagerly impatient to return to their homes, yet compelled to await more favourable weather.' Lady Falkland gave a ball in the Governor's Residence in Poona in the 1850s which she remembered ever after as the 'Blister Fly Ball'. Hordes of the flies (which have a painful sting) descended on the dancers and by the end of the evening the dance floor was black with squashed insects. 'One heard little else all the evening', she reported, 'but "Allow me, sir, to take off this blister fly that is disappearing into your neck-cloth"; or "Permit me, ma'am, to remove this one from your arm."'

The exiles relied more than their compatriots at Home on amateur performances to amuse themselves – concerts at which ladies sang and gentlemen did comic recitations, and theatricals. *Tableaux vivants*, in which the participants carefully posed a famous scene – 'Pygmalion in his Studio' or 'Home They Brought the Warrior Dead' – were popular. More ambitious groups put on full-length plays. 'Some of Shakespeare's deepest tragedies', wrote Mrs Ashmore from Cawnpore in the 1840s, 'gave rise to many a hearty fit of laughter.' On the whole, taste ran to light comedies on the lines of those nineteenth-century Calcutta favourites, 'High Life Below Stairs' or, for a change, 'High Life Above Stairs'. Some of the larger stations even had their own small theatres. Initially all parts were performed by 'gentlemen players', but by the middle of the nineteenth century it was generally considered acceptable for ladies to take part in performances. After all, a correspondent of *The Pioneer* in the 1880s wrote, 'The private stage is at once the most intellectual and the most widely appreciated diversion we possess.' A retired ICS officer still feared in the 1920s that the appearance of Englishwomen on the stage would hurt the Raj: 'it is up to us and to our women to do nothing to lower that prestige.' By then, however, the spread of the cinema was causing amateur theatricals to lose their appeal.

In the hot weather, social life came nearly to a standstill. Women who remained on the Plains ventured out only in the early morning or late at night. Sometimes they held quiet dinner parties, the table in the garden and the only light from candles. One consolation was the moonlight picnic. Kipling's story 'False Dawn' describes what happened in one small station. 'Saumarez gave a moonlight riding-picnic at an old tomb, six miles away, near the bed of the river. It was a "Noah's Ark" picnic; and there was to be the usual arrangement of quarter-mile intervals between each couple on account of the dust.' The picnic had a romantic purpose: it was generally expected that Saumarez would propose to the elder Miss Copleigh. Unfortunately in the confusion of a dust storm Saumarez proposes to the wrong Miss Copleigh, and although the matter is straightened out, there is a bitter taste left.

With the return of the cold weather, there was a renewed flurry of social activity. 'Lucknow en Fête' was how *The Pioneer* described the season of 1881. Different stations had their 'weeks', when people came in from the outlying districts to enjoy a concentrated whirl of pleasures.

The days and nights were crammed with dances, races, polo, dog shows, amateur theatricals, cricket, lunches. And almost always there was a *pagal* (mad) gymkhana for both men and women, including 'a costume race and other screamingly funny events, as well as trials of skill such as tent pegging, the Victoria Cross race, the Balaclava *mêlée*, a driving competition for ladies, and tilting at the ring'.

Planters, in particular, were famous for the ferocity with which they enjoyed themselves at their special three- or four-day 'meets', which were held whenever they could think of a good excuse. Sometimes they set up camps in the countryside, each with its mess tent and badminton and tennis courts. The days were filled with the usual games as well as excursions to nearby beauty spots, and the nights with dances, dinners, and campfire parties where the guests sat around the fire on comfortable chairs and sofas while a band played for their entertainment.

Monica Campbell-Martin went to a planters' meet in a town in North Bihar which drew planters from all over the province: 'Those of us with children took them along. An ayah went too, or a bearer, because we could not keep a watchful eye on the new generation and be a mile away at the club playing in tournaments. With the extra horses and cars, the children and their bearers, and sometimes the childrens' ponies, there was a lively collection that cheered you to look at it, just for the pleasant change of seeing so many in one place. Friends with insufficient accommodation put up tents in their gardens.' One evening there was a treasure hunt. The teams of 'a man and a girl' were sent out to find items on a list (the winners were the first ones to get back to the Club with their booty): 'One was a buck goat, the other was a hair from a redhead. In the middle of the night the bazaar was inundated by hilarious couples looking for buck goats. The bazaar folk enthusiastically entered into the spirit of the thing (they have a keen sense of humour), and rushed about trying to help. There was only one redheaded girl in Muzaffarpur that year. For days afterwards she went around with a hunted look.'

Christmas week was particularly gay; Lahore, for example, was famous all over the Punjab for its festivities. In 1880 a newspaper correspondent noted that 'the amusements which Calcutta has to fall back upon during the current holiday season are five days' racing, a few good cricket matches, a casual dance or two, Madame Carlotta Patti's concerts and the two circuses on the Maidan.' After Delhi had become the capital in 1911, its 'week' was the grandest of all; women calculated that they needed at least two trunkloads of clothes.

Christmas Day itself was a special occasion. The British decorated their bungalows and churches with wreaths of Indian flowers; for pine boughs they used palm branches, and for holly, poinsettias. In the morning they went to church, to sing 'Adeste Fideles' and 'Hark! the Herald Angels Sing' under the *punkahs*. After church, they received their Indian servants and employees who came to bring Christmas greetings and presents of *dalis* – baskets piled with flowers, cakes, sweets, fruits, toys for the little sahibs and memsahibs. In return, the employers handed over a tip, so that no one lost from the exchange of courtesies. Then, all over India, British families sat down to Christmas lunch. They pulled crackers and put on funny hats and tucked into roast turkey and plum pudding. (Sometimes, if they were in camp, they had to substitute roast peacock for the turkey.)

Perhaps the final word on the amusements that life in India offered to many woman should rest with Lillian Ashby, who grew up not in the excitement of Simla or Calcutta but on a small station in Bihar. As a young unmarried woman, her great treat of an evening was to drive five miles to the nearest railway station. 'We would enjoy the luxury of iced aereated drinks at Kellner and Company's Refreshment Room on the platform.' With her friends, she would watch the trains coming and going, bearing their passengers off to the wider world.

11

ON HOLIDAY

Hill stations, those peculiarly British contributions to imperialism, have tended to overshadow all the other sorts of holidays that were available. The best one of all was to go Home. With its gentle climate, its soft green countryside, Britain was such a pleasant contrast to India! For women, there was the opportunity to spend days, months, on end with the families they had so often missed while they were away. They could renew their acquaintance with European civilization, its books, its newspapers, and, always important, its fashions. If their husbands had managed to come with them, they might take a short sightseeing trip to the Continent (Switzerland was perennially popular). The only shadow on their happiness was the thought of their children who were going to be left behind when they returned to India.

If they did not go Home, they sometimes took a break from India by travelling to Ceylon – still oriental, of course, but with a pleasant climate and extraordinarily beautiful views. Or, by the late nineteenth century, they might go further afield to Australia. The sea voyage itself was said to be an excellent restorative for constitutions broken down by the Indian climate. (It was also a good idea to scout out future places for retirement; Home might prove too expensive, even uncongenial, after life in the colonies.)

Because of the time and money required for long trips outside the country, most women spent many of their holidays in India. The men never missed going Home as much as the women did: there were such wonderful opportunities for shooting and fishing close at hand. Some women shared the men's pleasure in sporting holidays. The boldest even tried pig-sticking (hunting wild boar), balanced precariously on their side-saddles. (Riding astride did not gain respectability until shortly before the First World War, when the three daughters of the Viceroy, Lord Minto, startled Simla by galloping down the Mall in divided skirts.) They went off into remote areas for long periods. One woman spent six months in wild Baltistan up on the Northwest Frontier, where, an acquaintance reported, 'she shot three bears and accompanied many of the stalks after ibex and markhor, sketched, sewed, washed, read, and wrote, and in spite of being far from strong, and recently recovered from a very terrible accident, did not know a day's illness.' Mrs Baillie, a great hunter in the early part of the twentieth century, once noted with interest that three hundred jungle ticks had burrowed beneath the skin on her arm between her wrist and her elbow. On another occasion she was charged by a bear which knocked her to the ground, chewed her topi and mauled her leg badly; she cleaned out the wounds herself, feeling 'rather faint'.

Monica Campbell-Martin, in the inter-war years, was another of the women who fell in love with *shikar*, as shooting game was called, on her first hunting trip into the jungle. Since there were not enough elephants available, the party – four British and thirty porters – walked. They carried food for ten days and some of the comforts of home, including a zinc bathtub. 'Four of the biggest coolies', she recalled, 'carried an enormous packing case, containing the beer, roped and slung on bamboos.' Her first outing was a success: the party bagged game birds, deer and a tiger, and she shot a bear. On subsequent expeditions, she learnt the art of shooting from the back of an elephant. She shot at crocodiles from a moving boat. She also learnt how to stalk game and, perhaps even more difficult, how to wait for it. 'Living with the wild life, I learned the signs that help a hunter; the crow in the tree looking down at something and cawing; the sudden chatter of a troupe of monkeys peering from the trees at something in the grass; the grazing herd of deer that gets a scent on the wind and scatters.' She was bitten and stung by an astonishing variety of insects and even by a creeper that 'if brushed against can penetrate an elephant's hide, leaving its soft hairs to fester and poison the skin'. She came down with malaria. But what compensations there were – the pair of leopards bagged or the king cobra eleven feet (3.5 m) long or simply the colours and sounds of the jungle. Her acquaintances took to calling her, possibly a touch disapprovingly, 'the Jungli Memsahib' (the wild woman).

Women also took up fishing. Monica Lang, who lived in Assam in the same period, went on holidays to the borders of Tibet. As she and her husband fished, they could see the snow-covered Himalayas in the distance; nearby, 'clusters of bluish pink orchids hung from the giant trees almost down to the water's edge'. Around their jungle rest-house were birds 'of every imaginable size and colour', and underfoot the tracks of tiger, leopard, buffalo, elephant, deer and pig.

If they did not care for sport, women could try sightseeing. It could not be denied that India had a great many picturesque ruins and natural wonders. By the end of the nineteenth century, it was almost mandatory to visit the Taj Mahal in Agra and the Red Fort in Delhi. (The rulers of India found the relics of their Mughal predecessors particularly interesting – and perhaps easier to comprehend than Hindu architecture.) Rajasthan also had some splendid sights, although the travelling was less convenient. Mrs King, who saw much of north India with her husband while he was in the ICS around the 1880s, was full of admiration for the Rajput state of Jaipur, renowned for the beauty of its people and its buildings. She kept her highest praise for the capital city: 'the streets are really noble, and the great open squares as fine as any European ones.' And the caves at Ellora had magnificent and ancient carvings. Most women did not like the caves; they did not know enough about the religions which had inspired them and they found the sexual significance of much of the carving disturbing. For the same reasons, few went to see the great Hindu temples.

Women of the generations before the Mutiny had been much more enthusiastic about sightseeing. Maria Graham, who toured India just after the beginning of the nineteenth century, Lady Falkland, whose husband was Governor of Bombay before the Mutiny, the Honourable Emily Eden, all of whom left lively accounts of their travels and observations, were not eccentrics. They simply had the Enlightenment's curiosity about the rest of the world. Fanny Parks, who travelled widely in the north of India in the 1830s, wrote a book – *Wanderings of a Pilgrim in Search of the Picturesque* – whose title in itself reveals its author's attitude.

In December 1834 Mrs Parks, whose husband was a Company official in Allahabad, set sail up the Ganges in a small boat towing a cook boat with the provisions – from sheep to chickens – for a month's journey. Her companions were her servants and her drawing materials. She was kept entertained by the riverside scenes – the crocodiles basking in the sun, the graceful Indian women carrying pots of water on their heads, even the half-burnt bodies shovelled into the river from the funeral *ghats* (landing places). The little expedition ran into adverse winds and rocks;

the weather turned cold and frosty and the boat sprang a leak. None of this seems to have bothered her unduly. The river itself was endlessly fascinating: 'high cliffs, well covered with wood, rising abruptly from the water: here and there a Hindoo temple, … a ruined native fort: clusters of native huts: beautiful stone ghats jutting into the river …' The boat could go no further than Etwah and here she was met by horses that had been sent on ahead. She travelled on towards Agra, passing through towns which she pronounced delightful because there were none of her countrymen there: 'a place', she declared firmly, 'is spoiled by European residence.' While she found Agra and the nearby deserted Mughal city of Fatehpur Sikri most interesting, she was disgusted by the local Europeans who hired a band to play while they danced on the marble terrace in front of the Taj Mahal. That was a foretaste of the attitude of later generations: the casual assumption that the country existed as a not particularly interesting setting for their activities.

By the end of the nineteenth century, British men and women who travelled for pleasure in India were in a minority, and of that minority most seem to have preferred natural beauty spots to man-made ones. It is strange, given India's long coastline, that going to the seaside was never fashionable; was it fear of what might happen to the Raj if the Indians saw sahibs and memsahibs in bathing suits? or simply fear of the heat? Trips along inland waterways, however, were comfortable, and the inconveniences of India intruded little. Ethel Savi looked back fondly on weekend outings with friends from the Bengal town of Barisal in house-boats towed behind a steam launch which took them down to where the delta of the Ganges and the Bay of Bengal met: 'I well remember the wildness of the scenery on the way, where primeval jungle grew down to the water's edge, the weird cries in the stillness of the night of the jungle-beasts, the howl of jackals, the roar of an angry tiger. By day we saw natural glades with deer grazing, their young gambolling around them.'

The Godden girls took a similar trip. Their father used the occasion of a journey to the dentist in Calcutta to take them back to their home in Narayanganj by steamer through the Sundarbans, an area of trees like mangroves which knot themselves into an impenetrable jungle along the Ganges' many mouths. The children spent hours on deck staring into the jungle's green depths, rewarded occasionally by a glimpse of a monkey or a deer. The river itself was alive with crocodiles, the larger man-eating *muggers* and the smaller *gavials*, with porpoises and water snakes, while a myriad of birds – ospreys, ibis, storks, kingfishers – darted about. The girls were depressed at the first cleared fields, the signs of civilization, and amazed when their aunt said in relief, 'I was tired of all that soggy green.'

Women also got a holiday of sorts if they accompanied their husbands on a working trip. Although the practice was dying out by the end of the Raj, district commissioners, for example, or forestry experts or estate managers were expected to spend part of their year out of their offices. For both men and women, going on an inspection tour meant a break in the usual routine of station life: they saw another, often more primitive, India. Rosamund Lawrence, always so eloquent, recalled a river trip in Sind when her husband was Commissioner there during the First World War: while he worked on his papers, she sat on the deck under an awning gazing out. 'The vast sky and the vast river are divided by one blinding line of mustard, sliding by. Great golden Sindi boats, laden with grain, with their huge rudders turning this way and that, dream past with idle sails, and there are little fishing craft with a spidery circle of net, and the graceful figure of some Mohana woman bent against the long steering pole.'

The grandest tours of all were those made by high officials to the Indian princes. Wives who accompanied their husbands got a chance to see the most exotic side of India. (Sometimes it was a bizarre mixture of East and West: Lady Dufferin visited a Punjabi chief who had a band of strapping Punjabi pipers, dressed in kilts, and, to add verisimilitude, pink silk tights.) The princes went all out to entertain their distinguished guests, building special guest houses, hiring French chefs, putting on lavish entertainments, and arranging hunts (often with the tigers carefully drugged so that there should be no awkward incidents). When Lady Willingdon, wife of the Viceroy between 1931 and 1936, went to Baroda, the Maharajah, knowing of her love for all shades of purple, even arranged to have the lavatory paper dyed; Lady Willingdon ungratefully complained, 'There is something wrong with your toilet paper because I am purple all over!'

On tour, indeed on any trips that took them off the beaten track, the British – certainly the nineteenth-century ones – travelled with an enormous quantity of baggage. To carry all they needed – and often they had to take provisions for several weeks – they took trains of porters as well as baggage animals, from camels to elephants. Anne Wilson described setting off in the 1880s to what she called 'a nomad existence in the wilds' with a string of twenty-eight camels loaded with chairs and tables, household linen, silver, china, glasses, clothes and books, and followed by men carrying beds on their heads. There were crates, too, of tinned food from the Army and Navy Stores and a veritable travelling farmyard with two cows and their calves and a dozen sheep. Children often went along; Norah Burke remembered travelling as a small child in a laundry basket tied to an elephant. Such expeditions were not carefree holidays for the women, who had the responsibility for making sure that everything ran smoothly.

Sometimes there were government bungalows where they could stay. These were often quite primitive. The wife of the Civil Surgeon of Manipur, who went on tour with him in the 1930s, sent vivid sketches to her family in England of rickety tables so oddly constructed that no human being could eat off them and of privies which consisted of a hole in the ground and a tripod made of branches lashed together, invented, she felt, 'by some chaste and unobservant bachelor'.

Not surprisingly, many women preferred to live in tents. A proper camp had separate tents for sleeping (with a corner partitioned off for a bathroom), for dining and for sitting. Sometimes, to avoid delays, arrangements were made to send ahead a duplicate set of tents and a body of servants to the next stopping place. The tents themselves were like good-sized rooms; with pictures hanging on the canvas walls and rugs on the floors, they looked almost like the inside of a bungalow. In their guide for British housekeepers in India, Steel and Gardiner stressed the importance of being comfortable in camp. They suggested, among other essentials, 'charming folding tables of bamboo and deodar'. When Emily Eden's sister Fanny went on a brief camping trip (with about 260 servants) in the 1830s, dinner was served, as befitted a Viceroy's sister, with silver dishes and candlesticks, on a table set up on a sandbank in a river. Later generations added luxuries like portable gramophones. Rosamund Lawrence danced the latest steps, which she had learnt only a few months before in Cheltenham, in the middle of the jungle with 'close netting over the windows to prevent panthers from coming in, and the moonlight so bright that my emerald engagement ring gleams *green*, not merely dark'.

British women tried to travel with as much of home as they could manage. If they were going to be in camp over Christmas, they brought along tinned plum puddings and crackers. They also tried to keep up standards in cooking. The guidebooks are full of advice on supplies and menus for life under canvas. In general, the memsahib was expected to overcome small obstacles, such as few or no fresh vegetables, and to keep a proper table with the usual number of courses. Special camping utensils included a portable water filter. Colonel Kenney-Herbert also recommended a mineral oil stove and something known as a 'Locomotive Boiling Set', which accelerated boiling.

Lucy Carne, author of *Simple Menus and Recipes for Camp, Home, and Nursery*, published at the beginning of the twentieth century, gave lists of dishes suitable for each meal in camp. A light breakfast, suitable perhaps for travelling in the hot weather, might be oatmeal porridge and boiled eggs, with toast and potted meat to follow, and hot cocoa to wash it all down. A more substantial breakfast in camp ran to kidney stew, pigeon potato pie, or even an Anglo-Indian curry. Luncheon was on the same lines: roast pigeons with bread sauce, potato wafers, stewed apple rings and cream, followed by cheese and potted meats for a savoury. In the late afternoon, tea in camp might offer sandwiches – even with cucumber and watercress – and cakes and perhaps a few confections such as toffee. Dinners were more elaborate still, especially if guests had ridden over to the camp. Ladies and gentlemen dressed with as much formality as they could manage, preferably in dinner jackets and long dresses.

A favourite expedition under canvas was through the mountains in the north. Sportsmen and women could find good shooting and fishing and, for those who were interested, plenty of opportunities for sketching picturesque scenes. The Hill people were cheerful and friendly; their women, unlike the Indian women of the Plains, did not hide their faces from strangers. The slopes were covered with pines and wild rhododendrons. Along the course of the sparkling mountain streams there were stands of giant ferns and tall slender bamboos. There was usually plenty of wildlife, such as green mountain parrots, gangs of monkeys, and giant spiders which wove webs fifteen feet (4.5 m) across. And in every direction there were wonderful views. Mrs King gives a description of one vista near Naini Tal: 'In the foreground are long grassy mountain spurs covered with fine Scotch firs; beyond these stretch out endless

ranges of hills, now faintly blue and purple with the evening mists –
while beyond them again, cutting the sky line and shining gloriously in
the sunlight, is the great snow range.'

The enterprising Mrs King made several trips in the northwest.
On one occasion she did a circuit with her husband from Srinagar in
Kashmir, west to Islamabad (now the capital of Pakistan), and then
southward towards Jammu, a city on the southern border of Kashmir.
The first leg of the journey was by boat, along the Jhelum River. From
Islamabad to Jammu, the party rode and walked for a total of nineteen
days. At first they traversed a plain planted with rice; wild iris bloomed
along the way. They slept in tents and, one night, in a guest house belonging to the local maharajah; under their bedroom window was a huge
octagonal pool with tame fish. Leaving the plain behind, they crossed the
9,000-foot (2,700 m) Banihal Pass, 'a fearful pull'. Towards the top, they
had to stop every ten yards to rest the horses. Their young son, too small
to ride, was carried by porters in a local litter, 'like a large butler's tray,
gaily painted'. Although there was luckily no snow, a bitter wind swept
the pass and they descended the steep road on the other side hurriedly.
That night they stayed in another native guest house, with elaborately
carved wooden windows – charming but cold. They kept on, stopping
during the day for lunch, once in 'a theatrically-arranged glen, forming
a *cul de sac* of high perpendicular rocks curtained with maidenhair,
into which a stream of water fell from a great height'. Another day they
crossed the rushing Chenab River on a rickety suspension bridge. Finally,
after passing through a field of strangely shaped rocks, they reached the
comparative comfort of Jammu.

These were not holidays for the faint-hearted. The mountain paths
were narrow and often steep, and the Hill ponies had a fondness for
walking on the very edge of sheer precipices. Mrs King found her own
way of coping: 'I hold my umbrella so as to keep out the sight as much
as possible, for I do not enjoy these bold and eagle-like positions.' Paths
might disappear in landslides, ponies dance nervously towards a sheer
drop, boulders suddenly hurtle down from above; the travellers had to
traverse high passes waist-deep in snow and step carefully across flimsy
bamboo bridges.

Some tried trekking once and once only. One woman went out
with her husband in Kashmir. When the horse carrying their kitchen

utensils fell over a precipice, he went to retrieve them; she took the two best remaining horses and fled back to civilization.

Of course their clothes did not make it any easier for the women on these expeditions. In the nineteenth century, they wore skirts slightly shorter than usual and stout boots rather than shoes; but while crinolines were fashionable they could only leave them off if they were far enough away from civilization. Early photographs show them standing on a glacier or a wild and precipitous mountainside, corseted and hatted and draped in yards of material. It was not until the end of the nineteenth century that a few bold souls wore bloomers (still voluminous but at least more comfortable) and not until after the First World War that they ventured into trousers.

Kashmir, that beautiful and remote native state up in the northwest, was one of the favourite spots for open-air holidays. The Vale of Kashmir was said to look just like Switzerland except for the local inhabitants, who, it was generally agreed, were dirty and often thieves but also extremely beautiful. In the nineteenth century, getting there was quite an undertaking, but by the twentieth the roads had been improved. A reasonable hotel had opened in the capital, Srinagar, and there were camping grounds nearby, one at Moorshi Bagh for married couples and ladies, the other at Chenar Bagh for men only. The most popular accommodations, however, were the gaily painted wooden houseboats – with names like Mon Repos and Sunnyside Up – on the lakes around Srinagar. Each had a cook boat attached and a small *shikari*, equipped with cushions and rowers to convey the tenants about. Sometimes, alas, the beds on the houseboats were infested with bugs, but otherwise their native owners fitted them out with chintz curtains, comfortable cushioned chairs, little tables and heavy sideboards. Not all were as luxurious as the one belonging to the British Resident, which Zoe Proctor stayed on in the 1880s: it had rose silk curtains and a *shikari* with sixty rowers who used heart-shaped paddles made of papier-mâché. Visitors could also rent simpler *doongas* – wooden boats about fifty feet (15 m) long with living compartments divided by thick straw mats on poles.

It was all very picturesque. Native merchants paddled by in their boats, selling fresh fruit, vegetables and flowers (Kashmir was famous for its gardens and orchards) and the local shawls and papier-mâché boxes. Snow-covered mountains ringed the lakes, whose clear waters reflected them back. There were plenty of interesting things to see: mosques and Hindu shrines, the quaint wooden bridges that spanned the rivers and canals of Srinagar, and, along the shores of Lake Dal, terraced gardens built by the Mughal emperors who also had loved Kashmir. In Srinagar, as well, were wonderful shops run by wily Kashmiri merchants with nicknames like Suffering Moses and Joyful Jacob. By the twentieth century, the city also boasted an amateur dramatic society, a golf course, and its own hill station – Gulmarg, also with a golf course which ran just below the snow line. (By the Second World War, Gulmarg offered skiing in the winter, with mules instead of lifts and porters to carry the skis.)

Men and women who wanted a more exciting holiday trekked up Kashmir's long and lovely valleys. A few women even climbed some of the local mountains. By 1900 there were two agencies in Srinagar run by retired army officers, which supplied camp outfits and porters. Food was usually not a problem: delicious wild mushrooms, strawberries, raspberries, mulberries, even rhubarb could be picked along the way, and meat, eggs and milk could be bought from the villagers.

As they wandered along, the holiday-makers came across remote villages whose inhabitants were invariably friendly and curious. They met travelling merchants from Central Asia who sold tea, wonderful silks, embroideries, printed cottons from Russia and strange barbaric jewelry. Everywhere the scenery was magnificent. The lower slopes of the mountains were covered with trees: blue pines, chenars (planes) like huge oaks, graceful poplars and birch, mountain ash, elders, buck-thorns, flowering viburnum, hawthorns, hazels. Above stretched the Himalayas. When the Godden girls trekked with their parents, 'Above the trees were green alps, where primulas and gentians grew and cows and goats were grazed in the summer; higher still was a world of rock, juniper and snow, where marmots whistled from the mouth of their burrows.' For women who liked flowers, Kashmir was a paradise. It was famous for the roses which grew wild everywhere in the valleys, filling the air with perfume. And there were wild iris, peonies, small delicate arabis and strawberry flowers, climbing clematis and honeysuckle. In the spring, wrote Marion Doughty, who was there at the end of the nineteenth century, 'Every step took one over tiny blue gentians, starry anemones, clusters of delicately striped pink and white tulips, violets, and countless other flowers.'

Most British women, however, wanted excitement of a different kind – that of the hill stations. Whereas the Mughals built palaces and mosques and gardens, the British in India left a legacy of railways, roads and hill stations. In the first part of the nineteenth century, the authorities discovered that sick and wounded soldiers recovered more quickly if they were sent up to camps in the Hills out of the summer heat. Gradually others followed suit and small settlements began to grow up. By the end of the century, the summer exodus to the Hills had become well established. Each government had its own hill station: Bombay went to Mahableshwar from April to June, then to Poona until October; the Madras government spent six months of the year in Ootacamund; the Northwest Provinces and Oudh, later the United Provinces of Agra and Oudh, removed itself to Naini Tal from 1 May until mid-October; Bengal went to Darjeeling for a mere four months; and the governments of the Punjab and of India itself went to the grandest hill station of all, Simla. In addition, the military had its depots and its summer homes for soldiers' families and the missions had sedate boarding houses where their workers could recover quietly from their labours.

Some thought the hill stations absurd. 'Fancy coming to these uttermost ends of the earth', remarked Constance Gordon Cumming, the Victorian traveller, 'to be pursued by the latest Paris fashions; satins, velvets, "the newest thing" in bonnets, which have just been sent direct to the wearer by pattern post – to say nothing of the last thing in white satin boots!' And cool air was all very well, but was it reasonable to carry on the government of India from isolated hilltops with rather inadequate communications? Every so often there were public meetings of protest, committees were formed and petitions instigated. There were complaints from both Indian nationalists and British businessmen about the expense of the annual move and the frivolity the rulers were presumably lapsing into when they should have been working. 'A deliberate attempt is being made', complained the *Statesman* of Calcutta in 1884, 'to carry on the Government by pic-nic.' Some dissenters even found fault with the Hills themselves. Lady Canning, wife of the Viceroy who presided over the aftermath of the Mutiny, found Simla 'very questionable': 'It is such a sea of hill tops, and the snow mountains are so far off, and the dryness makes all look wintery', and, as she added sarcastically, 'if one sees ten yards level one screams out "what a site for a house".'

Emily Eden complained that she could not sketch the mountains: they were too big to be picturesque.

None of the protests made the slightest impression. Even the sceptics had to admit that the cool air of the Hills was invigorating after the summer heat. Fanny Parks, who certainly cannot be accused of disliking India, exclaimed on her first visit to the small hill station of Landour, 'The delicious air, so pure, so bracing, so unlike any air I had breathed for fifteen years – with what delight I inhaled it!' And Lady Falkland, another woman not given to complaining about India, wrote after her first night in Mahableshwar, 'you think you have received a new set of bones: you get up refreshed, and your feet seem to run away with you'. Lady Dufferin found that she got into quite a 'tally-ho' frame of mind in the Hills. Mothers saw their listless pale children growing plumper and rosier and more energetic day by day. They themselves felt rejuvenated. After the sun-dried Plains, the very look of the Hills was refreshing, with streams, green grass, and flowers – and not just any flowers but the delicate flowers of Home. The air around her cottage, Anne Wilson noted with delight, was 'heavy with the scent of roses, verbena, mignonette and sweet peas'.

To women longing for Home, the Hills were the next best thing. They even smelled – except of course for the inevitable native bazaar – like Home. And if you did not look too closely at the scenery you might be able to imagine for an instant that you had been transported there. As one lady said of Ootacamund in the south ('Ooty', as it was known to generations of British in India), it was just like the Sussex Downs. 'Try to believe you are in India', she exclaimed: 'It is difficult.' Mrs Muter, an officer's wife who had survived the Mutiny in Meerut, found that the small Punjab station of Murree took her back to the days of her childhood: 'In fancy I was again in an English dell, with the trickling water rolling over the mossy stones.'

Going to the Hills was a duty to the race as well as a pleasure, and like all worthwhile duties, it involved a certain amount of hardship. Hill stations were not easy to get to, especially before good roads and railways were built. There was not even the most rudimentary road to Simla before 1856 and the small railway which still winds up there was not finished until 1903. Before that, women and children rode in carts or carriages, or they were carried up in a *doolie*, 'like a small four-poster

bed, with cotton curtains and feet only four inches [10 cm] high'. Each
doolie had four porters who chanted a monotonous song as they struggled
uphill. (Often they improvised rude verses about their burdens, which,
fortunately, the latter did not usually understand.) The ride was most
unpleasant for the passengers, as they were tilted uncomfortably backwards, and occasionally dropped by the porters, who perhaps panicked
at the sight of a snake or simply wanted to enforce their demands for
more money. (Another favourite trick was to hold the *doolie* out over a
precipice until the passenger gave in and agreed to pay more.) Constance
Gordon Cumming once had a dreadful journey at night up to Mussoorie;
her lead porter fell over a cliff, the others fled in a panic, and she had
to walk six miles (9.5 km) uphill in the pouring rain, feeling her way
along the cliff face with her hand.

Journeys to hill stations often took several days and the travellers were
obliged to stay in rest-houses along the way. When Annette Beveridge
travelled from her husband's station of Rangpur to Darjeeling, a distance
of some hundred miles (160 km) on the map, it took her four days by
dogcart, train, *dandy* (a sort of hammock carried by two men), and *tonga*
(a small two-wheeled carriage where the passengers sat facing backwards).
Even in the 1920s, it took two days to get from Calcutta to Darjeeling.

As the hill stations developed, enterprising Europeans, the widows
perhaps of British soldiers or, in one case, the former cook of a viceroy,
opened hotels and boarding houses. Families could take a suite of rooms
– bedroom, sitting room, and bathroom. Some were very good; there
was Peliti's in Simla, for example, with its comfortable sitting room and
'the well-ordered café', which, according to an observer at the end of the
nineteenth century, 'is of never-failing interest, for here in the groups
of laughing, faultlessly dressed English men and women, [the visitor]
finds the true Anglo-Indian'. Other hotels were like the one that Marion
Doughty found in Murree, with 'dirty, ragged, ceiling cloths, stained
walls, the plaster peeling off in great flakes, scraps of cotton carpets
… chairs with fragmentary legs, tables of unplaned wood, draped with
cotton cloths of another decade, a bed with furnishings that filled the
imagination with awesome phantoms, iron washstands and cracked
crockery, a glass minus its quicksilver, and a window dark with dust.'

Respectable ladies had their doubts about the clientele of the hotels.
When she was obliged to stay briefly at a hotel in Mussoorie, Mrs King

noted with some horror 'Such a curious set of people at table, and such curious English to be heard, a few ladies (save the mark!) looking and behaving as much like barmaids as they could.' The preferred course was to take a house for the season. Often, in order to cut costs, two or more women without their husbands would arrange to share. In the larger hill stations especially, rents were high, even for small, badly built houses.

If they took a house, the ladies then faced transporting not only themselves and their children but also their servants, their clothes, extra supplies (provisions in hill stations were notoriously expensive) and a good deal of their furniture, because even houses advertised as 'furnished' were very bare. *The Complete Indian Housekeeper and Cook* gives a list of the basic necessities for a party consisting of a lady, two or three children and an English nurse:

1st camel load:	Two large trunks and two smaller ones with clothing.
2nd camel load:	One large trunk containing children's clothing, plate chest, three bags, and one bonnet-box.
3rd camel load:	Three boxes of books, one box containing folding chairs, light tin box with clothing.
4th camel load:	Four cases of stores, four cane chairs, saddle stand, mackintosh sheets.
5th camel load:	One chest of drawers, two iron cots, tea-table, pans for washing up.
6th camel load:	Second chest of drawers, screen, lamps, lanterns, hanging wardrobes.
7th camel load:	Two boxes containing house linen, two casks containing ornaments, ice-pails, *angethis* [small charcoal stoves], door-mats.
8th camel load:	Three casks of crockery, another cask containing ornaments, filter, pardah bamboos [screens], tennis-poles.
9th camel load:	Hot-case, milk-safe, baby's tub and stand, sewing-machine, fender and irons, water-cans, pitchers.
10th camel load:	Three boxes containing saddlery, kitchen utensils, carpets.
11th camel load:	Two boxes containing drawing room sundries, servants' coats [because the servants were

> not used to the cold, British employers were
> obliged by custom to provide them with one
> warm coat each for the Hills], iron bath, cheval
> glass, plate basket.

Some items caused problems: pianos, which some musical ladies liked
to take with them, would not fit on camels and had to be provided with
a cart of their own or a set of coolies.

What sort of Shangri-la awaited them as they struggled upwards
with their trains of coolies and servants? Imagine a Victorian seaside
holiday town which had somehow acquired an Indian bazaar and a
temple or a mosque or two. Hill stations were strange places, trying to
be thoroughly British but somehow not succeeding. Most had a main
thoroughfare, usually called the Mall, where, by the end of the nineteenth
century, there were shops with European goods, hotels, cafés, libraries,
Clubs, stone churches with spires and Gothic arches, none of which
would have been out of place in a prosperous English spa. From the
centre of the station paths wound off through the trees to real houses,
not bungalows, built not of dusty mud bricks but of brick and timber,
with windows that actually had glass, with fireplaces, and with pitched
roofs. Their names were redolent of Aldershot or Bournemouth: Ivy
Glen, the Dovecote, Violet Hill, The Cedars, Ambrosia, Sunny Bank,
Mignonette. Occasionally an Eagle's Nest or a Rook's Nest made a faint
bow in the direction of its surroundings.

There were also, however, the unmistakable reminders that this
was still India. Indians were everywhere, waiting on their masters,
carrying the goods they needed, pulling them about in rickshaws. And
every hill station had its native quarter (in a neat piece of symbolism,
downhill – not, alas, always downwind – from the European part of
the station). Other touches marred the illusion of Home, such as the
monkeys clambering along the roof of the church. If you looked closely,
the buildings had a rough, unfinished look. Above all, there was the
location itself. Towns at Home did not sit perched crazily on a series
of jagged hills; they did not have the Himalayas floating silently in the
background to remind them of how small all human activity and bustle
was. The man responsible for designing much of New Delhi, Sir Edwin
Lutyens, found the whole mixture quite bizarre when he visited Simla

in 1912: 'if one was told the monkeys had built it all, one could only say, "What wonderful monkeys – they must be shot in case they do it again."'

The sociability of the hill stations was their main attraction; many women felt that they had spent far too long out of the company of their fellow-creatures. In Mahableshwar, Lady Falkland noticed with amusement that even a spectacular sunset, visible from a popular scenic lookout known as Bombay Point, did not distract the assembled ladies from their animated gossip. Perhaps to compensate for those dreary months on the Plains, women threw themselves into having a good time. A German doctor who visited Simla in 1845 was delighted by the ladies he saw 'galloping down the street, followed by a train of three or four elegantly equipped officers'. He also enjoyed a masked ball: 'It was a bright and merry party, for there are here a great many sprightly old ladies, who, loaded with perfect gardens of flowers, rush about in polkas with incredible zeal.' (Occasionally clergymen preached sermons in the hill-station churches about the frivolity they saw around them; for a week or two, the ladies might give up games on Sunday and go out to tea parties instead.)

The main social drawback was an unusual one for the British in India: there was often a shortage of men, so that women could not count on being invited to every dance. Sometimes, it was rumoured, desperate ladies bribed clerks to get invitations to official parties. Even bolder ones simply showed up at the door, asserting that they had lost their invitations.

The usual rules of behaviour were in force. Iris Portal described a viceregal picnic in the 1920s at which the ladies in their jodhpurs stood around a tablecloth laid on the grass and curtseyed. Precedence was as important in the Hills as anywhere else and newcomers were expected to make their rounds of calls. Wives were meant even on holiday to use their social activities to further their husbands' careers. A favoured type of dinner party in Simla, at least before the First World War, was the alphabetical: all the people with names A to B were invited to one, the Cs and Ds to the next – so that nobody would be excluded by mistake. As in the Plains, conversation concentrated on pay and promotion. Anne Wilson remarked, perhaps a little wearily, 'We are all so anxious in Simla to be in the right position for our position, in the right place, and talking to the right person at the right time.' Indians were discouraged from appearing on the scene, except as underlings. In 1890, the government of India worried over the proposed sale of a house in Simla to the Nizam of Hyderabad; in the general view it was undesirable even for princes to come to the Hills, where they might expect to join in the social round. By the inter-war years, thanks in part to social and political changes, Indians were rather more welcome as visitors.

Though life went on much as usual, with lunches and teas and dinners and dances, some things were different. The roads in most hill stations were so narrow and steep that ladies could not use carriages or, later on, cars. (In Simla only the Viceroy and the Commander-in-Chief of the Army were allowed to have such luxuries.) Some rode everywhere: according to Iris Portal, 'One used to ride out to lunch and to race meetings in one's best dress hitched around one's waist with a blanket tied around you, and a big floppy hat. You used a horse as you would a vehicle and the *syce* ran on ahead and waited for you and held your pony while you attended your function.' Less athletic women were carried by four porters in a *jampan*, a chair with a detachable canopy and curtains slung between poles. By the 1880s a new device from Japan which the British knew as the 'jennyrickshaw' (later merely 'rickshaw') began to make its appearance. The Indian version generally had an adjustable hood and four men who hauled it uphill with many loud groans, and then ran back downhill ringing the bicycle bell loudly. Well-to-do ladies hired their porters for the season and dressed them in liveries of their own design. Gaudy figures in 'purple and emerald with light blue trimmings' or 'bright yellow tunics and claret-coloured caps' puffed and grunted as they carried their mistresses about the Hills.

For adventurous ladies, there was the prospect of expeditions. Mrs Guthrie, who lived in western India in the 1870s, was amused by the pretty young ladies she encountered in the centre of Mahableshwar 'with high-heeled boots never meant for climbing, and poles of bamboo that might have sufficed to steady the steps of a member of the Alpine Club'. At Simla, you could climb up Jakko, with its monkeys and its old temple dedicated most appropriately to Hanuman, the Hindu monkey god, or down to one of the few pieces of level land – Annandale – to watch horse racing or perhaps a polo match. Short trips could be taken to Mashobra, which was a popular retreat from the formality of Simla. It was only six miles (10 km) away, but exciting enough for most tastes.

Ladies rode or took rickshaws, first through a long dark tunnel and then along a road which had a sheer drop of thousands of feet on one side. Later, when bicycling became fashionable, women rode out on their horses while their grooms took their bicycles; on the way back they exchanged and the women coasted back downhill to Simla. Lady Reading, who was always convinced that she was on the point of collapse, loved her escapes to the viceregal chalet in Mashobra in the 1920s. 'Most primitive', she described it with pride in her own hardiness; 'no hot water, iron tubs on zinc floors'. In Ooty, a great treat was to visit the aboriginal Todas in their villages, where the curious could examine, as one lady missionary put it, 'new types of faces and customs that have been preserved from ancient times'.

In every hill station there were favourite spots for picnics. Servants would be sent ahead with provisions and furniture, sometimes even tents, for the bold explorers. The ladies could walk with their escorts among the pines and ferns, admiring the masses of wild flowers, picking a few of the strawberries, barberries or raspberries that grew wild, possibly sketching a pretty waterfall, confident that the comforts of civilization were waiting to reward them. They could dine, sometimes even dance if there was someone along with a banjo or a guitar. They played childish games, such as egg-and-spoon races or a chasing game known as 'Tiggy, tiggy, touch wood'. In one of her short stories, Maud Diver gives a lyrical description of a picnic given by the bachelors of a hill station for their lady friends: 'The thing was perfect in detail: the menu, the natural glade framed in groups of noble old trees, their boughs hung with Chinese lanterns that glowed in the moonlit dusk like strange tropical fruits in some enchanted garden. At one end, a leaping bonfire crackled and laughed in flame, filling the open space with impish shadows. On a long trestle table, with cushions for seats, there were picnic delicacies worthy of a ball supper. Beyond – in deeper darkness, where lanterns flickered – khitmutgars kept jealous guard over "drinks" that ranged from innocuous "nemolade" to baskets of iced champagne. And over all, the unclouded moon of May wove her gossamer web of eerie light and shade.'

Ladies who had been too tired to do anything much on the Plains found in the cool air that they could take up sport again. It was usually possible to find a level spot for lawn tennis and badminton, 'the cause', wrote Mrs Guthrie, 'of much strife'. At Naini Tal the lake was the scene of ladies' rowing races. In 1867, young Barbara Kerr reported proudly, she was fortunate to be part of the crew of the Lieutenant-Governor's daughter, which had 'a very swell costume of dark blue stuff trimmed with scarlet braid and looped up with 15 scarlet anchors'. As the hill stations grew in sophistication they also acquired other sports. 'Rinking' (the nineteenth-century term for roller-skating) was very popular in Simla among the ladies in spite of – or perhaps because of – 'constant collisions', when young women were forced to throw their arms 'wildly round a stranger's neck'.

For those who sought more intellectual pursuits, the hill stations offered art shows – where, if they were confident enough, they could exhibit their watercolours of the native bazaar or their portraits in pastels. Clever ladies got up clubs with names like 'The Scribblers', which held readings of their members' work and gave prizes for the best compositions. Simla had 'Les Amis de la France', founded just before the First World War, whose members, ladies and gentlemen, spoke French to each other, listened to little talks on French culture, and put on the occasional play in French. Then there were concerts, sometimes even by professional artists on tour in India. The bigger hill stations like Simla and Darjeeling had real theatres. In Simla the Amateur Dramatic Society was very popular, at least until the First World War, when audiences began to decline in the face of competition from the new cinemas. It was a considerable coup for a woman to be offered a part in one of their plays. On the night of the performance, admirers sent bouquets to their favourites and there was much jealous comparing of piles of flowers. The Gaiety Theatre was pretty (even if the dressing rooms were a bit dirty) and proved a perfect setting for flirtations. Iris Portal recalled that 'hearts were broken and mended again on that stage and many riotous parties took place on it and in the Green Room.'

Flirting, of course, and gossip about it, were great pastimes in the Hills. There were unattached men up on leave to pay court to ladies without their husbands, and plenty of opportunities for them to do so. In fact those who did not manage to attach themselves to members of the opposite sex could find the hill stations very dull. Mrs Marryat complained in the 1860s that 'few enjoy them who have not the amusement of making love to fall back upon'. Val Prinsep, a fashionable artist from a family long established in India who visited Simla in 1877, said much the same thing: 'If you have not a pair, as in my case, you are likely to die of inanition.' Their critics said that the hill stations were very wicked indeed. But Lord Lytton, Viceroy at the end of the 1870s, who was perhaps used to a higher level of wickedness, found Simla quite disappointing in this respect. He wrote wistfully to Lady Salisbury in England: 'I envy you the pleasure of living amongst so many naughty people. Our social surroundings here are so grievously good … The young ladies are not allowed to dance lest they should dance to perdition, and I believe that moonlight picnics were forbidden last year by order of the Governor-General in Council lest they should lead to immorality. I wish I could report that our Empire is as well defended as our piety.'

By the end of the British stay in India, there were several dozen hill stations, some busy and crowded like Simla, others small and quiet. Some had a very military flavour, with summer barracks for the soldiers and homes for their wives and children. Each had its own character, military, sporting, even – in Almora near Naini Tal – Bohemian. (It was at Almora that a memsahib was introduced to an Englishman who had become a Hindu holy man: 'my hand was grasped warmly, saffron robes and caste marks and all, and "I think we met in Lucknow, Mrs Donaldson, playing tennis at Colonel T's."')

In south India, where it never got quite as hot as in the north, there were fewer hill stations. Kodai Kanal was a quiet place and attracted families with children as well as missionaries on leave. Coonoor was popular with invalids for its moderate climate, and nearby Wellington was appropriately enough a military sanatorium. The queen of the south Indian hill stations – some said of all India – was Ooty, 3,000 feet (900 m) above Wellington. Lady Canning compared the view of the Nilgiri Hills with 'the Highlands on a gigantic scale'. Ooty had all the standard features – church, Club, library – but it also had a lake and terraced botanical gardens.

Further north, the Presidency of Bombay had a handful of hill stations. Matheran, about sixty miles (100 km) from Bombay City, was small and fairly quiet. The big popular hill station was Mahableshwar, famous for its strawberry beds and its views. Poona was not exactly a hill station because it had been a city long before the British arrived, but here the British and rich Indians went to escape the heat of Bombay or the torrential rains of Mahableshwar.

Darjeeling was believed by many to be the prettiest of all the hill stations. It was also the wettest. *The Complete Indian Housekeeper and Cook* gave it a mixed recommendation: 'Most excellent hotels. Both living and house rent are dear, and the place is apt to be over-crowded. Society very gay. Leeches and ticks are a perfect pest. Scenery finest of all the hill-stations.' Steel and Gardiner's favourite was Dalhousie, right on the other side of India, which they described as 'prettiest and healthiest of all hill stations' with a 'good, but not very gay society'. Mussoorie was cheap, but society there was said to be 'rather mixed'; *The Pioneer*'s correspondent in 1888 found it a trifle Bohemian. Fifty years later there were complaints that it was too dull: 'the Margate of the mountains', one woman called it.

Simla was the grandest and gayest and most expensive of them all. 'No one should go up that has not a bag of rupees and many pretty frocks'. warned *The Complete Indian Housekeeper and Cook*. The women in Simla were the most flirtatious: 'that horrid Simla manner,' young Ruby Madden wrote home to Australia, 'the gush, the giggle and the repartee'. Simla men were the most powerful, or, if not that, the most elegant and dashing. The usual hill-station amusements were bigger and more elaborate than anywhere else. The fêtes for charities had more stalls and grander prizes for the raffles.

In the 1920s Simla witnessed Lady Reading's Moonlight Revel, where eight hundred guests enjoyed an Old English Fair that had been set up, complete with merry-go-rounds, fortune-tellers, freaks, and even a baked-potato stall, in the grounds of Viceregal Lodge. White canvas, waxed and powdered, was stretched across the lawn. The whole scene was illuminated with strings of red, white and blue lights. Lady Reading described it proudly in a letter: 'A full moon, the entire garden surrounded by walls of Dorothy Perkins in full bloom, all this made a fairyland of the scene.'

Lady Reading was also responsible in 1924 for a party that was remembered for years afterwards. In September she held a Feast of Lanterns in which the theme was Chinese – or at least the British version of it. Viceregal Lodge was disguised with hundreds of lanterns and Chinese panels, and the supper tables were decorated with chopsticks and birds' nests made of chocolate. The Viceroy's European staff were dressed in black satin jackets, blue satin trousers, pigtails and caps, and their eyes were made up to look slanted. The three hundred and fifty guests, also dressed in a vaguely Chinese fashion, greeted their hosts in what was felt to be authentic style, the men prostrating themselves on the floor and the ladies bowing with folded arms. The entertainment, according to Lady Reading, was a great success: 'A fanfare of trumpets and then to Chinese music [actually parts of the *Nutcracker*] 20 of Simla's prettiest girls danced charmingly. Then the lights went out and they each had a scarlet electric torch and danced in and out. A gong sounded, and through bright blue curtains emerged an enormous Dragon, about 7 feet [2 m] long, with motor lamp eyes, a marvellous creation made by Mr Bertram, our Estate carpenter.' The final excitement before the dancing started was the appearance of young Megan Lloyd George, daughter of the Prime Minister, who was pulled in by two other ladies in a rickshaw. Dressed in a Burmese costume, she bowed deeply before the Viceroy and presented him with a gold sunshade.

It was on glittering occasions such as this, or during the quieter diversions of picnics and walks, that women could forget they were in India. They could forget their homesickness, forget the families thousands of miles away, forget too that they were soon bound to head back down to the hot Indian Plains, to start again their perpetual struggle with the country.

12

UNCONVENTIONAL WOMEN

British society in India did not much like unconventional behaviour in women. Some variations of style were allowed; a woman could have enthusiasms – butterfly collecting, perhaps – of the proper genteel sort. She might even be mildly intellectual, as long as she did not overdo it. Senior memsahibs, who had served their time and proved their worth, were permitted some eccentricities. Careless women, however, faced the full disapproval of their peers, who did not hesitate to speak their minds: 'going *jungli*', they said, or worse, 'going native', or worse still, 'letting down the race and the Raj and the British Empire'. Yet even in the face of such pressure, certain women were prepared to bend or even ignore the rules. Sometimes they were forgiven; sometimes not.

Such women, and they existed even when the Raj was at its strongest and most confident, show that possibilities existed for British women in India other than the standard ones of good wife, mother, housekeeper. Moreover, they show that it was possible to go beyond the constraints of their time, their class and their sex in their reactions to India and the Indians. Sometimes women were unconventional by local standards because they came from backgrounds of such eminence at Home that they cared little for the conventions they found in India. Sometimes the difference lay in their characters: there were women, even from middle-class backgrounds, who were independent of mind and unafraid of disapproval. The writer Flora Annie Steel, for example, married into the heart of Raj society – her husband was in the ICS – but she went her own way with apparently no qualms. Other women were different because of their reasons for being in India: work, not marriage, had brought them there. They had chosen to come, perhaps as the result of a call to do mission work or simply in a spirit of adventure to take posts as governesses or nurses. Adventurous or restless women looked for something in India which they did not find at Home. By the end of the nineteenth century some radical women saw in India a chance for political activity: they wanted to improve the position of Indian women or even work to bring about the end of the Raj. Finally, and they could be pathetic figures, there were the women who married Indians, often without realizing the difficulties they were going to encounter.

The wives and families of viceroys and governors found it relatively easy to be unconventional if they chose. Lady Hailey, the noted shot who enjoyed picking flowers with her .22, gave Lahore society much to talk about when she lived there between 1924 and 1928: her explorations in the Himalayas (for which she eventually won the Royal Geographical Society's Gold Medal), her flying lessons (and her crash in 'such a jolly little aeroplane'), and her animals (including the pet bear she took with her for outings in a rickshaw). Guests who came to luncheon were obliged to watch her pack of Pomeranians being fed before they were allowed to sit down at the table. But her husband was Lieutenant-Governor of the Punjab and who would have dreamt of refusing invitations to Government House?

Women like Lady Dufferin or Lady Curzon also had an assured position in the highest circles at Home, and could afford to ignore many of the prejudices of local society. Lady Minto, whose husband was Viceroy just before the First World War, decided to make the acquaintance of Margaret Noble, an Irishwoman known in India as Sister Nivedita, in spite of the fact that Lord Minto's Indian Police were busy opening the letters and watching the activities of a woman who was regarded as a serious threat to the Raj. Sister Nivedita, as we shall see, was a strong supporter of radical Indian nationalism. Lady Minto visited her humble cottage in the heart of the Indian part of Calcutta, and later invited her to tea at Government House.

The women at the pinnacle of British society in India differed from most of the residents in not taking the whole thing very seriously. They laughed at local conventions in a way that would have been difficult for those who had to spend another twenty or thirty years in the country. Emily Eden, who accompanied her brother, Lord Auckland, to India when he was Governor-General for the Company in the late 1830s, later published the letters she wrote home; while they are among the most entertaining ever written about India, they strike a note typical among the great ladies who lived there for a short time. A snob about class more than about race, she found her fellow expatriates just as comical and alien as Indians. Local British society was simply a dreary shadow of circles which she would not have entered at Home. 'I never could take to the Calcutta society,' she wrote to a friend shortly after her arrival in India, 'even if there were any, but there is not.' When she left Calcutta to go on tour with her brother, she reported to her sister with amusement that the British residents were said to be sad to see them go. 'They liked our balls and parties, and whatever we did or said was the subject of an anecdote; and if we said or did nothing they invented something for us – and it all served to wonder at – which in a country where there is little society and few topics, was an advantage.' In fact, she found Indians slightly more interesting. If nothing else, they were picturesque, and some were themselves aristocrats. Ranjit Singh, the great Sikh ruler of the Punjab, was a 'very drunken old profligate.... Still he has made himself a great king; he has conquered a great many powerful enemies; he is remarkably just in his government; he has disciplined a large army; he hardly ever takes away life, which is wonderful in a despot; and he is excessively beloved by his people.'

The great ladies were also freer in the interests they could pursue. If they wished, they could be intellectuals without worrying about the local disdain for bluestockings. They could take a close interest in Indian matters. Who, after all, would dare accuse them of going native? The lively and beautiful Lady Falkland, who arrived in Bombay in 1848 with her husband, who was Governor, became fascinated with India. She inquired into the caste system, the customs, the habits of the people. She sketched busily to try to capture the flora and fauna. She was also something of a scholar: she read learned papers on India for amusement and she knew the Latin names of most of the plants she came across. As the illegitimate daughter of William IV, her background, although perhaps not impeccable, was undoubtedly aristocratic.

More interesting than these, because the obstacles they had to overcome were greater, were the women who were more permanently part of British society in India, who were born or married into it but who managed to get around its more tiresome restrictions. They did not always heed the accumulated wisdom of their society. They might stay in the Plains during the hot weather, for example, in spite of the warnings and the discomfort; they travelled with their husbands in parts where, it was said, no white woman should go; they read more than light novels; they often learnt to speak one or more Indian languages fluently. A granddaughter of Honoria Lawrence's, who was married to a member of the Madras Council, was famous in the 1930s for her fluency in Tamil, a particularly difficult language; she was able to swear at her washerman with both the proper insults (usually references to his incest or impotence or both) and the correct terms for his status. Some women called willingly on Indian ladies and, more difficult, were able to talk to them normally. Iris Portal had a friend in *purdah* in Hyderabad before the Second World War: 'She was a witch of moderately benign practices, some of which she demonstrated to me when we were alone together chewing *pan* and talking about our neighbours and our children in a womanly sort of way.' Certain women managed somehow to keep a foot in different camps. David Symington, who was in the ICS just before Independence, had a mother-in-law who came from a thoroughly official background; she was also, however, a close friend of Gandhi, of Jinnah, the leader of the Muslim League, and of scores of other Indian politicians. Since she had a reputation as an astrologer, she was often asked to cast their horoscopes.

It was easier for women to be unconventional in the eighteenth and early nineteenth centuries than later on, partly because standards of acceptable behaviour were more elastic, partly because they had already shown themselves to be out of the ordinary simply by coming to India. One of the more dashing characters of the late eighteenth century was Mrs James Hall, the Spanish-born wife of a Madras barrister, who had served at one time in the military service of the Nizam of Hyderabad. Dressed in a Mughal-style flowing robe over loose trousers, and with a sabre and plumed helmet, she had commanded a battalion of women who guarded his seraglio. She was a woman of strong passions and she spent some years in prison for beating a thief to death. Other European women of that period wandered around with a freedom and with an openness of mind that would have been hard to imagine when the Raj reached its full pomp and dignity.

Emma Roberts, a writer and journalist, lived in India between 1828 and 1832 with her sister and brother-in-law. She occupied herself with studying the country and its people and writing learned books and articles as well as editing a Calcutta paper, the *Oriental Observer*. She found much to admire in Indians – their honesty, for example, and their religious sense. Benares, the holy city of the Hindus, impressed her favourably: 'Amid much that is strange and fantastic, there are numerous specimens of a pure and elegant taste, and the small antique pagodas which abound in every direction, are astonishingly beautiful.' The racial arrogance of many of the local British worried her: 'Want of urbanity, a too common trait in the English character, will, it is to be feared, retard the good understanding which ought to exist between natives of rank and the servants of their foreign rulers.' On her second visit to India, in 1839, she wrote another book describing her voyages and edited the *Bombay United Service Gazette*. She was compiling statistics for a book on western India when she died in 1840.

Another woman who was delighted with India was the beautiful, energetic, and, by her middle years, rather fat Fanny Parks. With no company but her servants, she toured across India in the 1820s and 1830s. Her mild and long-suffering husband was in the Company's service in Allahabad, but she had no intention of letting that slow her down. As Fanny Eden, sister of Emily and of Lord Auckland, explained, 'She has a husband who always goes mad in the cold season, so she says it is her duty to herself to leave him and travel about.' Fanny Parks wanted to know everything: she went to see Indian dancing at nautches ('some of the airs were very pretty'); she took lessons on the sitar; she learnt Persian and Hindustani; she measured the trunks of baobab trees; she collected information about *thugs*; she played the Indian version of chess with a native gentleman. In her accounts of her travels she writes about everything from elephants to Islam. Her response to hook-swinging (one of the more curious Hindu practices, in which devotees put hooks into their flesh and swing from them) was characteristic: 'I was much disgusted, but greatly fascinated.' Unlike later ladies who tasted Indian dishes with a squeamish reluctance, Fanny Parks found the native cuisine delicious. *Pan*, that mixture of betel leaf, betel nut and spices which Indians chew as a digestive, she thought 'very refreshing'. She was willing to try anything once. When she had a headache, she took opium given her by an Indian friend and reported that she felt extremely well 'and talked incessantly'.

Fanny Parks was rarely bored in India. 'How much there is to delight the eye in this bright, this beautiful world! Roaming about with a good tent and a good Arab, one might be happy for ever in India.' And she had none of the inhibitions imposed by belonging to the ruling race, which made later memsahibs so awkward in their dealings with Indians. She took people as she found them. One of her great friends was Colonel James Gardner, one of those European adventurers who had made their fortunes in the service of Indian princes. He had married into an upper-class Muslim family and his household was run on Indian lines. Fanny Parks spent many happy weeks staying there, talking to her host, gossiping in the *zenana*, and assisting at the wedding of one of his daughters.

Another of her friendships that would have been unusual fifty years later was with the ex-queen of Gwalior. She pitched her tent in the Gwalior camp and found the ladies of the court most entertaining. And no doubt they were amused in turn, especially when the large Mrs Parks put on Mahratta dress and gave them a demonstration of riding side-saddle. She said her farewells sadly: 'I had passed so many happy hours, amused with beholding native life and customs, and witnessing their religious ceremonies.'

As the nineteenth century wore on, the limits of ladylike behaviour were drawn more tightly; even a Fanny Parks might have found it difficult to wander around and poke her nose in everywhere. But the strong characters still managed to live their own lives. Annette Akroyd may have married a member of the ICS but that did not turn her into a conventional memsahib. Perhaps it helped that she came from a Nonconformist religious background and that she had obtained a solid education at Bedford College in London. Perhaps it helped also that she had come to India originally to work for the education of Indian women. When she first set foot in the country, at the age of thirty, her opinions – and they were decided ones – were already formed. Her first contacts in India were not with the British but with progressive Indians. In 1873, with some help from her Indian friends, she opened a school for Hindu girls.

Those first years were difficult for her. She was lonely and found that she did not get as much help from Indian reformers as she had expected. She was also greatly disillusioned when Keshub Chunder Sen, the great opponent of child marriage, married his young daughter to the

Maharajah of Cooch Behar. It was a relief, in a way, when Annette met her future husband. Henry Beveridge was also serious-minded and also wanted to help the forces of progress in India. (Their son William was to write the report which became the foundation of the welfare state in Britain after the Second World War.)

Their marriage was a great success. In one of her letters before they were married, Annette foresaw quite accurately what it would be like: 'We will stay at home and you shall read French and I German to one another ... Are you willing to do that when we go into banishment with only the frogs in the tank for our companions?' They often had to live in small, dreary stations in Bengal, but Annette always found enough to occupy her mind. She remained determinedly intellectual, and she learnt Bengali and, later on, Persian and Turki. She was never predictable in her views: she did not much like Bengalis as a race, which was standard among the British in India, but she did have many individual Indian friends (including Bengalis), which was not usual. She did not like India either, but she gave her first child, Laetitia, the Sanskrit name Santamani (meaning 'the jewel of tranquillity').

Another strong-minded and independent lady was Flora Annie Steel, who was in India between 1867 and 1889. While she came from a more conventional background than Annette Beveridge (her family, in spite of financial difficulties, could claim to be upper-middle-class) and married when she was only twenty, she never allowed herself to be turned into the standard memsahib. Her interests were wider than those of most other British women in India. Although her own education had been sketchy, Mrs Steel was used to the company of intellectuals, as her father had counted men like Thackeray among his friends, and one of her sisters married Henry Nettleship, professor of Latin at Oxford. It also must have helped that Mrs Steel had a strong sense of her own abilities: as she wrote in her autobiography near the end of her life, 'It has been so evident, all my life, that I was gifted at my birth with unusual – what shall I call it – charm, vigour, personality, influence.'

Although she was conventional in believing British government was the best thing for India, she knew far more about the country than was considered necessary for a woman. Her husband was posted for several years in a small town in the Punjab near Lahore where there was 'literally *no one* but the natives', so she learnt to read and write in the vernacular. She ran English classes for local boys, and sang them sentimental ballads as a reward for hard work. She shared, perhaps to excess, her husband's work: years later an ICS officer was scandalized to find an official order signed by 'F.A. Steel'. The local Municipal Council, made up of Hindu and Muslim notables, met under her supervision in her garden, where she fed them iced melon and plum pudding. When Kasur needed a new town hall, Flora Annie Steel designed an elaborate tiered structure which must have looked rather like a wedding cake.

The Punjab government, perhaps in self-defence against the critical editorials she was writing for a Lahore newspaper, appointed her Inspectress of Girls' Schools in the Punjab. When she discovered that degrees were being sold at the Punjab University, she made such a fuss that the government first tried to silence her by transferring her husband to a remote post. She refused to move, and when a hard-pressed official asked Mr Steel to keep her in order, his answer was, 'Take her for a month and try.' Not surprisingly, it was the government which capitulated and set up the inquiry she had demanded.

In her spare time, Flora Annie Steel collaborated on that essential book, *The Complete Indian Housekeeper and Cook*, which is full of exhortations about coping with India in an enthusiastic and cheerful spirit. She had no patience with women who whined about the hardships of life in India or who complained of boredom. She also wrote short stories and novels, some about Europeans, others, more unusually, with Indians as their main characters. Her novel about the Mutiny, *On the Face of the Waters*, which she published in 1896, stands out from other novels of the same period in its attempt to see the event from an Indian perspective. She tried, as she said in her preface, to give a picture 'in which the differentiation caused by colour is left out'. In some ways she was rather like Annette Beveridge, sure enough of her own opinions and not overly worried about consistency. Flora Annie Steel said firmly that she preferred Muslims to Hindus – but she had many Hindu friends. She held that East and West could never meet – but when she came back to India after her husband's retirement to do her research on the Mutiny, she stayed in the native quarters, often with native friends.

Writing was an occupation that attracted ambitious women in India. It was cheap and portable (always an important consideration).

Local society was quite proud of its successful lady writers. They were not full of strange ideas like some of the women writing at Home; indeed they almost invariably expressed the highest admiration for the Raj and its cohorts. Nor were they at all Bohemian: usually they came from the most respectable circles. Ethel Savi's family had been connected with the East India Company for several generations; her brothers were civil servants or planters, and her son went into the Imperial Police. Alice Perrin was the daughter of a general in the Bengal Cavalry and married into the Indian Medical Service.

Perhaps the most unconventional of them all was the poet Adela Florence Cory, who wrote as 'Laurence Hope'. In 1889 she fell madly in love with Malcolm Nicolson, a dashing colonel in the Bengal Cavalry. She married him after a whirlwind courtship, and in 1890 disguised herself as a Pathan boy to follow him on an expedition through the wild, lawless country on the frontier between India and Afghanistan. In 1902, she published *The Garden of Kama*, a collection of poems with exotic oriental themes, which instantly became popular. The most famous poems, the 'Indian Love Lyrics', were set to music by Amy Woodforde-Finden, whose husband had also been in the Bengal Cavalry. 'Laurence Hope' did not live to enjoy her success: romantic to the last, she committed suicide shortly after her husband died in 1904.

Over the years these women writers churned out hundreds of novels and short stories, many set in India (the British version), but others in a world as far removed from India as possible, of green lawns and butlers and stately houses, a world that was firmly upper-class. Today their books, with titles like *Captain Desmond, V.C.*, *The Autobiography of a Spin*, *The Ayah and the Lady*, sit unread on the shelves of former station libraries in India. Occasionally a copy can be picked up in a second-hand bookstore or on the remoter shelves of a big library, perhaps by a student looking for a research topic or by a connoisseur of nostalgia who finds in them humour never intended by their authors. In their time, though, Maud Diver, Alice Perrin, Ethel Savi and Flora Annie Steel all wrote books that sold well – and not just in India.

Writing may have served as an escape from loneliness, but it was also a mild rebellion against the role of wife and mother that society decreed for women. If they were successful, the women writers even achieved a measure of financial independence from their husbands.

The Canadian Sara Jeanette Duncan was another popular novelist. She came to India on holiday and stayed to marry Everard Cotes, who was first a curator in the Indian Museum in Calcutta and then a journalist and editor in Calcutta and Simla. She had been a successful journalist before she married, and soon discovered that she disliked being an ordinary memsahib. E. M. Forster, who met her in Simla a dozen years after her marriage, found her clever but difficult and, as he wrote in his diary, 'I fancy unhappy'. She found the society she had to live in dull and philistine, and she did not much care for India either. Unfortunately her husband, who was a gentle scholar, was in no position to compensate her with power, position or wealth. And so she continued writing to be able to buy temporary escape. Her books and articles gave her the money to travel frequently to Europe and Canada.

Another group of women who went much closer to the limits of what society considered permissible were those who came to India not to get married but to work for British families. Some, nannies for example, were definitely lower-class, but others looked like ladies. Governesses and companions were generally treated as members of the family. They sometimes came to India because they had had no choice of jobs, sometimes because they liked the adventure. The governess for Anne Wilson's son had left England because she found standards slipping, even in grammar. She was upset by the 'restlessness' of the times – this was the early 1900s – and so chose to spend her last years in a more conservative society.

By the second half of the nineteenth century, a number of European women worked as secretaries, governesses or simply companions in Indian princely families. It was a mark of distinction to have European servants, and the more progressive princes also realized that it made sense for their children to be educated in the ways of their conquerors. C. C. Dyson had a friend who, in the years before the First World War, was guardian to the twelve-year-old wife of a chief in western India. Like many women in similar posts, Miss Boyd often went for months without seeing another European. She remained cheerful and busy, however, looking after the girl's education, supervising her household and taking care of the jewelry. In her spare time she took an interest in the state's schools. It was not always possible for women like Miss Boyd to make Indian friends: conservative Indians, who were especially powerful in the Indian states, disliked the break with tradition that their presence represented. On the other hand, such women had an opportunity to see a side of Indian life which most of the British never saw.

Edith Tottenham, who worked for the Maharani of Baroda from 1911 to 1920, became the trusted confidante of the family. She was admitted to rites like the Nag Panchmi festival, when the women of the court worshipped the cobra as their protector. (It must be admitted that her description makes it sound like a church bazaar: 'all the ladies joined hands and walked around the dais singing sweet little songs.') She also grew to resent bitterly the slights and suspicions of the British towards her employer. On one occasion the Resident in Baroda complained, unjustly in Miss Tottenham's opinion, that the Maharani had been rude to some memsahibs: 'Loyal as I wished to be, of course, to my race, nevertheless I insisted to the Maharani that she was not to apologize.'

Some of the nannies ended by becoming an enduring part of the family. The 23rd Maharajah of Bikaner, who was born in 1924, was looked after by Nanny Dent: 'She was there from the time we were born and we loved her more than we loved our parents. In time she looked after our own children and then the grandchildren and when she got old and retired that was our saddest day. When she died we built a cenotaph for her in England.' A few old nannies chose to live out their days in India.

Towards the end of the nineteenth century women began coming to India as doctors and nurses. Some had started out as missionaries but their experience of India had persuaded them that they might be of more use if they knew how to save bodies as well as souls. There were few women doctors at first because the obstacles that stood in their way were formidable. It was difficult even to get medical training. In Madras, the exceptionally determined wife of a barrister managed to win the support of the Governor and Surgeon-General for herself and three other women to receive training in the Madras Medical College. The first morning they appeared for instruction in a hospital they received a poor welcome: the male surgeon told them that it was folly to educate women as doctors and that, although he could not prevent them from walking around the wards with him, he was determined not to teach them. The medical establishment in India, which was a branch of the government, had much the same attitude for a number of years. When a generous Bombay businessman in the 1880s offered to build a hospital for women, to be run by women doctors, the Bombay government objected. It was willing to maintain such a hospital only if the women doctors acted 'under the instruction and guidance of the male superior staff.' And when a series of hospitals for women was built in India under the supervision of the Dufferin Fund, the senior Civil Surgeon (a man of course) had responsibility for inspecting them. This produced tension, especially when the Civil Surgeon was younger and less experienced than the women he was supervising. There was also trouble over the question of operating: conservative doctors felt that women were not suited to surgery and some senior surgeons insisted that they do all major operations even in the women's hospitals.

At first, the local British were not sure what to make of women doctors or nurses, and Indians were reluctant to use their services. Indian women were traditionally cared for by midwives, who not unnaturally resented the new competition; Indian men worried that their wives would break *purdah* even if they went into a women's hospital. A woman doctor's reputation frequently depended on luck; if she delivered lots of male babies, for example, she was sought after.

Medical women frequently worked on their own. While they were generally admired, they were often not seen in the Clubs or at the grand dinner parties. They preferred to live close to their patients in the native town rather than in the spacious British quarter and had little time for the usual amusements of the Raj. They were generally tough and dedicated women, like the matron of the Peshawar hospital, whose doctor husband was shot dead by the father of a patient who had died. In spite of this tragedy, Mrs Starr went back to work in the hospital. In 1923, Afghan tribesmen raided across the border, killing an officer and taking his wife and daughter back with them as hostages. Mrs Starr, who spoke fluent Pushtu among her other abilities, volunteered to go and negotiate for their release. She was successful and was later decorated by Lord Reading for her courage.

The largest single group of women who worked in India were the missionaries. In 1911, for example, the census counted 1,236 European women in religious work throughout the country, as compared to

1,943 men. Usually the missionaries came from modest middle-class backgrounds; their fathers were mill-owners or bank managers, rarely country gentlemen. Exceptions existed, of course – women like the Luce sisters, who came from a solid upper-middle-class family and whose private incomes allowed them to live like the upper crust of British society. Ella Luce belonged to the Club, dined with local official society, served alcohol at her own dinner parties – all unmissionary-like behaviour; but Miss Luce, as she pointedly observed, did not draw a salary from the Zenana Bible and Medical Mission, which sponsored her.

The British community were never entirely comfortable with missionaries. The official view, especially after the Mutiny, was that enthusiastic Christianity was a mistake in India. Evangelical work would only upset the natives. Thoughtful people felt, moreover, that the sort of Christianity so many of the missionaries preached was narrow and intolerant. And besides, missionaries were excessively earnest for a society that believed in jollity and games. Even on the liners going out to India they kept apart, reading their Bibles together and holding what seemed like far too many services. In India, few were ever seen in the Club; nor did most missionaries care for sport. And they also talked about God in an extraordinarily familiar way: to those who believed that religion was little more than the obligatory attendance at the station church on Sundays this seemed in bad taste. Still worse, some missionaries were quite undignified in their behaviour – and it was somehow worse in women – and so far forgot themselves as to preach in the bazaars, to live in an Indian style, and even to wear Indian dress.

The missionary societies, run by men, encouraged their female workers to concentrate on Indian women, through special *zenana* missions. It was also felt that women missionaries should refrain from confronting the forces of darkness too vehemently. The Church of England Zenana Missionary Society insisted that its members should exemplify in their work 'the sweet womanly graces of quietness, patience, carefulness, undistractedness and simplicity'. Many ended up marrying other missionaries; it was useful for the men to have women to help them in their work. (Over the years there also developed missionary families whose children were drawn into the life.)

43   Simla in its infancy, in 1867: outside Oakaver – a particularly grand
house – the memsahib contemplates some of her many plants in pots,
which may have travelled up to the Hills with her (43).

44   Hill-station holidays offered coolness, scenery reminiscent of Home, and sometimes
        lavish entertainments. At Simla (44) the Mall – seen here in the 1890s – led past
        buildings in a sort of Indo-Swiss style up to a little Gothic church. The memorable Feast
        of Lanterns (45) was organized by Lady Reading at Simla in 1924 (see pp. 234–35).
        She sits resplendent like the Empress Dowager; the Viceroy is beside her in the
        shadows, the young Megan Lloyd George on his lap.

45

46   Sports and tourism were other diversions. Mrs Pratt and Mrs Ward Smith, standing
beside their elephant on *shikar* near Hardwar on New Year's Day, 1900 (46), are as
well armed as their husbands. Hindu monuments were visited relatively rarely, and
then perhaps on a special occasion; the party posed in front of a temple at Gwalior
(47) were guests at the installation of Lord Elgin as Viceroy in 1894.

47

48   Strange vehicles with which the women had to come to terms included inflated bullock hides (48), here on the Ganges near Hardwar, propelled by rather alarming raftsmen. Lady Elgin, the Viceroy's wife, kept her composure in an ornate ceremonial litter (49) carried by liveried porters and shaded by an umbrella-bearer.

The best adventure for an enterprising woman was to accompany her husband on a tour of inspection (50). Mildred Archer remembers with joy setting out across a flooded river in Bihar in the 1940s with her two children, their *ayah*, a turbaned *chuprassi*, and her husband the Deputy Commissioner (who took the picture).

49

50

Among the faces that emerge are those of individuals who belonged to the team – their husbands were dutiful civil servants or soldiers – but who never chanted its slogans mindlessly.

Between 1837 and her death in 1854, Honoria Lawrence (51) looked on India with a humane, fascinated eye (see pp. 48, 55–56, 88 and 157).

Annette Akroyd (52) founded a school for Hindu girls in 1873, before marrying Henry Beveridge (see pp. 80 and 241–42).

51

52

Adela Florence Cory, or 'Laurence Hope' (53), became famous for 'Pale hands I loved beside the Shalimar'. A romantic in life as well, she dressed as a boy to follow her husband, a Bengal Cavalry officer, to the Northwest Frontier, and later committed suicide after his death (see p. 244).

Flora Annie Steel (54), in India between 1867 and 1889, wrote *The Complete Indian Housekeeper and Cook* and much else, including this masque performed at Dalhousie in 1883; she appears bottom right, in a tall Welsh hat, with her husband seated behind her and their daughter on the grass at their feet (see pp. 242–43).

53

54

55

56

Women on the fringe of the British community included
missionaries and others who chose to work for a living, like this
solitary schoolmistress in Clarkiabad (55). Frankly outside
it was Madeleine Slade, or Mirabehn (56), who followed Gandhi
to bring about the end of the women of the Raj (see p. 265).

But women missionaries did not come to India primarily to get married. They came to do good, to fight wickedness in all its manifold forms. They had had a call, a sudden crisis in their lives, as they were listening to a missionary back in Britain on leave perhaps, when they knew that they must dedicate themselves to saving Indian souls. Some were feminists as well as Christians: they wanted to save souls and to save women – from child marriage, from ignorance, from disease.

The trouble, as they all discovered, was that it was very difficult to persuade Indians that they needed saving. They visited the women in *purdah* day after day, trying to tell them little stories with a message. They also (and this took courage) preached in public to curious and sometimes hostile Indian crowds. Like the district officers, they went on tour, moving with their tents from village to village. 'Sometimes', reported Irene Barnes in *Behind the Pardah* (a history of the Church of England Zenana Missionary Society published in 1897), 'the novel contrivance of an open-air magic lantern is employed for sowing the seed in these dark hearts.' The message was a simple one: 'First a picture of her Majesty, the Queen-Empress; next a few English scenes; and then a series of pictures illustrating the Life of our LORD.' The missionaries made few converts, for all their work. Most Indian Christians came from the lowest castes and had little to lose: the new religion might make their miserable lives better and, at the very least, the missionaries might feed them. One lady spent eighteen years preaching to *zenana* women in Lucknow without making a single convert. A fellow missionary wrote, 'One can only admire the wonderful patience, courage and faith which enabled her to go on day after day and year after year with no visible results.' (The *zenana* ladies might have described her persistence differently.) Faced with the reality of India, many of the missionaries settled for less than winning the whole battle. They continued to preach but they also ran schools for Indian girls, they did medical work, and they looked after orphans.

No matter how well they came to know India, women missionaries could rarely admit to themselves that there was any good in the Indian traditional beliefs. *Behind the Pardah* said firmly, 'We cannot stain our pages with the detestable doings of these Hindu deities, or wade through the mire of Indian theology.' As usual, it was the Indian propensity to mix sex with religion that was particularly upsetting. Marie Christlieb, who worked in India in the 1920s, was appalled by the pictures of the gods at play which she noticed in the houses of Indian women she was visiting: 'How these gentle and modest women could endure them I could not think. They were so unpleasantly obtrusive that I could not keep my attention off them.' Over the years, however, a few missionaries came to a reluctant admiration for the spirituality which pervaded Indian life – although there do not seem to have been any female equivalents of C. F. Andrews, who came to India as a missionary but ended by becoming a Hindu and a disciple of Gandhi.

The great majority of women missionaries were adventurous only in wanting to work in India at all. They were expected to behave with the utmost propriety, not only because of the fears of their own community about the spiritual and physical threat that India posed to women but also because of strict views of Indians on what constituted female modesty. They were not supposed to ride, or, if they did, only on the quietest of ponies. They lived simply but in a European way: indeed two Australian women who lived in Delhi 'like natives' before the First World War were generally despised by their fellows. Missionaries, male and female, often shared the racial attitudes of the British community; as one Indian convert complained to Margaret Harkness, a memsahib who was often critical of the Raj, 'They expect us to do all the drudgery.' If missionaries lived too austerely, it was again bad for the ruling race. They must not get too close to India; Amy Carmichael, who worked in south India for over fifty years, caused much comment in the 1890s by taking some Indian children to stay with her in Ooty for a holiday. When she actually started to wear Indian dress she was criticized for damaging British prestige.

It was unfortunate that the Indians, men particularly, did tend to get the wrong idea about women missionaries. They were objects of great curiosity, especially in the villages; the villagers crowded round them debating loudly with each other. Were these women at all? Perhaps they were a sort of prostitute? They were questioned closely about their social habits. 'May you go to anybody?' an English missionary was asked in the 1920s; and she answered 'of course' before she realized that her questioner was not talking about accepting invitations to dinner parties. Missionaries tried to explain patiently that they were doing God's work;

this also caused difficulties because in India the temple women did this by acting as prostitutes. Occasionally it all got too irritating: when an Indian passerby referred rudely to one missionary as a dancing girl, she jumped out of her carriage and thrashed him with her umbrella.

There was much to dishearten them – a British society which did not really want them, Indians who did not listen to the message they brought, lives which were difficult, sometimes even dangerous. In some areas, crowds of men followed them shouting insults. 'I confess I am very frightened,' wrote one woman from the Punjab in the 1890s, 'but GOD is ever faithful and keeps us from harm.' They could not help being lonely. Worse, they sometimes had doubts. Were they really accomplishing anything at all? India was so big, so ancient, so resistant to change. There is a sad passage in Amy Carmichael's diary, written after she had been working as a missionary for twenty years: 'January 15. I never knew spiritual assaults could be so tumultuous. They are like a noise of shoutings within me.' And on 20 January: 'The taunting voice this morning said, "Wast thou not a fool to wreck thyself thus on thy God?" Some broke down, physically and spiritually, and had to be sent Home. Others kept on doggedly, sustained by willpower and an unshakable faith.

Lady Dufferin, for example, knew a Miss Angelina Hoare, daughter of a well-to-do English family, who 'slaves among the natives in the paddy-fields, almost as one of themselves, wearing a sari, and tramping up to her knees through the marshy rice-fields.' She and her sister, who was also a missionary, were thought to look 'odd' by a more conventional memsahib. Mrs Brown, a friend of Rosamund Lawrence, was the daughter of a rich Australian family who had married a missionary in spite of their opposition. The couple worked with the lowest and most miserable outcastes, and Mrs Brown was both forthright and amusing about the work. 'I've told Mr Brown I can't really LOVE them as he does. You see, my dear, they do *stink* so.' At her husband's urging, the couple had given up all worldly possessions; they lived hand to mouth with their children on gifts or money from their missionary society. One day, she told Rosamund Lawrence, there was nothing in the house: 'All my faith went. "It will be all right," said Mr Brown, but I was crazy with fear. He spent the night in prayer, and I cried and cried. The next morning came a hundred pounds from a sympathiser in England. I've never troubled since that day.' As she told the story, she laughed, 'looking into space all rapt and delighted as though she were seeing something hidden from the rest of the world'.

Missionaries, doctors and teachers were unconventional by British standards but they were still, if they chose, considered part of that society. Some women, however, did not worry about whether they were in or out, for they had other, greater concerns. Ursula Graham Bower, who came from an upper-middle-class background in England, was like this. She fell in love with the Nagas, a partly Mongolian people, and their country on the Indo-Burmese border, eventually learning their language and their ways. She was adopted by a Naga tribe and even taken for the reincarnation of a goddess by a small and fanatical sect. During the Second World War, she helped to organize and lead Naga scouts in V Force, a guerrilla unit under General Slim, which was on the front lines against Japan.

She had come out to India in the summer of 1937 when she was twenty-three to spend a holiday with friends in Imphal on the Northeast Frontier. She lived the usual cantonment life: golf at the Club, tennis, dining out, shopping, watching polo twice a week. Something happened to her, though, when friends took her up into Naga country in the hills above Imphal. When she came back ten days later, she had changed: 'It was as though I had rediscovered a world to which I had belonged the whole time; from which, by some accident, I had been estranged.... Not yet of the hills, but already divorced from my own race, I wanted nothing now but the lovely, wild reality of mountain and jungle.'

Reluctantly she returned to England at the end of her holiday, but she continued to dream of the Naga country and the following summer she managed to scrape together enough money to go back with the excuse of making a photographic record of the Naga way of life before it disappeared. The local Political Agent, extraordinarily, gave her permission to travel alone into the hills. As she was short of money she travelled with only two native companions, a servant and a compounder, sent out to dispense medicines in the remoter villages. She borrowed a tent and some cooking gear, and bought a few cheap cotton shirts, a pair of shorts, and some native sandals which she wore with army socks. That, apart from her cameras and film, was the extent of her luggage.

The journey was difficult (at this point she did not even speak much of the local language), but also enchanting. 'For the first time I had known responsibility, loneliness, worry and exhaustion. I'd been revolted by wounds and filth, hampered by lack of the language, but nevertheless I was going back to it if it killed me. And I couldn't have given one sane reason why.' She went back, again and again, and sometimes it did come close to killing her. Once when she came down badly with fever, her cook had hysterics and her other servant was too drunk to bring her medicine. Yet there were other moments, when the hills were unbearably beautiful, or when she witnessed the ancient Naga rituals and the villagers dancing by torchlight through the night. More and more she saw with Naga eyes, and her own world looked strange. When she descended to the Plains a party of fellow Europeans seemed alien creatures: 'how odd, how knobbed and craggy they were, after the smooth Mongol faces; how pallid the woman was, like a plant left in the dark!' The Europeans in turn called her, perhaps with a touch of malice, 'the Naga Queen'.

Ursula Graham Bower remained British, at least in her desire to help out when the war started, but she did it in her own way, in Naga country with Naga companions. For over two years she patrolled her section of the frontier. At night, she slept with a Sten gun handy. When the big Japanese advance came in the spring of 1944, her small force of 150 scouts suddenly found itself between the advancing Japanese and the Allied front lines with one rifle, one shotgun, and seventy muzzle-loaders. Luckily they were not called upon to use them.

As the war wound down, she met a rare Englishman who actually wanted an unconventional wife. Colonel Betts, also in V Force, liked the sound of the Naga Queen. He decided to call on her in the Hills; he took his butterfly net along so that the trip would not be wasted if the two of them did not hit it off. On the fourth day after his arrival, he proposed and was accepted, at least by Ursula Graham Bower herself. That was not the major hurdle; her staff of Nagas, by now close friends, if not relatives, had to pass judgment. They all assembled and demanded to speak to her. 'The Sahib', said the most senior, to her relief, 'is all right.' The couple had a Western wedding with cake, wedding dress, and guard of honour at the church door. Some months later, they were given a Naga wedding by Ursula's tribe. The elders explained that the marriage could not really be recognized until the proper rites had been performed. The celebrations lasted from four in the afternoon until the following morning. 'We danced,' she remembered, 'we sang till the sun went down. We danced the noon down, too; all three cockcrows and sunrise, we danced them by.'

Ursula Graham Bower did not so much reject British society as simply ignore it. What of those who wanted to belong but could not because they had committed the great sin, in the eyes of their com- patriots, of marrying Indians? Such women were relatively rare; in the early nineteenth century, the best-known was Mrs Meer Hassan Ali, who left a lively account of her marriage into a noble Lucknow Muslim family. Nothing is known of her background or maiden name, but she apparently met her future husband while he was a professor of Hindustani in England between 1812 and 1816. After living in India for some twelve years, she left for England, according to later reports because she could no longer tolerate her husband's other wives. In her *Observations on the Mussulmauns of India*, however, she says nothing of the difficulties of interracial marriage and indeed has little but praise for the domestic habits of the Muslims. In 1843, Honoria Lawrence, who was visiting Lucknow, heard that she was still alive, and acting as the matron of a boys' school in England.

By the late nineteenth century the obstacles to interracial marriages were much greater, but they still occurred. Often what happened was that an Indian studying in England married while he was there; or an Indian prince took an extra wife when he ran into an attractive woman in his travels: one young prince married the stepdaughter of a Dutch balloonist who was touring India. The Maharajahs Holkar of Indore in the twentieth century made a family habit of taking American wives. Tukoji Rao II, who was deposed by the British in 1903 after a series of scandals, married as his third wife the convent-educated Nancy Miller from Seattle. The marriage was a highly successful one and she managed to win over both his family, including the senior wives, and his former subjects. She died in Indore in 1995.

There does not seem to have been much difference between Muslim or Hindu men when it came to choosing foreign wives. Hindus, because they pursued Western education earlier, were perhaps more likely to meet girls in Britain, at least in the nineteenth century.

Women who married Indians outside India often found their hopes of an easy, carefree life dashed when they reached India and faced the reality of living in an extended family with a domineering mother-in-law. They had also assumed, mistakenly, that they would be able to mix with British society. Instead they found themselves, members of the same race as the rulers of India, treated as any native might be. Even on the voyage out, fellow passengers avoided them when news of their unfortunate marriages got around, and in India respectable hotels and boarding houses did not want them as guests. The Maharani identified only as 'Florence' by the civil servant who met her was 'a homely, gentle Irishwoman', who would sit night after night in her drawing room waiting for the European visitors who were staying in her palace to pay her a call; they never came. The government of India showed what it thought of such marriages by refusing, in the case of Indian rulers, to recognize the wives as legal or the children as legitimate until the very end of the Raj.

The thought of a European woman married to an Indian disturbed many of the British in India. As 'Boxwallah' wrote in his memoirs during the early 1900s, 'Unless she is sexually perverted, she has violated her own nature in marrying a man of coloured race.' Captain Clive Somerton, the hero of Alice Perrin's popular novel *The Anglo-Indians*, reacts to the love of a young Indian prince for the heroine Fay Fleetwood with 'that primitive sense of repulsion innate in white-skinned humanity towards the notion of race admixture with a dark-skinned people – a repulsion arising from Nature's tendency to breed upwards, not downwards'. Ethel Savi devoted an entire successful novel to the topic. *The Daughter-in-Law* has as its heroine Kathleen, 'the spirit of an exquisite lily in human shape', who is degraded by her marriage to Hurri Mohun Dey: after a quarrel, 'he apologized in the only way his bestial mind could suggest as a proof of his sincerity, and Kathleen passed the night in sleeplessness and tears for her humiliation and the outrage she had endured.'

Objections came from the Indian side as well. It was a terrible blow to most Indian families when one of their sons married a foreign woman. In the case of orthodox Hindus, there was the added complication that the woman was Untouchable; no one could eat with her or accept food from her hands. She often found to her dismay that she was expected to conform to the ideal of the Indian daughter-in-law, observing *purdah* with the rest of the women and treating her husband's parents with the greatest deference. An Englishwoman who married into a strict Muslim family in 1937 found that she was accompanied everywhere, even in the *purdah* quarters, by a female relative or servant. If she went into the bathroom, one of them waited outside. When her husband was away she was guarded by two *ayahs* who slept across the door. If their husbands tried to take their foreign wives' part, the women were blamed for their bad influence. When children came, there were fresh problems. Should they be brought up as Indians or as Europeans? Often the mothers-in-law firmly took over the children's upbringing, leaving the mothers lonely and resentful.

In spite of the obstacles, some of the marriages were very happy. Women with enough strength of character and the right sorts of husbands made a satisfying, if restricted, world for themselves. Henry Beveridge once called on a large blonde lady married to a Muslim in a small town in Bengal; she seemed, he reported to Annette, 'to maintain her place very well'. (It may have helped that she had borne her husband ten children.) Some women threw themselves wholly into Indian life: they followed the rules of *purdah*, they wore Indian dress, they sometimes converted to their husbands' religion. (Sometimes indeed they unnerved the women of their husbands' families by the fervour and punctiliousness with which they followed all the rules.) And they were repaid with devotion. When the Maharani Florence lay dying, her bed was covered with toys, jewelry, music boxes – anything her distraught husband could think of to amuse her. At her death, as a mark of particular respect, he ordered the sacrifice of white peacocks.

Another successful marriage was the one between Morag Murray, a Scottish girl, and the son of a Pathan chieftain after the First World War. She met her future husband when he was at university in Glasgow. Both families disapproved strongly when they announced their intention of getting married. (Her future father-in-law's main concern was whether she would be able to hold the family fort when the men were away fighting; as it turned out, she was.) Nevertheless, the couple were married, and it proved to be several years before she saw her husband's home in the wild country beyond the Khyber Pass. His family, in spite of their initial reservations, welcomed her warmly and married them again with Pathan rites. Hundreds of tribesmen came in from the surrounding country for the ceremonies, bearing lavish gifts of carpets, saddles, gold cloth, jewels and shawls. That night the hills around the fort were ringed with bonfires of celebration. Morag Murray Abdullah, as she now was, went a long way to meet her in-laws. In return, her new relations also made compromises: contrary to local custom, the young couple were given their own fort to live in.

Finally, among the unconventional women there were the restless souls who sought in India something they did not find in their own civilization. They did not mind the cold shoulders of British society because they had no intention of being accepted into it; indeed they were rejecting everything it stood for. Madeleine Slade, the admiral's daughter who as Mirabehn became a devoted disciple of Gandhi, ritually burnt all her smart Paris dresses on her voyage to India and put on Indian dress.

What these women sought often led them to take a deep interest in an Indian religion, usually Hinduism; some virtually disappeared from sight, like the woman Lord Curzon's private secretary, Sir Walter Lawrence, heard of who was one of a band of yogis living in a sacred cave. Others were visible enough, in their writing and lecturing, to irritate the British profoundly.

One of these was Lady Minto's acquaintance Sister Nivedita, who had been born Margaret Noble in 1867. She had grown up in a God-fearing, genteel and relatively poor household, her father a Congregationalist minister, her mother very devout. From her parents, she learnt to have a social conscience and to do good works. Her young adult years were devoted first to one cause, then to another. She was not a dilettante, but she was obviously a woman who had not yet found what she wanted. She became a teacher in a mining town in England, then a journalist who wrote about the sufferings of the poor and of women. She became a socialist, she lost her belief in God, she was attracted towards Buddhism.

In 1895, her quest came to an end when the well-known Indian holy man and social reformer Swami Vivekananda came to lecture in London about his work. She went to hear him and decided almost at once to go to India to work for him. As she described it later in a letter to a friend, 'Suppose Swami had not come to London at that time! I would have been like a headless torso. For I always knew that I was waiting for something. I always said a call would come and it did.'

She arrived in Calcutta just before the turn of the century and started transforming herself from a British bluestocking into a model Hindu woman. She studied Bengali and was initiated as a novice into Vivekananda's religious order. 'It was all like a birth into a new world', she recalled happily later. She opened a little school for Hindu girls, but teaching increasingly took second place to lecturing and writing about India. In 1904 she published *The Web of Indian Life*, which sought to explain to the West the strengths of Indian life. (At the same time, the book made frequent and unfavourable comparisons with the West.) In the years that followed, she stressed the same points: Christianity paled beside Hinduism (as she told a group of Indians in a lecture in 1902, 'in religion you have a great deal to give, and nothing to learn from the West'); whereas a Hindu wife was all purity and steadfastness and womanly virtues, Western women were egoistic and greedy for power. The West, unlike India, was jettisoning all the finer things of life in its mad drive to make money.

Increasingly her work took a political turn. Once she had admired the Empire but now she called the British in India 'a gang of robbers'. She became friends with many of the leading nationalists, some, like G. K. Gokhale, moderates and others, like Aurobindo Ghosh, closer to terrorists. When Lord Curzon aroused fury in Bengal in 1905 by dividing the province (a decision widely perceived by Indians as an attempt to destroy the unity of Bengali nationalism), she sided with those who advocated the most radical measures of protest. The authorities had been watching her since 1902, and it was even rumoured in 1907 that she was about to be arrested; perhaps by coincidence she left on a lecture tour of Britain and the United States. By 1908 she was openly talking of the need for insurrection. The British of the Raj were appalled by her; the missionaries had hated *The Web of Indian Life*; *The Englishman* called her a traitor to her race. It all rolled off her back. She died in 1911 after a severe attack of dysentery, convinced to the end that she was doing the right thing.

Annie Besant was a more flamboyant version of Sister Nivedita. She was notorious at Home before she ever came to India for the fervour and energy with which she advocated one controversial cause after another, from radical socialism to the rights of women and of workers, to birth control. At the beginning of the 1890s, when she was in her early forties, a new enthusiasm, this time for India, seized her. She made the acquaintance of Gandhi, then a young law student in London, and, more significantly, met Madame Helena Blavatsky, a rather dubious character who had founded the Theosophical Society in 1875. Madame Blavatsky and her equally mysterious colleague, the American Colonel Henry Olcott, claimed to be in possession of revelations from dead Tibetan mahatmas called Koot Hoomi and Morya. (The mahatmas made their presence known with a smell of sandalwood and exotic spices, and their messages came sometimes written on prettily coloured paper, more often whispered into Madame Blavatsky's ear.) In 1879 the Society decided to work in India, home of so much ancient wisdom. Not surprisingly, many educated Indians welcomed it; on the other hand, most of the British did not, since the enthusiasm for things Indian implied a criticism of Western civilization and of themselves. When Madame Blavatsky died in 1891, Annie Besant succeeded her as leader, and in 1893 she moved from London to the Society's colony at Adyar in Madras.

Spiritual matters were not enough, however, to occupy her energies and increasingly she became involved with Indian nationalism, especially its most significant manifestation, the Indian National Congress. She tried to prod what was at the time an association of moderate nationalists drawn from across India and from all religions into demanding home rule; during the First World War, she and other radicals formed Home Rule Leagues. The government of India, alarmed at the danger to the Raj posed by this elderly lady of sixty-nine, arrested her in the summer of 1917. She was released some months later, on the intervention of the new reform-minded Secretary of State for India, Edwin Montagu, who was trying to conciliate Indian nationalist opinion. She was of course a heroine to the nationalists; Congress promptly elected her its president. (She was the first woman to hold the post.) That year was the peak of her political career – and the start of its decline. Gandhi was now taking Indian nationalism in hand and the older leaders like Mrs Besant were about to become irrelevant. She was not popular with her compatriots in India. 'A shameless political huckster', said *The Englishman* in 1918. When the government decided to release her from prison, there were furious telegrams and letters of protest, and all over India meetings passed resolutions of censure.

Women whose unconventional behaviour threatened the Raj were not easily forgiven. Often the memsahibs were loudest of all in their condemnations. When Mary Carpenter came to India in 1866 to work for the improvement of women's education, she reported that 'Scarcely any ladies here come near me, partly perhaps from fearing that I should meddle with their plans, chiefly probably because they were afraid of my heterodoxy.' If there were many women, like those in Paul Scott's *Raj Quartet*, who questioned the British mission in India, they kept very quiet about it.

13

WOMEN IN A CHANGING WORLD

Even while the Raj was at the height of its glory, in the last quarter of the nineteenth century, the pressures were beginning to build up from below. And this time the discontented Indians were not a ragbag of reactionaries, hereditary rulers, holy men, simple peasants: they were businessmen, newspapermen, lawyers, speaking the language of their foreign rulers and turning their own ideals of democracy and fair play against them. This was a new sort of nationalism and ultimately it was to sweep aside the world of the Raj, with its polo and parties, its Clubs and its hill stations.

At first it was not very alarming. The early Indian nationalists were few, and they sang 'God Save the Queen' at their meetings. By the First World War, however, Indian nationalism was turning into something rather formidable. By the time of the Second World War it was shaking the Raj to its very roots. Simultaneously the British, first at Home and then even in India, were beginning to lose faith in the whole giant confidence trick. They were no longer sure that they had the right to rule India, or indeed if they even wanted it any longer.

The British in India at first dismissed the nationalists as harmless cranks. (It surely says something about the attitude of British men to their own women that one of the charges against Indian nationalists was that they were 'effeminate'.) But by the start of the twentieth century, the cranks were growing more numerous and insistent. At the end of the First World War, when it appeared that the politicians at Home were actually going to give in to the nationalist demands for Indianization of the public services and for self-government, the British in India were bewildered and resentful.

Not surprisingly, women remained the Raj's staunchest supporters. As we have seen, some felt differently, and considered that the Indians might be capable of looking after themselves, that, in any case, European ways of doing things were not necessarily the best; but most were very proud of Britain's role. From 1978 to 1983, some thirty years after India obtained its independence, women who had once been memsahibs were interviewed by the Cambridge South Asian Archive. They were asked, among other things, for their views on the Raj, and their answers followed the same lines:

- One of the most wonderful achievements ever known.
- We put more into India than we took out.
- The peasant always loved the Raj.
- I took it for granted that our rule was fair & just & beneficial.

Women's views on Indian nationalism usually echoed the most conservative among the men: it would be years, centuries, before India would be ready to govern itself. How could Indians expect to govern when they had, as one lady said tactfully, 'certain defects' of character? It was well known, said another, that Orientals were deficient in both industry and initiative. Perhaps because their knowledge of Indians was usually confined to servants, the memsahibs tended to see all Indians as childlike creatures in need of constant supervision. Generally, of course, the women of the Raj were not supposed to take much interest in politics. In moments of crisis, however, they were used by the men as a reason why the Raj could not compromise with the nationalists and they themselves were moved to speak out in their own defence.

The first such crisis after the Mutiny came, curiously enough, in 1883 when the law member of the Viceroy's Council introduced a bill to tidy up some loose ends in the administration of justice in India. Sir Courtney Ilbert was a quiet, hardworking man with a dislike of inconsistencies. He had noticed, among other things, an 'anomaly', as he described it, in the fact that, under existing law, Europeans living outside the big cities could elect to be tried in criminal matters by a European rather than an Indian judge. In fact, before the 1880s the privilege had not been exercised because the district judges were members of the ICS and therefore invariably European. By the time Ilbert introduced his bill, however, a few Indians had managed to get to England and pass the examinations for the ICS. A couple of them had even been appointed judges. To Ilbert, to the Viceroy Lord Ripon (a Liberal of a mildly reforming nature), and to the majority of officials who were consulted, it seemed absurd not to give Indian judges, who possessed the same qualifications as their European colleagues, jurisdiction over Europeans brought before the court. It seemed an unimportant change and no one expected the storm of protest, of rage, even of hysteria, which welled up among the British population, especially in Bengal, where relations between the races were already cool. There were mass meetings, petitions, letters to the British press in India, wild rumours, burnings of effigies of Ilbert and Ripon, even plots to kidnap the Viceroy and spirit him out of the country. Memories of the Mutiny were revived, especially the dreadful threat to women and children. 'To make their grievance a general one,' reported the head of the Criminal Investigation Department cynically, 'they raised the cry of danger to European women.' Stories circulated, none of them ever verified, that in Calcutta Indians, emboldened by the liberal policies of Lord Ripon, had tried to rape European women. In a crowded meeting at Allahabad, a speaker assured his audience that the government in fact intended that Europeans should intermarry with Indians. This news was greeted, said the newspaper account, with 'prolonged groans and hisses'.

Women had put up with quite enough already, it was said; the fresh indignities of the Ilbert Bill were intolerable. Why, already they had to come into court while Indian women in *purdah* did not. And now, a barrister in Allahabad pointed out, 'our gentle young women, no matter how beautiful and young, no matter how refined and modest and delicate, must be compelled to appear in a native court before a native judge with a raised veil'. An engineer in Bengal said that English gentlewomen, such as his wife and daughter, were going to be subjected to the rulings of 'polygamists'. Even women of lesser refinement were going to suffer, said a civil servant in Chota Nagpore: no Indian magistrate could deal with cases of adultery involving the lower classes because he would not understand the 'apparent coarseness and brutality in those relationships' which is often combined 'with real affection and good will'. Emotions never ran as high in Bombay, where relations between the races were notably easier. When Ripon passed through on his way back to Britain at the end of his viceroyalty, Nora Scott noted to her family, 'The feeling here towards Lord Ripon is so different to what it is in Calcutta that

I hope everything will go off well and give him some comfort, after all he has had to hear from the Bengal planters and their confrères.'

The Ilbert Bill was expected by its opponents to be the ruin of India. The threats to European business and to European women were all tied up together. Planters complained that they would not be able to get wives to solace their lonely lives because no woman would dare to come out to the *mofussil*. A prominent Calcutta businessman painted a grim picture: 'the planter absent in Calcutta, the neighbouring zemindar [landowner] with an old grudge trumping up false accusations against the defenceless wife, with hired witness before a hired judge, and the consequences'.

The ladies were not slow to take up their own defence. 'Have we not enough to endure in India, isolated as we often are, suffering from the climate and separated from our children,' wrote 'Indignation' pathetically to *The Pioneer*, 'without the addition of a constant fear of personal attack?' Some ladies were careful to point out that they were not objecting to Indian judges on racial grounds: 'It is not the colour of their skins, it is the colour of their minds which we object to', wrote 'An Englishwoman'. Even Annette Beveridge, liberal in so much else, argued that until Indian men emancipated their own women they were not fit to judge 'civilized women'. The memsahibs forsook their usual reticence to take concerted action. They held public meetings and drew up petitions. Seven hundred ladies in Bihar sent a petition to the House of Commons. Nearly six thousand addressed Queen Victoria herself, confident that she would understand the indignity they faced.

Perhaps the women's activities had effect. At any rate, the governments of India and of Britain decided they had had enough. The Ilbert Bill became law, but in such a watered-down version that no apprehensive memsahib could have any objection to it. Unfortunately for their peace of mind, however, the victory had an unforeseen result. Indian nationalists who, up till then, had confined themselves to the politest of requests for the mildest of reforms watched and learnt from the storm. They learnt how to organize an effective protest; they discovered that the government of India did not like a fuss; they saw the utility of appealing to opinion in Britain. Shortly after the Ilbert Bill agitation, the Indian National Congress held its first meeting. Indian nationalists went on being polite but they also began to make larger and firmer demands.

In Bengal, Lord Curzon's decision in 1905 to divide the province provoked the first boycott of British goods; it also produced the first crop of violent protests. The British community was horrified when an assassination attempt on a judge resulted in the deaths of two British women. *The Pioneer* warned angrily that ten terrorists must die in future for 'every life sacrificed'. A member of the Viceroy's Council wrote in 1910 that it was no accident that Indian nationalism was strongest in Bengal, where 'the most licentious and degraded forms of Hindu superstition are most practiced'. One paper reassuringly reported that 99 per cent of British women could use small arms.

Although the First World War was to hasten the disappearance of the Raj, at first the British noticed little difference in their lives. Military wives saw their husbands leave with their regiments for France or for the ill-fated expedition to Mesopotamia, but civilian wives did not always have to face such partings: men in official positions were not allowed to join up without special permission, which was given reluctantly. And women in India still had plenty of servants, not like Home, where the domestic help were rushing off to well-paying factory jobs. They did some knitting for the troops, and they looked after their children, who had to stay in India for the duration (often that simply meant sending them off to schools in the Hills). Most kept up their usual social rounds. There were complaints that society was not what it had been: some lower-class men had inevitably been promoted to officers and their wives, said one memsahib, were 'shoddy-looking goods' who cared only for pleasure, a vice which, alas, was starting to infect solid members of the middle classes who should have known better.

The British in India were also insulated from the terrible sense of hopelessness and futility that the war engendered in Europe as it dragged on. They remained secure in their sense of superiority, while at Home thoughtful people were beginning to wonder whether Western civilization had any value at all. The women also missed the shock that their contemporaries at Home felt at working in a man's world – the drain of men to the trenches meant that women had to take on jobs which no one had thought them capable of doing – and, moreover, succeeding. When the war ended, the old joke that it took years for ideas to travel out to India had never been truer.

They expected the Raj to run on, just as it always had. It was not a reasonable belief but they had failed to realize how much their world had changed. The war had shown a great many Indians that their white masters could be as irrational and savage as anyone else in the world. The confidence trick had depended on the faith of the ruled just as much as on that of the rulers. The mud of France, the incompetent muddle in Mesopotamia, the English and French girls who saw nothing strange in going to bed with Indian soldiers, all helped to destroy the myth of the invincible and inviolate white man. Indians wanted more than paternalism, no matter how benevolent; and they grew more effective at demanding power. Congress was turning into a mass movement; in Gandhi, who had come back to India just before the war started, it had an organizer who could reach the illiterate peasant masses. His weapons of 'soul-force' and 'passive resistance' were to baffle and enrage the British in India until they made mistake after mistake. What they failed to realize at first was that the government at Home had decided that the time had come to give in to some of the nationalist demands. In August 1917, the Secretary of State for India announced in the House of Commons that the government intended to take 'substantial steps as soon as possible' to prepare India for responsible self-government. It was not clear how long that would take, but the important thing was that the promise had been made. After six months in India, talking not only to officials but to all the main Indian political leaders, Montagu announced a complicated scheme of constitutional reform (which soon proved to be unworkable and far short of what Indian nationalists wanted).

The government of India, never as enthusiastic about reform as its masters in London, was convinced that it needed repressive measures in reserve in case of trouble; in March 1919 it forced through, over the unanimous opposition of the Indian members on the Viceroy's Legislative Council, the Rowlatt Acts, which extended several wartime emergency powers of government. Gandhi at once announced a *hartal* to oppose what he considered an immoral action. (The *hartal* was a traditional Indian version of a general strike, the souls of the strikers being too shocked by evil to engage in worldly activities.) All over India, in the first week of April, Indians stopped work for a day. As was to happen again with Gandhi's non-violent protests, some Indians proved unable to resist the temptations of violence. Crowds turned into bad-tempered mobs; stones were thrown, windows broken. Touching on a theme that was to become a favourite one, 'An Englishwoman' wrote from Calcutta to *The Englishman*, 'If the authorities cannot control the mob let the ladies band together and show that they at least have some British pluck.'

The worst trouble of all came in the Punjab. Riots broke out on 10 April in Amritsar, the holy city of the Sikhs. Mobs attacked European banks and killed three European employees. Miss Frances Sherwood, a missionary who had worked in Amritsar for fifteen years with the Zenana Missionary Society, was dragged from her bicycle and beaten by a mob which left her for dead. (Her life was saved by a Hindu family, who took her in and nursed her, at considerable risk to themselves, a fact which the more rabid British tended to overlook.) Another lady, a doctor, narrowly escaped death in her hospital; her Indian colleagues hid her from the mob. The other European women and children were hastily gathered together in a crumbling mud fort.

Troops under General Reginald Dyer were sent to the city to restore order. Here, on 13 April, Dyer took an action which, more than any other single event, convinced moderate Indians that the British must go. A crowd assembled, in spite of Dyer's ban on public meetings, at a place called Jallianwalla Bagh. The crowd was either entirely peaceful or full of agitators bent on trouble – depending on whose version you listened to afterwards. At any rate, Dyer ordered his troops to fire straight into the gathering – fearing, as he said later, that an order to disperse would simply provoke a direct attack on his greatly outnumbered force. At least four hundred Indians were killed. Two days later, the Lieutenant-Governor imposed martial law over the whole Punjab. Both he and Dyer remained convinced until they died that they had prevented a second Mutiny.

When the news of events in the Punjab began to filter out, most British in India agreed with them. The women had a particular cause for gratitude because yet again, so it appeared, Indians had been intent on violating them. Rumours, very like those which had followed the Mutiny, flew around the community about 'Ravishment Proclamations' calling on Indian nationalists to assault European women. Their newspapers dwelt with horror not on the deaths at Jallianwalla Bagh but on the attack on Miss Sherwood and the murder of the three European men.

General Dyer, member of a well-known British family in India, avenged the attack on Miss Sherwood to the best of his ability. Under his notorious 'crawling order', all Indians passing the spot where she had been set upon (and some had no choice if they wanted to get to their homes) had to go on their hands and knees in the dust. Nothing could have been more typical of his milieu than his subsequent explanation: 'We look upon women as sacred or ought to. I was searching my brain for a suitable punishment to meet this awful case.'

Most of his compatriots understood Dyer's feelings and approved of his actions in the Punjab. Their sense of shock and betrayal was therefore all the greater when the government of India appointed a committee of inquiry which criticized the way martial law had been administered in the Punjab and censured Dyer, who was forced to resign his command in 1920. As during the Ilbert Bill agitation, women had a good deal to say on the subject. Throughout 1920 they filled the press with their letters; over six thousand signed a protest, pointing out that Dyer had saved them from 'unspeakable horrors', which was sent to the Prime Minister; and a thirteen-woman committee organized the Dyer Appreciation Fund to present the 'Saviour of the Punjab' with a Sword of Honour and a purse for saving them all from 'murder, torture, arson, looting and wholesale anarchy'. Some sold their jewelry in gratitude. Altogether £26,000 was raised. Miss Florence Holland, principal of a girls' school in Mussoorie, who headed the Dyer Appreciation Fund, expressed the prevalent view when she said that Britain no longer seemed to care about its glorious heritage. 'The Indian agitators who strove to wreck their country's weal, go unscathed – free to carry on their fiendish schemes (who can tell with what dread results?). The British General, *who kept the peace of India*, is pilloried and degraded!'

A few women dared go against the current of emotion. Three lady missionaries bravely signed a letter in which fellow missionaries and educators condemned the 'Prussianism' and the assumption of racial superiority on the part of the authorities, and called for a spirit of Christian forgiveness and cooperation. Annie Besant spoke at a public meeting in Bombay to condemn the commanding officer's actions. (*The Englishman* was beside itself at her 'malicious and mischievous campaign against her own kith and kin'.) But the overwhelming majority of letters to the papers from women showed no doubts at all about the rightness of Dyer's actions.

The British community as a whole enjoyed a unity they had not known since the exciting days of the Ilbert Bill. Women were even admitted to the European Defence Association for the first time, and the Domiciled Europeans and Eurasians were temporarily encouraged to stand with the group that usually preferred to ignore them. But although they had supporters at Home, notably the Conservative *Morning Post*, they failed to sway the government in Britain either from disgracing Dyer or from carrying on with reforms in India. When it had to listen to millions of Indians, it was no longer prepared to pay much attention to the shrill voices of a tiny minority. In any case, most people at Home had other things to worry about besides an empire which was coming to seem old-fashioned and irrelevant.

The end of the First World War marked the end of the political importance of the British in India. Some of them probably realized it at the time, but for most the realization took much longer. There was some difficulty for a few years in recruiting young men to work in India. Among those who lived there, however, the old convictions were shaken but not destroyed.

Life itself went on much in its usual pattern, even though the old hands grumbled that their society was losing its standards. The wrong sort of people were coming out from Home; the new memsahibs were not used to the standard of living they enjoyed in India and it went to their heads. In fact, most changes were of a superficial sort. The spread of electricity brought with it electric fans, lights, refrigerators, and even luxuries like electric shoe-warmers to keep mildew at bay during the monsoon. By the 1930s many households had radios so that they could listen to the transmissions of the Indian Broadcasting Company or, if they had short wave, fuzzy, static-ridden broadcasts from Home. (Delhi radio station had a popular Children's Hour, which sent out special birthday messages to little sahibs and memsahibs, such as 'Greetings to Gillian Dench of the North West Frontier Province. If she will look in Mummy's wardrobe she may find a surprise.') Many houses now had running water and bathrooms equipped with what were called 'pull-the-plugs'; yet the sweeper and the water carrier did not disappear entirely, even in the cities, until after the Second World War. Cars were beginning to replace horses. The memsahib now needed a smaller establishment of servants, which was just as well because servants were becoming expensive, although not of course as dear as at Home.

Holidays in hill stations continued to be popular but women were increasingly going Home for the summer to see their children when they could. By the 1930s there was an air service from Karachi and the P&O built some faster liners. Wives of civil servants had subsidized passages, thanks to the Lee Commission of 1924. On the smaller stations, the number of Europeans shrank because the civil service was taking in increasing numbers of Indians. This, it was felt, was very hard on European women, who would not be able to find congenial companionship in the Indian wives. In fact, as some of them discovered with relief, Indian women were changing too, giving up *purdah*, going to Western-style schools (sometimes indeed even at Home), and taking up such arts of civilization as bridge and golf.

New fashions made their slow way out from Home. The cocktail party began to replace some of the elaborate long dinners. Many of the young found Club life boring; they preferred going out dancing or to 'Beat it Up' parties in bars where they stood each other exotic cocktails. The new jazz from America arrived; in 1924 it received a viceregal imprimatur with the Readings' Jazz Band. In Calcutta, Firpo's Restaurant, which opened after the war, was enormously popular; it had a jazz band, and did not serve drinks by the glass but simply left a bottle on each table (at the end of the evening a waiter estimated how much had disappeared); the authorities did not allow it to have a cabaret for some years, lest the sight of scantily dressed European showgirls should give Indians the wrong ideas. Even remote Kashmir had its Bright Young Things who shattered the silence of the mountains with loud gramophones and who scandalized their elders with mixed bathing by moonlight.

Women's style changed too. By the 1920s it was quite acceptable for ladies to wear jodhpurs; only the very old-fashioned used side-saddles. Topis were still worn in the sun, however; they did not disappear altogether until the end of the Raj. Women's skirts gradually got shorter, which made golf and tennis easier. (As always in India it took time for the fashions of Home to make the voyage out: in 1925 Princess Arthur of Connaught caused a sensation by appearing in short skirts – 'just like a flapper', said the conservatives.) Women shingled their hair and the more daring took to smoking cigarettes in public. More women took up volunteer work. It became quite fashionable, for example, to lead Brownies and Girl Guides. (In deference to Indian sensitivities, the authorities renamed the Brownies the Bluebirds and the Brown Owl became the Wise Bird.)

Although the patterns of life seemed unchanged, the people themselves were becoming irrelevant. In Britain, they were regarded widely as a curious community left behind by time. Good liberals who had read *A Passage to India* found them rather appalling – or quite simply comic. As Rose Macaulay wrote in her review of the book, which appeared in the *Daily News* of 4 June 1924, 'Never was a more convincing, a more pathetic, or a more amusing picture drawn of the Ruling Race in India.' The exiles discovered, when they went Home on holiday, that they were strangely out of tune. A furious retired colonel said that the place was filled with 'emasculate tenors and husky women crooning what pass for love-songs; young gentlemen at Oxford ranting that they "will not fight for King and Country"'. They were hurt and bewildered that people at Home no longer seemed to value the things they held dear. 'There are things worse than war', wrote the wife of the Civil Surgeon in Manipur in 1936: 'cowardice, disloyalty, to betray a great trust and to fail in one's duty to people one has undertaken to administer and protect – are all worse than war.'

In spite of the last-ditch fight put up by a group of diehards led by Winston Churchill, successive administrations in the 1920s and 1930s continued to move India towards home rule. In 1935 the Government of India Act extended the franchise and gave the provinces greater, indeed virtually autonomous, powers. In 1937 the first elections for the new provincial legislatures were held, and ministries composed of Indian politicians took office.

The growing power of Indians in their own country often made it easier to have friendships with them. There was less of the difficulty caused by feelings of superiority or inferiority. Anne Symington, who came from an impeccable official background and who married into the ICS, had many friends in the Congress party. During the Quit India troubles in 1942 she would have tea with her friend Sarojini Naidu: 'I met everybody that was anybody in the political world there and they used to say, "Is it all right to speak in front of Anne?" and she'd say, "Oh yes, perfectly all right."' The day before Sarojini Naidu was to be arrested, along with the other Congress leaders, she had a farewell dinner – with her favourite champagne and roast duck – with the Symingtons.

British men and women in India had to adjust slowly to the idea that independence must come, but many never reconciled themselves to what they saw as excessively rapid change. They grumbled in their Clubs and at their private dinner parties. They complained that the old deference among the Indians was vanishing. On her tour in 1929, Ethel Savi had a run-in with a *dhobi* at Maiden's Hotel in Agra. When she ticked him off for charging too much, 'he showed a truculent and independent spirit and was disposed to be impertinent – thus giving me a sidelight on the New India'.

The outbreak of the Second World War startled many of the Raj. In their snug world with its apparently unchanging patterns, they had failed to realize the significance of the rise of Hitler. The news of Britain's declaration of war on Germany arrived in Simla on the night of a viceregal ball. A woman who was there remembers trying to absorb the news in that unreal atmosphere: 'In the dark of the night, the endless procession of rickshaws wending their way towards Viceregal Lodge, each with its own wavering lantern, looked to me wonderfully beautiful, a trail of glow-worms flitting past the trees as the road twisted and turned.' Like most Europeans living in Asia, the British had also failed to take the growing power of Japan seriously. The successful Japanese attack on Pearl Harbor in December 1941 was therefore all the more unexpected. The usual round of Christmas parties took place but inwardly, said Enid Candlin, an American woman living in Bengal, people were numb with 'unbelief and consternation'. The extraordinary string of Japanese victories brought the war increasingly close to the borders of India. For a time, in 1942, it looked as though Japan might be on the point of mounting an invasion. The bewildered, pitiful refugees from Burma who straggled into India throughout the spring and summer and the December air raids on Calcutta shook the confidence of the Raj as it had not been shaken since the Mutiny. Some wives and children went up to the Hills for safety, though they ran the risk of being cut off if the Japanese should come. Other women thought of desperate subterfuges, such as staining their children's faces with walnut juice to make them look like little Indians and sending them off to hide in the villages with their *ayahs*. There was a certain amount of unseemly panic. In Madras unfounded reports of a Japanese fleet on its way across the Bay of Bengal produced a flight inland. The Governor of Madras reported to the Viceroy, 'I am sorry to say that some Europeans, even in the hills, gave way to sheer terror and were demanding to be evacuated from Ootacamund of all places.'

Such behaviour and, more important, the relentless Japanese advances finished off the myth of white superiority throughout Asia. In August 1942, Gandhi found an enthusiastic response when he launched his 'Quit India' campaign. Again things got out of hand: a few Europeans were beaten up by mobs and the railways had to have guards along their lines to protect trains from sabotage. In the cities, especially, some women met with insolence or open hostility. Iris Portal was riding her bicycle to work in a hospital one day when she was confronted by a crowd of boys in the road shouting 'Quit India', 'so I put my head down and rode straight at them on my bicycle, ringing the bell violently'. Strangely enough, the usual stories of the rape of European women did not surface this time. Could it be that the British were now seeing Indian nationalists as a coherent (if misguided) force rather than an irrational horde?

Many women did not follow the political developments in India closely. They were busy worrying about their husbands and children. They felt a vague distrust of Congress: it was said that its leaders were negotiating secretly with Japan. Gandhi aroused mixed feelings then and later. Some of the former memsahibs questioned by the Cambridge South Asian Archive thought him simply a charlatan – 'a politician dressed up as a prophet'. Others had a grudging admiration – 'half saint, half crafty politician'.

Women were also busy with war work. This time they were needed to replace men who had gone off to war. They worked in offices, edited newspapers, and helped out in hospitals. Many joined the armed forces as cipher clerks, drivers, or nurses. The Indian Medical Service was forced to recruit women doctors for the first time in spite of objections from some of the male doctors. Women also ran canteens for the troops along the railways and at the big depots. Ursula Graham Bower, the 'Naga Queen', who managed one at a railway junction in Assam during the dark days of 1942 when the dispirited Indian and European troops were pulling back from Burma, remembered above all the sheer physical exhaustion of working eighteen-hour days: 'Let no one suppose that dealing with thousands of uprooted and demoralized human beings, against time, and with improvised equipment, is a kind of Church Tea. It is a dirty, sweaty, frantic navvy's job; one is hewer of wood and drawer of water, coal-heaver, stoker, scullion, constable, nurse, all by turns and all at once, and dustman to wind up with. One's taskmaster, the hardest I know, is the crying need of hundreds of fellow-beings, displayed daily in all its nakedness.' All over India, women went to classes to learn about first-aid and ARP (air raid precautions). They rolled bandages and knitted. They put on concerts to entertain the troops – both British and American – pouring into India and invited lonely soldiers home to meals.

The expansive way of life was necessarily somewhat curtailed, although newcomers, just arrived from wartime Britain, were still impressed by its lavishness. In Delhi, a housing shortage meant that some women married to civil servants had to live in tents – but they had three tents apiece, each with its own brick fireplace and separate brick kitchen. Up in the hill stations, the summer seasons followed their usual pattern, as if there were no war in progress. In Calcutta, while the streets filled up with starving Indians fleeing the great Bengal famine of 1944, the European restaurants were serving 'lobster, caviare, champagne, the lot'. It is true that prices went up and that there was some mild rationing (Europeans got larger rations than Indians). There were also shortages of chocolate and cloth. It became almost impossible to buy stockings and women discovered for the first time in over a century the comfort of going barelegged in the hot weather. They also started to wear much lighter underwear and some abandoned their topis, with no obvious ill-effects.

There were so many rude stories in the British press about high living in India that the Secretary of State for India asked the Viceroy, Lord Linlithgow, to look into it. Linlithgow sent an indignant telegram to Britain, pointing out: 'Need for relaxation greater in tropics more especially under the heavy pressure at which Europeans in India have been working without leave for some years.' The telegram went on to paint a picture of austerity which cannot have aroused much sympathy at Home: 'Social functions almost entirely discarded. Late hours in hotels and restaurants are prohibited. Use of cars greatly limited, consumption of liquors very substantially reduced and the only relaxations which Europeans generally permit themselves are occasional visits to early dances or cinema performances.'

Still, they did suffer. Many women did not know for several years whether their husbands were dead or alive; others knew only that their husbands were in prisoner-of-war camps. India was not a restful place with the threat of invasion – which did not really vanish until the end of 1944 – and the turbulent political climate. They showed the strain by becoming irritable over small details. Enid Candlin lost the friendship of a neighbouring memsahib when she took the side of a gardener who felt he was owed a tiny sum of money: 'Now, she contended, was the time for all the white people to stick together and uphold the honour of their country.'

When the war started, women who had bothered to think about the future of the British in India assumed, by and large, that they were there indefinitely. By the war's end, even the stubbornest had come to realize that the Raj was dying. 'We were not wanted in India', wrote the wife of a man in the Indian Police. 'It was made clear, politely by some, less politely in slogans and demonstrations by others, at worst in rioting.' One watershed was Sir Stafford Cripps's trip to India on behalf of the British Government in March 1942 to promise India political freedom once the war was won. While in India, he had an interview with leaders of the British community in which he told them bluntly that he could do nothing to protect their position in an independent India. In 1945, the newly elected Labour Government was pledged to the immediate handing over of power in India. It sent Earl Mountbatten of Burma out as Viceroy to wind up the Raj, which he did with ruthless efficiency by 1947.

British women, like their men, felt that Britain was betraying India by pulling out so quickly. Those who loved the country were saddened by its partition into India and Pakistan and by the terrible events of 1947 when Hindus, Muslims and Sikhs turned on one another. 'I really think what troubled one most', wrote one woman years later, 'was the growing tension between people we had known, liked, and trusted – a feeling that everything was falling apart *between them*.' Lady Corfield, who had been born in India and whose husband was a high-ranking civil servant, stood in Simla and listened to screams and explosions from the coolies' quarters down the hill: 'you felt helpless, there was nothing you could do.' Women and children in the parts of India where the violence was worst had to be taken down to the ports in military convoys. Lady Henniker, the wife of an army officer, was up in Gulmarg in Kashmir when the troubles started, and missed the military escort that had come for the Europeans in Srinagar. Her husband managed to send up a couple of trucks with some soldiers for her and the other Europeans, mainly retired, stranded there; most of the elderly residents refused to leave because they could not abandon their dogs.

The Raj, apparently so secure forty years earlier, crumbled surprisingly quickly at the end. The women, on the whole, did not waste much time worrying about it. They busied themselves, as they had always done, with packing up, with selling off the furniture they could not take with them, and with paying off the servants. They were apprehensive at leaving a familiar way of life and adjusting to post-war Britain. Where would they find houses for their families? Would their husbands find jobs? What was it going to be like to do their own cooking?

They left their bungalows, emptied for the last time of the Benares brass, the little wooden tables from Kashmir, the photographs, the thousand knick-knacks with which they had made them home-like. They left the gardens with their rows of flowers in clay pots, their tennis courts, the swings hanging from the trees where the little sahibs and memsahibs once played.

Many women stayed on for a few years because their husbands had been invited by the new rulers of India and Pakistan to help with the transition. If their husbands were in business, Independence in fact made little difference to their lives. For many missionaries Independence was a relief: as one woman missionary said, 'we were no longer regarded as part of the ruling power but were accepted for what we were'. Miss Tomlinson, an old missionary in a small hill town, paid no heed to the changes at all. She continued, as she had always done, to terrorize the local officials, ordering them to limit the loads donkeys could carry, sending for them to see the poor who came to her clinic, and scolding them mercilessly. The head of the local administration complained gently to an Englishman: 'When you British made our country free, sir, ... someone forgot to tell Miss Tomlinson.' A few women never left India at all. They had nothing to go Home for.

CONCLUSION

The memsahibs went home in 1947 as so many had done before them. After all, that was what they had wanted during those long months and years in India – wasn't it? They had talked of Home, read its newspapers and magazines, copied its fashions, and followed its gossip. They had held it up as a standard by which India was found wanting. Nevertheless, when the time came for them to go, some of them were secretly anxious: 'We loved England dearly,' said one, 'and had longed all these years for home, yet, faced with the uprooting, I found myself scared of leaving a way of life that had grown so familiar.'

The trip back by boat kept alive the world they were abandoning just a bit longer. Up to the Suez Canal, the old social hierarchy still held. *Burra memsahibs* could still make lesser women shake in their shoes. It was at Port Said, when their boats slid into the Mediterranean, that the changes started. Ceremonially, generations of British who were leaving India threw their topis into the sea, but as they watched them bob away on the waves, they were jettisoning something of themselves as well – the certainties and the confidence that came from being part of a ruling race. The docking completed the shock. The European porters showed little of the deference that Indian ones did; men and women who had been great figures in India were now jostled aside and put, a final indignity, into second- and third-class railway carriages.

Nevertheless, the returning exiles revelled in the green fields, the cool breezes, and the cosy villages. Maria Graham, who arrived back in 1811, spoke for later generations as well: 'The figures of the hills, the varied colours of the fields, the village towers and spires, all belong to my own home, and make me forget, in the happiness they seem to promise, all the dangers, and toils, and difficulties, I have encountered since I left them.' Not everyone was as enthusiastic; England was often smaller and greyer than they remembered. Fanny Parks thought that Plymouth looked 'so wretchedly mean' and 'cold and gloomy', and she found her compatriots unappealing. 'What can be more ugly than the dress of the English? I have not seen a graceful girl in the kingdom.'

Moreover, life in Britain was not always what they had imagined all those miles away in India. English servants were expensive and not nearly so obliging as Indian ones. Houses and lodgings were smaller than they had remembered. The countryside was lovely – but almost too cosy; there was not the spacious feeling of India with its endless horizons. 'England presses on one rather hard', said one retired memsahib: 'it's very close, confined.' They found also that no one at Home was much interested in India: stories about trekking in Kashmir or shooting tigers were not nearly so fascinating as the latest village gossip, and Indian politics, as the House of Commons had always known, produced the most tremendous boredom in listeners.

Many of the women realized then that they could never forget India. Iris Portal felt that 'India was my home and I have left half of myself behind.' Their thoughts, as Julia Curtis found, turned often to those days of the past: 'In the damp of a murky December fog, I always think of a crisp and sunny morning in the cold weather; of the lovely green of the paddy fields; of the violet tints on the Western Ghauts, and of a garden where roses, heliotrope and tuber-roses grow in profusion, and the fragrance of violets scents the air.' They remembered the smoke rising from cooking fires at dusk, the great dusty Plains, the cries of birds and animals, the jingling of bells on Indian carts, the colours and the light, the sound of rain crashing on the roof during the monsoon, and they remembered the people, their comforting *ayahs*, their loyal servants, the graceful women, the beggars, the priests. They tended to forget the unpleasant side of India: the squalor, the cruelties and the terrible poverty. They forgot the dust storms when they could not see a foot in front of themselves; the dreadful nights sitting by a child that seemed to be dying of fever; the loneliness of life on a small station; and the fears, of poisonous snakes and insects, of mad dogs, of disease, of India itself.

Saddest of all were the women who had not wanted to leave but had been forced out by circumstances. Ursula Graham Bower made one last tour on her beloved Northeast Frontier after Independence. She knew that the new government did not want her and her husband to stay: 'Our days in Eden were numbered and the desolation beyond loomed frighteningly close, a grey desert of days at which we could hardly bear to look.' When she arrived in England, her first heartbroken reaction was that 'home was no longer home, that it was utterly foreign, that home was in the Assam hills and that there would never be any other, and that for the rest of our lives we should be exiles.'

Curiously, few of the women who looked back on India with fond nostalgia wanted to return even for a short visit. Perhaps, having been disillusioned with a homecoming once, they did not want to risk it again. India, their India, was better in their memories. Perhaps, too, they did not want to go back as ordinary tourists to a country where they had once been important.

It is now long enough after the Raj to see the women with some objectivity. They went out to a difficult, alien country, usually when they were young and unformed. They found a cosy, reassuring British world on one side and India on the other. Is it any wonder that they fled to the security of the former? What is impressive is how some women, once they got past their initial terror, did put out feelers, by learning Indian languages and trying to meet Indians.

It should be remembered, too, that the women of the Raj worked with what they had: a collection of inherited wisdom about India; the convictions and prejudices of their own culture towards others that it considered to be less developed; and rigidly defined roles as women, as wives, and as mothers. They were also subject to the temptations of being part of an elite – and one that was felt to be of a superior race.

Nevertheless, they did not always take the Raj seriously; true, they were part of it, but they were also relegated to a secondary role. There were women who resented that, who laughed a little at some of the solemn pretensions of their men, and who had a certain sympathy for some of the Indian hurts and demands. Some admired Gandhi and the Indian nationalists, and told their husbands (perhaps not publicly) that they should try to understand the Indian point of view.

If a balance sheet is to be drawn up for the women of the Raj, let it be remembered to their credit that they so often loved their servants and were loved in return. (That they found it more difficult to establish contact with Indians of their own status is another matter.) Let it be remembered that they lived in a difficult country with bravery and competence. Even today India can be menacing; think of it before antibiotics and modern communications. They travelled miles on their own, endured hardships and dangers as a matter of course. And they tried to be ladies in all circumstances, like the woman who amused herself when her husband was on tour by shooting tigers and then returning to camp and sitting down to do exquisite needlepoint; or the woman who, when things became tense before Independence, refused to alter her daily routine – but slipped a revolver into her handbag just in case.

Today they tend to be remembered as dim, comic figures or as vicious harridans who poisoned relations between the Indians and the British. Neither memory does them justice. They were living women, with worries, happinesses and sorrows like anyone else. Their world has gone now, with its insular little community and its glory reflected from the Raj. They probably would not have worried much about how posterity regards them. They had a duty to do and they did it to the best of their abilities. Most of all, they simply got on with living.

NOTES

References are given in shortened form to works which will be found in the Select Bibliography. Other abbreviations are:

CSAA   Cambridge South Asian Archive
NAI   National Archives of India
IOL   India Office Library, London

PREFACE
p. 11 Anglo-Indian attitudes: Macfarlane 123–25, 127–28 — p. 14 new avenues of scholarly focus: Eaton 73; Ghose 3–4 — p. 15 fancy dress balls: Shope 376 — p. 15 Lady Curzon's maternity dress: Thomas 388 — p. 16 Anglo-Indian domestic culture: Procida 125 — p. 16 craze for curry: Chaudhuri

INTRODUCTION
p. 21 eighteenth-century attitudes: Mukherjee 81; p. 21 Hastings: Marshall 12

CHAPTER 1: THE VOYAGE OUT
p. 30 early women travellers to India: quoted in Mickelson 34; D. Kincaid 44 — p. 31 voyage in sailing ships: Caunter 4, 5, 7–8; p. 32 Sherwood, ed. Darton 228; Fay 218, 105, 108; p. 33 Sherwood quoted in Bamfield 29; [Blane] 38; p. 34 Mackenzie I, 15; [Ashmore] 13 — p. 35 crossing the Egyptian desert: Fay 96 — voyage in steamships: p. 36 *Indian Outfits* 29, 27; Steel and Gardiner 220 — p. 37 partings: Hinkson 15 — p. 37 Malta: *Indian Outfits* 30 — 'pickled monks': Wallace-Dunlop I, 13 — sightseeing: *Indian Outfits* 30 — p. 38 Red Sea: *Indian Outfits* 32 — shipboard romances: Hinkson 20–21 — games: D. Kincaid 303; Savi (1947) 195 — p. 39 Aden: *Indian Outfits* 32 — Indian Ocean: Campbell-Martin 1–2

CHAPTER 2: FIRST IMPRESSIONS
p. 41 Bombay: Hinkson 26; Guthrie (1877) I, 44–45; p. 42 Guthrie (1877) I, 52; R. Lawrence 28, 29–30; Guthrie (1877) I, 48, 56; Falkland I, 6 — p. 43 Ceylon: [Metcalfe] 95 — Madras: [Ashmore] 41; [Maitland] 34; Graham (1812) 124; p. 44 Hickey 107; [Maitland] 17; [Ashmore] 43; Fay 161–62 — Calcutta: [Metcalfe] 96; p. 45 [Blane] 44; Fay 171 — European quarters: Lang 49 — Europeans a minority: Wilson (1911) 4 — p. 46 Indians: Guthrie (1877) I, 140; Campbell-Martin 5; p. 47 Fane 139–40 — p. 48 English: Fane 63, 87, 58 — first journeys: [Metcalfe] 117; [H. Lawrence] 53; p. 49 [Blane] 156; Curtis 93–94; p. 50 Lang 56; Campbell-Martin 10; Macfarlane 123–25 — new customs: Hinkson 25

CHAPTER 3: THE SOCIETY OF THE EXILES

p. 52 the élite: *Pioneer*, 27 Dec. 1881 — p. 53 numbers of Europeans: *Report on the Census of British India ...* 1881, Form X, 8–9; *Report, Census of India*, 1921, I, pt. 1, Subsidiary Table IV, 97; *Report on the Census of Bengal*, 1881, I, 148; NAI, Foreign Dept, Internal Branch, 1895, 122–23, B Proceedings — p. 54 Parsees: Scott 90, 181 — p. 55 impermanence of British society: R. Godden (1942) 10; Steel and Gardiner 26 — p. 56 problems of moving: [H. Lawrence] 122; *Indian Outfits* 63 — sociability of British: Thompson 117; Wilson (1911) 56; p. 57 Fraser 84 — boredom: *Pioneer*, 21 Jan. 1890 — p. 58 nature of British community: MacLeod 136 — p. 59 hierarchy: *Pioneer*, 11 Sept. 1885 — p. 60 precedence: Rivett-Carnac 92; Russell 14; NAI, Home Dept, Public Br., Mar. 1896, 267–68 Deposit; p. 61 NAI, Home Dept, Public Br., Oct. 1890, 419 Deposit — nature of community: Thompson 207; Wilson (1911) 99; Kipling (1964) 88, 89 — attitudes to India: *Report of the Census of the Punjab ...* 1881, I, 2; C.A. Kincaid 205; p. 62 Darling 118; Savory 339; Ackerley 19, 87 — religion and British: [Madden] 193 — conversation: Dufferin I, 57: Falkland 2; Prichard II, 26 — p. 63 openness: Wilson (1911) 66 — high spirits of British: Baden-Powell 74; de Warren quoted in Dewar 221; Wilson (1911) 107 — p. 64 languid ladies: [Maitland] 19 — the Club: R. Lawrence 27; Macfarlane 3 — p. 73 women: [Greaves] 74; de Warren quoted in Dewar 223; Diver, *Englishwoman* 25; p. 74 E. Bell 95; IOL, Oral Archives Coll., Lady F. Smyth — weakness of women: Hull and Mair 235 — standards for women: Diver, *Captain Desmond* 146; *Englishman*, 28 June 1918 — prostitutes: NAI, Home Dept, Police Br., Jan. 1892, 63–65 B Proceedings — pornography: NAI, Home Dept, Public Br., July 1888, 384 Deposit; NAI, Home Dept, Judicial Br., Apr. 1913, 193–204 A Proceedings — p. 75 Serpentine Dance: NAI, Home Dept, Political Br., Feb. 1917, 82–110 — Maud Allen: NAI, Home Dept, Police Br., Nov. 1913, 59–79

CHAPTER 4: THE LAND OF EXILE

p. 76 conformity: Wilson (1911) 107 — p. 77 knowledge of India: [Maitland] 26; IOL, Oral Archives Coll., Lady F. Smyth — pre-Mutiny attitudes: [Metcalfe] 143; p. 78 Clemons 66; Login 38–40; Parks I, 60, 383; Graham (1814) 87 — p. 79 attitudes to Indians: Paget 104 — duty of British: Lovat Fraser 38; p. 80 Sir A. Fraser 213 — obstacles to friendship between races: Savi (1947) 147; Cotton 39; Beveridge 210; *Pioneer*, 28 Dec. 1885; p. 81 Webb 6–12, 84; p. 82 Wilson (1911) 33–34; Diver, *Englishwoman* 83 — p. 83 visits to Indian women: Savory 367; Masani 58; Ashby 86; Scott 86–87, 71 — social occasions: C. C. Dyson 282; p. 84 Parks I, 74; *Pioneer*, 28 Jan. 1881; Tottenham 314; Butler [Portal] 17 — distance between races: W. S. Blunt 262; p. 85 Keene 203; Dawson 353; Beveridge 88 — women's views on Indians and India: [Blane] 103; King I, 24; Diver, *Siege Perilous* 58; E. Bell 109; p. 86 Mackenzie I, 167; Wilson (1911) 22; C. C. Dyson 235; p. 87 Sherwood quoted in K. K. Dyson 178; King I, 204; King II, 17 — fear of India: R. Lawrence 63 — p. 88 idealizing Home: [H. Lawrence] 41

CHAPTER 5: FACTS OF LIFE

p. 89 baggage: *Indian Outfits* 1; *Real Life in India* 144; p. 90 Steel and Gardiner
215 — p. 91 clothes: [Blane] 149; p. 92 *Hartley House* 155; Steel and Gardiner
216; Wallace-Dunlop I, 231; Kerr 210; Steel and Gardiner 211 — p. 93 topis:
Parks I, 55; Dewar 57 — miscellaneous advice: Steel and Gardiner 216; *Indian
Outfits* 12, 13, 14 — p. 94 household goods: Lang 183; Curtis 42; *Indian Outfits* 15;
The Englishwoman in India, 37–38 — travel: Bombay Archives, General, 1907,
vol. 79, com 101; *Englishman*, 9 Feb. 1920; p. 95 [H. Lawrence] 131; Login 50; p.
96 Wallace-Dunlop I, 98; [H. Lawrence] 123; p. 97 Postans, *Cutch* 6; Marryat,
'*Gup*' 185–86; J. and R. Godden 158; p. 98 Billington 326; p. 99 Hinkson 35;
Eden (1930) 102–3; p. 100 [H. Lawrence] 98, 132 — houses: *Indian Outfits* 57;
p. 101 Wallace-Dunlop I, 132–33; CSAA, Women in India; p. 102 Steel and
Gardiner 27; Savory 337 — *punkah:* Parks I, 25 — p. 103 verandahs: [Cuthell]
(1910?) 5 — bathrooms: Savi (1947) 68 — shopping: p. 104 *Hartley House*
50; Duncan 58; Savi (1947) 23; p. 105 Curtis 119; Wallace-Dunlop I, 197; R.
Lawrence 46 — *mofussil* life: Campbell-Martin 40–41 — p. 106 Indian climate:
Real Life in India 149 — hot weather: R. Lawrence 266; King I, 105, 106; p. 107
Campbell-Martin 134; [Cuthell] (1910?) 272; *Indian Outfits* 83; Parks I, 303; R.
Lawrence 144 — p. 108 ice: King I, 33–34 — coping with hot weather: *Indian
Outfits* 75; p. 109 Steel and Gardiner 204, 211; Billington 333 — monsoon: p. 110
R. Lawrence 56 — insects: Curtis 109; Clemons 60; Falkland 149; p. 111 Parks I,
61; Dufferin II, 154; Falkland 15 — health: Lang 114; p. 112 Lawrence 221, 255,
259; Tilt 34, 56–57, 84; *Pioneer*, 18 Nov. 1888; *Pioneer*, 7 July 1883; p. 113 CSAA,
Women in India; Parks II, App. xviii, 501–2; Savi (1947) 93; Mrs H. Reynolds
50; Ashby 180 — p. 114 earthquake: Campbell-Martin 157–58 — menaces:
CSAA, Bayley Papers; Lang 195, 107 — boredom: Kerr 215; p. 115 Marryat 54;
Wallace-Dunlop I, 206; Wilson (1911) 50; Darton 249; Ashmore 81 — love of
India: CSAA, Women in India; IOL, Oral Archives Coll., Lady F. Smyth; R.
Lawrence 99

CHAPTER 6: WOMEN IN DANGER

p. 118 start of the Mutiny: Hibbert 84; p. 119 Muter I, 18; Hibbert 101–2;
Chick 69; Hibbert 116; Chick 106; Hibbert 230; p. 120 quoted in Bamfield
101 — Lucknow: Inglis 61; Hibbert 250, 247; Chick 248; p. 121 Chick 257;
Bartrum 36; Hibbert 249; Chick 260; Inglis 100–101, 116 — Cawnpore:
Hibbert 183, 186, 192; p. 122 Chick 184; Hibbert 195; 207; p. 123 Chick 176;
quoted in Smailes 82 — revenge: Hibbert 355; Russell 21; [Blane] 123–24
— memories: Surtees 245; Trevelyan 67; [Cuthell] (1910?) 76–77; A. Blunt
413; p. 124 Savi (1947) 35; Allen 57; p. 125 'Civilian' 135–43; Grey (eds) 237;
Darling 116 — sexual threat: Marryat 6; *Anglo-Indian Guardian*, 7 June 1889;
Swabey 238; p. 126 Diver, *Englishwoman* 77; Whitehead, preface xi; Daly, 24
May 1856; Ballhatchet 115; p. 127 Ackerley 28; NAI, Home Dept, Medical
Br., Mar. 1914, 34–42 A Proceedings; Fuller 129; p. 128 Allen 124; R. Godden

(1982) 41; Ballhatchet 116, 50; Mrs G. H. Bell 161 — p. 129 *A Passage to India*:
Forster, Intro., 20, 186–87, 153, 236; p. 130 Furbank II, 124, n.2; Furbank II,
128 — p. 131 *The Raj Quartet: Jewel in the Crown* 311 — security: Savi (1947) 74

CHAPTER 7: COURTSHIP AND MARRIAGE
p. 133 raised to be memsahibs: Macfarlane 58 — Indian mistresses: Curtis
112, 113 — education of girls: Savi (1947) 14, 142; p. 134 J. and R. Godden
213; Dawson 351; Jacquemont I, 360 — chastity: Savi (1947) 14; NAI, Home
Dept, Medical Br., Feb. 1883, 45–49 B Proceedings — p. 135 courting:
CSAA, Donaldson Papers 3 — p. 136 engagements: [Blane] 172; C. C. Dyson
12; Marryat 50; Allen 44–45 — p. 145 flirting: *Hartley House* 22, 36; Prichard
235 — p. 146 motives for marriage: de Warren quoted in Dewar 224; 'Aliph
Cheem' 225; p. 147 King II, 55 — qualities for wives: King II, 59; D. Kincaid
224; Church Missionary Soc. Letters, 1882, N. India, #273; Kipling, *Plain
Tales*, 106–9 — p. 148 courtships: Mackenzie I, 278; [Gray] 244–47; Curtis
137; p. 149 Hamilton 187 — weddings: Beveridge 112; [Blane] 153–54 — p.
150 introduction to marriage: R. Lawrence 23; Savi (1947) 66; p. 151 Smith
7–8; Steel (1929) 122; Lang 53; Smith 13 — coping with marriage: Curtis
104; p. 152 R. Lawrence 90; Wilson (1911) 39–40 — strains on marriage:
Steel (1929) 122; *Pioneer*, 19 Sept. 1881; Daly, 17 July 1855; p. 153 IOL, Oral
Archives Coll., Iris Portal; Butler [Portal] 17; Macfarlane 119–20; p. 154
Savi (1947) 100–101; C. C. Dyson 121; p. 155 Aberigh-MacKay 109; [Blane]
105, 146, 173, 181 — p. 156 soldiers' marriages: Guest 31–32; Interview with
Mrs W. T. Atkins; Punjab High Court, Divorce Proceedings 3–21 — p. 157
happy marriages: Mackenzie III, 175 — adultery: *Pioneer*, 24 Feb. 1882;
p. 158 Savi (1947) 117; Diver, *Englishwoman* 24; Richards 151; Blood 171;
[Cuthell] (1892) 39

CHAPTER 8: CHILDREN: OUTPOSTS OF EMPIRE
p. 159 children: E. Bell 199; Wilkinson 107–8 — p. 160 contraception: Smith
35; Bamfield 26 — pregnancy and childbirth: *Birch's Management* 15–16; p.
161 Lang 162; [Blane] 69, 76, 112, 152, 155 — p. 162 wet nurses: Steel and
Gardiner 163 — children's health: Steel and Gardiner 177–82; Wilkinson
110; Tytler 78; p. 163 *Birch's Management* 13; Platt 133; *Birch's Management*
358; Platt 135 — *ayahs*: CSAA, Women in India; p. 164 *Birch's Management*
10 — spoiled children: Ashby 49; Steel and Gardiner 87 — training of children: Macfarlane 51–52; *Pioneer*, 4 Oct. 1880 — p. 165 children's parties: R.
Lawrence 263; Dufferin I, 54 — dangers to children: *Birch's Management* 10,
9–11; p. 166 Richards 151; Diver, *Englishwoman* 42; Platt 139 — p. 174 education: Nathan 332; p. 175 J. and R. Godden 13; p. 168 Kipling, *Wee Willie Winkie*
99, 131; Diver, *Englishwoman* 41; Curtis 156; Scott 116; p. 169 Wilson (1911)
176; Curtis 157; Campbell-Martin 153

CHAPTER 9: HOUSEKEEPING

p. 170 household management: Steel and Gardiner 9, 7; 'Chota Mem' 4; R. Lawrence 34 — difficulties: [Blane] 70; p. 171 Lang 110; Campbell-Martin 24–25 — supervision: Steel and Gardiner 2; *Indian Outfits* 69; p. 172 'Chota Mem' 4; Fay 181 — Indian character: Platt 37; 'Chota Mem' 56 — p. 173 testimonials: Campbell-Martin 99 — servants: Steel and Gardiner 5; p. 174 'Chota Mem' 55 — numbers of servants: Buck 39; [Cuthell] (1910?) 210; Parks I, 120; Beveridge 150, 195 — p. 175 storeroom: Steel and Gardiner 14 — p. 176 meat: Daly, 29 May 1856 — tinned food: Steel and Gardiner 12 — water: Beveridge 263 — p. 185 kitchen: Wilson (1911) 8 — cooks: CSAA, Hall Papers, ch. 10, 36; Curtis 115; p. 186 Steel and Gardiner 72; Savi (1947) 146 — servants: Steel and Gardiner 73; [Aitken] 81; p. 187 *Indian Outfits* 47; p. 188 Steel and Gardiner 84, 4 — relationship with servants: Beveridge 206; p. 189 Bamfield 135; Allen 81, 135; Interview with Mrs D. Berringer; CSAA, Women in India; CSAA, Donaldson Papers 3 — gardening: p. 190 Campbell-Martin 161; Parks I, 78; [Cuthell] (1910?) 69, 12; King II, 47; p. 191 Temple-Wright 9; King II, 140; Campbell-Martin 93 — women's conversations: 'Chota Mem' 7

CHAPTER 10: SOCIAL LIFE AND AMUSEMENTS

p. 192 social life: CSAA, Donaldson Papers 5; Wilson (1911) 292; p. 193 C. C. Dyson 132; Allen 151; Nicolson 158 — calling: C. C. Dyson 95; p. 194 Curtis 100; *Pioneer*, 20 Feb. 1882; *Madras Mail*, 13 Apr. 1883 — p. 195 hierarchy: E. Bell 43; R. Lawrence 209; Wilson (1911) 48; *Pioneer*, 23 Sept. 1881; Savi (1947) 136 — p. 196 pageantry: [Harkness] (1912) 136 — chits: Maitland 137; p. 197 D. Kincaid 160 — daily routine: Maitland 138 — riding: Allen 111; p. 198 Curtis 99 — sports: Bence-Jones 181; Ashby 152; Kipling, *Plain Tales* 56–57, 59; p. 199 Campbell-Martin 39 — tennis parties: CSAA, Women in India; Steel and Gardiner 48 — garden parties: p. 200 Bence-Jones 161; Nicolson 124–25 — the Club: Starr 33–34 — p. 201 evening outings: Fay 164 — dinners: Fay 189 — Anglo-Indian cooking: Kenney-Herbert 1; p. 202 Steel and Gardiner 47; Gordon 5; Carne 27; Cumming 399; Kenney-Herbert 336; p. 203 Kenney-Herbert 112, 15 — dressing for dinner: Wallace-Dunlop I, 300; J. and R. Godden 89 — dinner parties: Diver, *Englishwoman* 55–56; p. 204 Wilson (1911) 49; p. 205 *Pioneer*, 7 Sept. 1881; *Pioneer*, 28 Sept. 1881; *Indian Outfits* 88; p. 207 *Pioneer*, 17 Sept. 1881 — card parties: Fay 189 — balls and dances: CSAA, Women in India; Curtis 123; [Ashmore] 62–63; p. 208 IOL, Ussher Papers, 3 July 1934; Curzon I, 224; p. 209 [Blane] 156; Hamilton 40; p. 210 Hamilton 41; D. Kincaid 269–70; Bence-Jones 73; Falkland 153 — p. 211 amateur theatricals: [Ashmore] 228; *Pioneer*, 19 Feb. 1881; Horne 23 — picnics: Kipling, *Plain Tales* 43 — Lucknow: *Pioneer*, 3 Feb. 1881 — 'weeks': p. 212 Savi (1947) 142 — planters' meets: Campbell-Martin 138 — Christmas: *Pioneer*, 27 Dec. 1880 — p. 213 Lillian Ashby: Ashby 143

CHAPTER 11: ON HOLIDAY

p. 214 Lord Minto's daughters: Buck 58 — p. 215 hunting: Doughty 225;
Baillie 76, 204–6; Campbell-Martin 61, 113–15 — fishing: Lang 239 — p. 216
sightseeing: King I, 182; p. 217 Parks I, 333, 340, 355 — holidays on water:
Savi (1947) 127; p. 218 J. and R. Godden 169 — on tour: R. Lawrence 221;
Dufferin I, 103; Allen and Dwivedi 247; p. 219 Wilson (1911) 1; Burke 11;
CSAA, Taylor Papers 7–8 — in camp: Steel and Gardiner 148; Dunbar 63;
R. Lawrence 88; p. 220 Kenney-Herbert 449–50; Carne 6, 15, 19 — trek-
king: King II 8–9; p. 221 King II 215, 216, 221, 86; Hunter 196–97 — p. 222
Kashmir: Bamfield 131; p. 223 J. and R. Godden 188; Doughty 31 — p. 224 hill
stations: Cumming 305; *Statesman* quoted in *Pioneer*, 20 June 1884; Buck 34;
Eden (1919) 297 — p. 225 mountain air: Parks II, 228; Falkland 95; Dufferin
II, 137; Wilson (1911) 38; Savory 331; Muter I, 125 — journey to Hills: Wilson
(1911) 37; p. 226 Cumming 485–86; Beveridge 159 — accommodation: D.
Kincaid 252; Doughty 253; p. 227 King I, 141 — baggage: Steel and Gardiner
195–96 — p. 229 Simla: Lutyens 37 — social life of hill stations: Falkland 98;
Buck 205; Portal 1585; Wilson (1911) 303 — p. 230 Indians in hill stations:
NAI, Home Dept, Public Br., Apr. 1890, 327 Deposit — riding: Allen 132 —
rickshaws: Cumming 302 — expeditions: Guthrie (1881) I, 103; p. 231 Butler
31–32; Duncan 68 — picnics: Diver, *Siege Perilous*, 98 — hill-station amusements: Guthrie (1881) I, 103; p. 232 Kerr 210–11; Prinsep 251; Butler 139
— flirting: Marryat 100; p. 233 Prinsep 262; Buck 41 — types of hill stations:
CSAA, Donaldson Papers 8; Surtees 257; p. 234 Steel and Gardiner 43, 44;
Pioneer, 30 Mar. 1888; Baker 252 — Simla: Steel and Gardiner 43; [Madden]
179; Butler 111; p. 235 Butler 141

CHAPTER 12: UNCONVENTIONAL WOMEN

p. 236 unusual women: Bence-Jones 181; p. 238 Eden (1919) 273; Eden (1930)
2–3, 209; Trevelyan 134–35; p. 239 Butler 187; [Symington] 79; Guthrie (1877)
I, 94–95 — Emma Roberts: p. 240 Roberts I, 225–26, III, 86 — Fanny Parks:
Dunbar 114; Parks I, 29, 28, 445; II, 45; p. 241 Parks II 191; Parks I, 293 —
Annette Beveridge: p. 242 Beveridge 121 — Flora Annie Steel: Steel (1929)
287, 104; p. 243 CSAA, Women in India; Steel (1929) 173; Steel (1896) 11 — p.
244 women writers: p. 245 Fowler 290 — governesses: Wilson (1911) 150; C.
C. Dyson 281 — p. 246 secretaries: Tottenham 77, 153 — nannies: Allen and
Dwivedi 42 — medical women: p. 247 Balfour and Young 29, 25 — mission-
aries: p. 248 Luce 62; p. 257 Barnes 10, 93; Luce 90; Barnes 29; Christlieb
36; p. 258 [Harkness] (1912) 207; [Harkness] (1909) 194; Houghton 184;
Christlieb 65–66; [Harkness] (1909) 195; p. 259 Barnes 105; Houghton 191;
Dufferin II, 127; Reynolds 169; R. Lawrence 145, 147 — p. 260 Ursula Graham
Bower: Bower (1952) 7–8, 21 p. 261 Bower (1952) 84, 217, 226 — p. 262 mixed
marriages: [H. Lawrence] 139; Younger 147–59; p. 263 Irvine 107; 'Boxwallah'
289; Perrin 271; Savi, *Daughter-in-Law* 153, 291; Cottrell 404; p. 264 Beveridge

345; Irvine 107 — Morag Murray Abdullah: Abdullah *passim* — p. 265 Sister
Nivedita: Foxe 34; Noble 16; p. 266 Foxe 130, 126 — Annie Besant: p. 267
Englishman, 19 Apr. 1918; *Englishman*, 27 Sept. 1917 — Mary Carpenter: Kerr
205

CHAPTER 13: WOMEN IN A CHANGING WORLD
p. 270 women on Raj: CSAA, Women in India; C. C. Dyson 210; Wilson
(1895) 155 — Ilbert Bill: p. 271 D. Kincaid 213; Gopal 147; *Pioneer*, 1 Nov. 1883;
Pioneer, 8 Mar. 1883; *Parliamentary Papers*, 1884, lx, 388, 298; *Madras Mail*,
24 Mar. 1883; Scott 72; p. 272 *Pioneer*, 3 Mar. 1883; *Pioneer*, 18 July 1883;
Beveridge 227–28; *Parliamentary Papers*, 1884, lx, 591; *Pioneer*, 28 Mar. 1883
— p. 273 partition of Bengal: quoted in Wolpert 282; Rees 180; [Harkness]
(1909) 257 — First World War: E. Bell, 220–21 — p. 275 Amritsar: *Englishman*,
16 Apr. 1919; p. 276 *Report of the Committee … to Investigate the Disturbances
in the Punjab* III, 120; Draper 237; *Englishman*, 5 July 1920; *Englishman*, 13
July, 1920; *Englishman*, 10 July 1920 — p. 277 inter-war years: CSAA, Dench
Papers 66; p. 278 D. Kincaid 308; Butler 14 — p. 279 Home: Irvine 351; CSAA,
Taylor Papers 17 — Indian nationalism: Allen 207; [Symington] 216; p. 280
Savi (1947) 202 — Second World War: CSAA, Bayley Papers 50; Candlin 89;
p. 281 Mansergh I, 801 — Quit India movement: Allen 204; CSAA, Women in
India — war work: Bower (1952) 155 — p. 282 impact of war: CSAA, Women
in India; Mansergh I, 765; p. 283 Candlin 200 — Indian independence:
CSAA, Bayley Papers 126; CSAA, Women in India; IOL, Oral Archives Coll.,
Lady Corfield; p. 284 CSAA, Women in India; [Symington] 243

CONCLUSION
p. 285 going Home: CSAA, Bayley Papers 130; Graham (1812) 183; Parks II,
330–32; p. 286 IOL, Oral Archives Coll., Lady F. Smyth; IOL, Oral Archives
Coll., Iris Portal; Curtis 165–66; Bower (1953) 211, 238

SELECT BIBLIOGRAPHY

UNPUBLISHED SOURCES

Bombay State Archives. General Department, Proceedings
British Library, London. Ripon Papers
Centre of South Asian Studies, University of Cambridge. Bayley Papers; Dench Papers;
 Donaldson Papers; Hall Papers; Haig Papers; Taylor Papers; Women in India:
 Replies to Questionnaires, 1978–83
Church Missionary Society, London. Correspondence from missionaries in India
India Office Library, London. Oral Archives Collection: Interviews with Lady Corfield,
 Mrs Betty Diamond, Mrs Irene Edwards, Mrs Lee, Mrs Lakshmi Mazumdar,
 Mrs Iris Portal, Mrs S. Ralli, Lady Frances Smyth, Mrs Marjorie and Mr James
 Williamson; Ussher Papers
Mickelson, Joan Marie. *British Women in India 1757–1857*, PhD, University of Michigan,
 1978
National Archives of India, Delhi. Foreign Department, Internal Branch, Proceedings;
 Home Department, Judicial, Medical, Police, Public, and Political Branches,
 Proceedings
Punjab State Archives, Lahore. Records of the Punjab High Court, Divorce Proceedings

NEWSPAPERS

Anglo-Indian Guardian (Calcutta)
Calcutta Review
Civil and Military Gazette (Lahore)
Englishman (Calcutta)
Madras Mail
Pioneer (Allahabad)
Statesman (and Friend of India) (Calcutta)
Times of India (Bombay)

BOOKS AND ARTICLES

Abdullah, Morag Murray, *My Khyber Marriage* (London, 1934)
Aberigh-MacKay, George, *Twenty-One Days in India*, 2nd edn (London, 1880)
[Aitken, E. H.] EHA (pseud.), *Behind the Bungalow*, 14th edn (London,
 Calcutta and Simla, 1929)
Aldis, Janet, *A Girl Guide Captain in India* (London, 1924?)
Ali, Mrs Meer Hassan, *Observations on the Mussulmauns of India*, 2nd edn, ed.
 W. Crooke (London, 1917)

Aliph Cheem [Walter Yeldham], *Lays of Ind* (Calcutta, 1875)

Allen, Charles (ed.), *Plain Tales from the Raj* (London, 1975)

— and Dwivedi, Sharada, *Lives of the Indian Princes* (London, 1984)

An Anglo-Indian: see *Indian Outfits*

Ashby, Lillian Luker, *My India* (London, 1938)

[Ashmore, Mrs], *A Narrative of a Three Months' March in India; and a Residence in the Dooab* (London, 1841)

Atkinson, Capt. George F., *Curry and Rice (on Forty Plates) or The Ingredients of Social Life at 'Our' Station in India* (London, n.d. [1859])

Baden-Powell, Lt.-Gen. Sir Robert, *Indian Memories* (London, 1915)

Baillie, Mrs W. W., *Days and Nights of Shikar* (London and New York, 1921)

Baker, Amy, *Six Merry Mummers* (London, 1931)

Balfour, Margaret I. and Young, Ruth, *The Work of Medical Women in India* (London and Bombay, 1929)

Ballantyne, Tony (ed.), *Debating Empire.* Special issue of the *Journal of Colonialism and Colonial History*, 3:1 (Spring 2002)

— and Burton, Antoinette (eds), *Bodies in Contact: Rethinking Colonial Encounters in World History* (Durham, NC, 2005)

Ballhatchet, Kenneth, *Race, Sex and Class under the Raj* (London, 1980)

Bamfield, Veronica, *On the Strength* (London, 1974)

Barnes, Irene H., *Behind the Pardah* (London, 1897)

Barr, Pat, *The Memsahibs* (London, 1976)

— and Desmond, Ray, *Simla: A Hill Station in British India* (London, 1978)

[Bartrum, Katherine], *A Widow's Reminiscences of Lucknow* (London, 1818)

Bayly, C. A., *Empire and Information: Intelligence Gathering and Social Communication in India, 1780–1870* (Cambridge, 1996)

Beames, John, *Memoirs of a Bengal Civilian* (London, 1961)

Becher, Augusta Emily, *Personal Reminiscences in India and Europe 1830–1888* (London, 1930)

Bell, Evelyn, *Memory Be Good* (London, 1939)

[Bell, Mrs G. H.] John Travers (pseud.), *Sahib-log* (London, 1910)

Bence-Jones, Mark, *Palace of the Raj* (London, 1973)

Beresford, Leslie, *The Second Rising* (London, 1910)

Besant, Annie: see Nethercot, Arthur H.

Beveridge, Henry, Lord, *India Called Them* (London, 1947)

Biddulph, John, *The Pirates of Malabar and An Englishwoman in India Two Hundred Years Ago* (London, 1907)

Billington, Mary Frances, *Woman in India* (London, 1895)

Birch's Management: see Green

[Blane, Minnie], *From Minnie, with Love*, ed. J. Vansittart (London, 1974)

Blood, Gen. Sir Bindon, *Four Score Years and Ten* (London, 1933)

Blunt, Alison, 'Embodying war: British women and domestic defilement in the Indian "Mutiny", 1857–8', *Journal of Historical Geography*, 26:3 (July 2000), pp. 403–28

Blunt, Wilfrid Scawen, *India Under Ripon: A Private Diary* (London, 1909)

Bower, Ursula Graham, *The Hidden Land* (London, 1953)

—, *Naga Path* (London, 1952)

Boxwallah, *An Eastern Backwater* (London, 1915?)

Bradley, Shelland, *The Adventures of an ADC*, 2nd edn (London, 1910)

Bremner, Christine S., *A Month in a Dandi* (London, 1892?)

The British in India (Colne, 1971)

Brown, Hilton, *The Sahibs* (London, 1948)

Buck, Sir Edward, *Simla Past and Present*, 2nd edn (Bombay, 1925)

Buckland, C. T., *Sketches of Social Life in India* (London, 1884)

Buettner, Elizabeth, *Empire Families: Britons and Late Imperial India*
(Oxford and New York, 2004)

Burke, Norah, *Jungle Child* (New York, 1955)

Burton, Antoinette M., *Burdens of History: British Feminists, Indian Women,
and Imperial Culture, 1865–1915* (Chapel Hill and London, 1994)

— (ed.), *Gender, Sexuality and Colonial Modernities* (London and New York, 1999)

Butler, Iris, *Viceroy's Wife* (London, 1969) (See also Portal, Iris)

Cable, Boyd [Ewart, Ernest Andrew], *A Hundred Year History of the P. & O.
(Peninsular and Oriental Steam Navigation Co.) 1837–1937* (London, 1937)

[Caldwell, R. C.], *The Chutney Lyrics*, 2nd edn (Madras, 1889)

Campbell, Helen, *An Eastern Diary* (privately printed, Tenby, S. Wales, 1913?)

Campbell-Martin, Monica, *Out in the Midday Sun* (London, 1948?)

Candler, Edmund, *Abdication* (London, 1922)

Candlin, Enid Saunders, *A Traveller's Tale* (New York and London, 1974)

Canning, Charlotte: see Surtees, V.

Carne, Lucy, *Simple Menus and Recipes for Camp, Home and Nursery*, 2nd edn
(Calcutta, 1919)

Caunter, Rev. Hobart, *The Oriental Annual, or Scenes in India* (London, 1836)

Census: see *Report. Census of India*

Chaudhuri, Nupar, 'Shawls, jewelry, curry, and rice in Victorian Britain', in Nupur
Chaudhuri and Margaret Strobel (eds), *Western Women and Imperialism:
Complicity and Resistance* (Bloomington, 1992)

Chick, Noah, *Annals of the Indian Rebellion, 1857–58*, ed. David Hutchinson
(London, 1974)

Chirol, Valentine, *Indian Unrest* (London, 1910)

Chota Mem [Mrs C. Lang], *The English Bride in India, Being Hints on Indian
Housekeeping*, 2nd edn (London and Madras, 1909)

Christlieb, M. L., *Uphill Steps in India* (London, 1930)

Civilian, 'The Tree-Daubing of 1894', *Calcutta Review*, 106 (January 1898)

Clemons, Mrs Major, *The Manners and Customs of Society in India* (London, 1841)

Collingham, E. M., *Imperial Bodies: The Physical Experience of the Raj,
c. 1800–1947* (Cambridge, 2001)

Cooper, Frederick and Stoler, Ann Laura, *Tensions of Empire: Colonial*

Cultures in a Bourgeois World (Berkeley and London, 1997)

Cotton, Sir Henry John Stedman, *New India* (London, 1904)

Cottrell, Ann Baker, 'Outsiders' Inside View: Western Wives' Experiences in Indian Joint Families', *Journal of Marriage and the Family*, 37:2 (May 1975), pp. 400–07

Cox, Sir Edmund C., *My Thirty Years in India* (London, 1909)

Cumming, C. F. Gordon, *In the Himalayas* (Edinburgh, 1884)

Curtis, Julia, *Mists and Monsoons* (London and Glasgow, 1935)

Curzon, Lady: see Nicolson, N.

Curzon, Lord, *British Government in India: The Story of the Viceroys and Government House*, 2 vols (London, 1925)

[Cuthell, Edith H.] An Idle Exile (pseud.), *In Tent and Bungalow* (London, 1892)

[—], *My Garden in the City of Gardens* (London and New York, 1910?)

Dainty Dishes for Indian Tables (Calcutta, 1879)

Daly, John (comp.), *Letters from India*, unpublished

Darling, Sir Malcolm, *Apprentice to Power* (London, 1966)

Darton, F. J. Harvey (ed.), *The Life and Times of Mrs Sherwood (1775–1851), from the Diaries of Captain and Mrs Sherwood* (London, 1910)

Dawson, J. E., 'Woman in India: her influence and position', *Calcutta Review*, 83 (July 1886), pp. 347–57

Dewar, Douglas, *Bygone Days in India* (London, 1922)

Diver, Maud, *Captain Desmond, V.C.* (Edinburgh and London, 1909)

—, *The Englishwoman in India* (Edinburgh and London, 1909)

—, *Siege Perilous and Other Stories* (London, 1924)

Doughty, Marion, *Afoot Through the Kashmir Valleys* (London, 1901)

Draper, Alfred, *Amritsar* (London, 1981)

Dufferin and Ava, Marchioness, *Our Viceregal Life in India*, 2 vols (London, 1890)

Dunbar, Janet, *Golden Interlude* (London, 1955)

Duncan, Jessie, *Life in India* (Toronto, 1944)

Duncan, S. J., *The Simple Adventures of a Memsahib* (New York and London, 1893). See also Fowler, M.

Dyson, C. C., *From a Punjaub Pomegranate Grove* (London, 1913)

Dyson, K. K., *A Various Universe* (Delhi, 1978)

Earl, Barbara, *Trekking in Kashmir* (Lahore, 1930)

Eaton, Richard M., '(Re)imag(in)ing other²ness: a postmortem for the postmodern in India', *Journal of World History*, 11:1 (Spring 2000), pp. 57–78

Eden, Emily, *Miss Eden's Letters*, ed. V. Dickinson (London, 1919)

—, *Up the Country* (Oxford, 1930)

Edwardes, Michael, *Bound to Exile* (London, 1969)

EHA: see Aitken, E. H.

Emanuel, Louis, *Jottings and Recollections of a Bengal 'Qui Hye!'* (London, 1886?)

The Englishwoman in India, by a Lady Resident, 2nd edn (London, 1865)

European and Anglo-Indian Defence Association (after 1912 European Defence Association), *Annual Reports*

Faber, Mary Anne, *Recollections of Indian Life* (privately printed, London, 1910)

Falkland, Viscountess, *Chow-Chow*, ed. H. G. Rawlinson (London, 1930)

Fane, Isabella, *Miss Fane in India*, ed. J. Pemble (Gloucester, 1985)

Fay, Mrs Eliza, *Original Letters from India (1779–1815)* (London, 1925)

The First Years of a Little Girl in Bengal (Calcutta, 1829)

Fitzroy, Yvonne, *Courts and Camps in India* (London, 1926)

Forster, E. M., *A Passage to India* (London, 1984). And see Furbank, P. N.

Fowler, Marian, *Redney: A Life of Sara Jeanette Duncan* (Toronto, 1983)

Foxe, Barbara, *Long Journey Home: A Biography of Margaret Noble* (London, 1975)

Fraser, Eugenie, *A Home by the Hooghly: A Jute Wallah's Wife* (Edinburgh, 1989)

Fraser, Lovat, *India under Curzon and After* (London, 1911)

Fraser, Sir Andrew H. L., *Among Indian Rajahs and Ryots*, 3rd and rev. edn
          (London, 1912)

Fuller, Sir Bamfylde, *Some Personal Experiences* (London, 1930)

Furbank, P. N., *E. M. Forster: A Life*, 2 vols (London, 1977–78)

Gaughan, Joan Mickelson, *The 'Incumberances': British Women in India, 1615–1856*
          (New Delhi, 2013)

Geofry, [?], *Ooty and Her Sisters, or Our Hill Stations in South India* (Madras, 1881)

Ghose, Indira, *Women Travellers in Colonial India: The Power of the Female Gaze*
          (New Delhi, 1998)

Ghosh, Durba, *Sex and the Family in Colonial India: The Making of Empire*
          (Cambridge, 2006)

Godden, Jon and Rumer, *Two Under the Indian Sun* (New York, 1966)

Godden, Rumer, *Breakfast with the Nikolides* (London, 1942)

—, *The Lady and the Unicorn* (London, 1982)

—, *A Time to Dance, No Time to Weep* (London, 1987)

Gopal, S., *The Viceroyalty of Lord Ripon, 1880–1884* (London, 1953)

Gordon, Constance E., *Anglo-Indian Cuisine (Khána Kitâb) and Domestic Economy*,
          2nd edn (Calcutta and Bombay, 1913)

Graham, Mrs Maria, *Journal of a Residence in India* (Edinburgh, 1812)

—, *Letters on India* (London, 1814)

[Gray, James], *Life in Bombay, and the Neighbouring Out-Stations* (London, 1852)

[Greaves, Gen. Sir G. R.], *Memoirs of General Sir George Richards Greaves*
          (London, 1924)

Green, C. R. M. and Green-Armytage, V. B., *Birch's Management and Medical
          Treatment of Children in India*, 5th edn (Calcutta, 1913)

Greenfield, Rose, *Five Years in Ludhiana* (London, 1886)

Grey, F. and C. (eds), *Tales of Our Grandfather, or India Since 1856* (London, 1912)

Guest, Freddie, *Indian Cavalryman* (London, 1959)

Guthrie, Katherine Blanche, *Life in Western India*, 2 vols (London, 1881)

—, *My Year in an Indian Fort*, 2 vols (London, 1877)

Halliday, James: see Symington, David

Hamilton, Gen. Sir Ian, *Listening for the Drums* (London, 1944)

[Harkness, Margaret Elise] John Law (pseud.), *Glimpses of Hidden India*
    (Calcutta, Simla and Bombay, 1909)

[—] John Law (pseud.), *Indian Snapshots*, 3rd edn (Madras, 1912)

Harrison, Irene, *Agatha Harrison* (London, 1956)

Hartley House, Calcutta (London, 1789; repr. 1908)

Hauswirth, Frieda, *A Marriage to India* (London, 1931)

Hibbert, Christopher, *The Great Mutiny: India 1857* (London, 1978)

[Hickey, William], *Memoirs of William Hickey*, ed. P. Quennell, new edn (London, 1975)

Hill, Sir Claude H., *India – Stepmother* (Edinburgh and London, 1929)

Hinkson, Pamela, *Indian Harvest* (London, 1941)

Horne, W. O., *Work and Sport in the Old I.C.S.* (Edinburgh and London, 1928)

Houghton, Frank, *Amy Carmichael of Dohnavur* (London, 1953)

Hull, Edmund C. P. and Mair, R. S., *The European in India; or, the Anglo-Indian's*
    Vade-Mecum (London, 1871)

Hunter, Isabel Fraser King, *Land of Regrets* (London, 1909)

An Idle Exile: see Cuthell, E. H.

Indian Outfits & Establishments: A Practical Guide for Persons About to Reside in India;
    Detailing the Articles Which Should Be Taken Out, and the Requirements
    of Home Life and Management There, by An Anglo-Indian (London, 1882)

Inglis, Lady Julia, *The Siege of Lucknow* (London, 1892)

Irvine, Lt-Col. A. A., *Land of No Regrets* (London, 1938)

Jacob, Violet, *Diaries and Letters from India, 1895–1900*, ed. Carol Anderson
    (Edinburgh, 1990)

Jacquemont, Victor, *Letters from India*, 2 vols, 2nd edn (London, 1835)

Keene, H. G., 'The Indian Services', *Calcutta Review*, 74 (1882)

Kennedy, Dane, 'Imperial history and post-colonial theory', *Journal of Imperial*
    and Commonwealth History, 24:3 (July 2008), pp. 345–63

—, 'Imperial history wars', *Journal of British Studies*, 54:1 (January 2015), pp. 5–22

—, *The Magic Mountains: Hill Stations and the British Raj* (Berkeley, Los Angeles,
    Oxford, 1996)

Kenney-Herbert, Col. A. R., *Wyvern's Indian Cookery Book, Being a New and Revised*
    Edition of Culinary Jottings for Madras, 7th edn (Madras and London, 1904)

Kerr, Barbara, *The Dispossessed* (London, 1974)

Kincaid, C. A., *Forty-Four Years a Public Servant* (Edinburgh and London, 1934)

Kincaid, Dennis, *British Social Life in India, 1608–1937* (London, 1938)

King, E. A. [King, Mrs Robert Moss], *Diary of a Civilian's Wife in India, 1877–82*,
    2 vols (London, 1884)

Kipling, Rudyard, *Plain Tales from the Hills* (London, 1964)

—, *Wee Willie Winkie and Other Stories* (London, 1914)

Lang, Monica, *Invitation to Tea* (London, 1953)

Law, John: see Harkness, M. E.

[Lawrence, Honoria], *The Journals of Honoria Lawrence: India Observed, 1837–1854*, ed.
    J. Lawrence and A. Woodiwiss (London, 1980)

Lawrence, Lady [Rosamund], *Indian Embers* (Oxford, 1949)

Leonowens, Anna Harriette, *Life and Travel in India* (London, 1884)

Levine, Philippa (ed.), *Gender and Empire* (Oxford and New York, 2004)

[Login, Lena (Campbell)], *Lady Login's Recollections*, by E. Dalhousie Login
        (London, 1916)

Luce, Ella, *Glimpses of Christian India* (London and Edinburgh, 1933)

Lutyens, Mary, *The Lyttons in India* (London, 1979)

McClintock, Anne, *Imperial Leather: Race, Gender and Sexuality in the
        Colonial Contest* [sic] (New York and London, 1995)

Macfarlane, Iris, *Daughters of the Empire: A Memoir of Life and Times in the
        British Raj* (New Delhi, 2006)

Mackenzie, Mrs Colin [Helen], *Life in the Mission, the Camp, and the Zenana*,
        3 vols (London, 1854)

MacLeod, R. D., *Impressions of an Indian Civil Servant* (London, 1938)

[Madden, Ruby], *A Season in India: Letters of Ruby Madden*, ed. H. Rutledge
        (Sydney, 1982)

[Maitland, Julia], *Letters from Madras, During the Years 1836–1839, by a Lady*
        (London, 1843)

Mansergh, Nicholas (ed.), *The Transfer of Power 1942–1947*, vols 1 and 2
        (London, 1970–71)

Marryat, Florence, *'Gup', Sketches of Anglo-Indian Life and Character* (London, 1868)

Marshall, Peter, 'Warren Hastings as scholar and patron', in Marshall, *Statesmen,
        Scholars and Merchants* (Oxford, 1973), pp. 242–62

Masani, Zereer, *Indian Tales of the Raj* (London, 1987)

Mason, Philip: see Woodruff

Massey, Montague, *Recollections of Calcutta for over Half a Century* (Calcutta, 1918)

Mayer, J. E. (ed.), *The Humour and Pathos of Anglo-Indian Life* (London, 1895)

[Metcalfe, Emily], *The Golden Calm: An English Lady's Life in Moghul Delhi*,
        ed. M. M. Kaye (Exeter and New York, 1980)

Metcalf, Thomas, *Ideologies of the Raj* (Cambridge, 1995)

Miln, Louise, *When We Were Strolling Players in the East* (London, 1894)

Mitchell, Mrs Murray, *In India* (London, 1876)

Moorhouse, Geoffrey, *Calcutta* (London, 1974)

—, *India Britannica* (London, 1984)

Mudford, Peter, *Birds of a Different Plumage: A Study of British Indian Relations
        from Akbar to Curzon* (London, 1974)

Mukherjee, S. N., *Sir William Jones: A Study in 18th-Century British Attitudes
        to India* (Cambridge, 1968)

Muter, Mrs D. D., *Travels and Adventures of an Officer's Wife in India, China,
        and New Zealand*, 2 vols (London, 1864)

Napier, Philip, *Raj in Sunset* (Ilfracombe, Devon, 1960)

Nathan, R., *Progress of Education in India, 1897–98 – 1901–02*, 2 vols (Calcutta, 1904)

Nethercot, Arthur H., *The First Five Lives of Annie Besant* (London, 1961)

—, *The Last Four Lives of Annie Besant* (London, 1963)

Nichols, Beverley, *Verdict on India* (London and New York, 1944)

Nicolson, Nigel, *Mary Curzon* (London and New York, 1977)

Noble, Margaret E., *The Web of Indian Life* (London, 1904). And see Foxe, B.

O'Hanlon, Rosalind and Washbrook, David, 'After Orientalism: culture, criticism,
        and politics in the Third World', *Comparative Studies in Society and History*,
        34:1 (January 1992), pp. 141–67

An Old Indian, 'Social life in Bengal fifty years ago', *Calcutta Review*, 73 (July 1881),
        pp. 378–400

An Old Resident, *Real Life in India* (London, 1847)

The Onlooker [Alastair MacRae, ed.], *The Onlooker Book of Verse* (Bombay, 1944?;
        Delhi, 1968)

Paget, Mrs Leopold, *Camp and Cantonment: A Journal of Life in India in 1857–1859,
        with Some Account of the Way Thither* (London, 1865)

Panter-Downes, Molly, *Ooty Preserved: A Victorian Hill Station* (London, 1967)

[Parks, Fanny], *Wanderings of a Pilgrim in Search of the Picturesque*, 2 vols
        (London, 1850 cit.; repr. 1975). And see Dunbar, J.

Parliamentary Papers 1883, vol. LI: Correspondence on the subject of the proposed
        alteration of the Provisions of the Code of Criminal Procedure with respect
        to Jurisdiction over European British Subjects

— 1884, vol. LX: Further Correspondence and Papers

Perrin, Alice, *The Anglo-Indians*, 3rd edn (London, 1912)

Pierson, Ruth Roach and Chaudhuri, Nupur (eds), *Nation, Empire, Colony:
        Historicizing Gender and Race* (Bloomington, 1998)

Pinch, Trevor, *Stark India* (London, 1930?)

Platt, Kate, *The Home and Health in India and the Tropical Colonies* (London, 1923)

Pollard, Eliza F., *The White Dove of Amritzir* (London, 1896?)

Portal [Butler], Iris, 'The Sahibs at play', *Country Life*, 1 Dec. 1977 (See also Butler, Iris)

Postans, Mrs Marianne, *Cutch; or, Random Sketches, Taken During a Residence in
        One of the Northern Provinces of India; Interspersed with Legends and Traditions*
        (London, 1839)

—, *Western India in 1838*, 2 vols (London, 1839)

Prichard, Iltudus, *The Chronicles of Budgepore*, 2 vols (London, n.d.)

Prinsep, Val C., *Glimpses of Imperial India* (repr. Delhi, 1979)

Procida, Mary, 'Feeding the imperial appetite: imperial knowledge and Anglo-Indian
        domesticity', *Journal of Women's History*, 15:2 (Summer 2003), pp. 123–49

Rae, Mrs Milne, *A Bottle in the Smoke* (London, 1912?)

Reading, Lady: see Butler, Iris, *Viceroy's Wife*

Rees, Sir J. D., *Modern India* (London, 1910)

Report, Census of India, 1921, by J. T. Martin, vol. 1

*Report of the Census of the Punjab Taken on the 17th February, 1881, by Denzil Charles
        Jelf Ibbetson*, 3 vols (Calcutta, 1883)

Report on the Census of Bengal, 1881, by J. A. Bourdillion (Calcutta, 1883)

Report on the Census of British India Taken on the 17th February 1881, 3 vols
          (London, 1883)

*Report of the Committee Appointed by the Government of India to Investigate the
          Disturbances in the Punjab, etc.*, 3 vols (London, 1920)

Reynolds, Charles, *Punjab Pioneer* (Waco, TX, 1968)

Reynolds, Mrs Herbert, *At Home in India* (London, 1903?)

Richards, Frank, *Old Soldier Sahib* (London, 1965)

Rivett-Carnac, J. H., *Many Memories of Life in India, at Home, and Abroad*
          (Edinburgh and London, 1910)

Roberts, Emma, *Hindostan* (repr. Delhi, 1972)

—, *Scenes and Characteristics of Hindostan, with Sketches of Anglo-Indian Society*,
          3 vols (London, 1835)

Rowe, A. D., *Everyday Life in India* (New York, 1881)

Russell, William Howard, *My Indian Mutiny Diary*, ed. M. Edwardes (London, 1957)

Satow, Michael and Desmond, Ray, *Railways of the Raj* (London, 1980)

Savi, E. W., *The Daughter-in-Law* (London, 1913)

—, *My Own Story* (London, 1947)

Savory, Isabel, *A Sportswoman in India* (London, 1900)

Scott, Nora, *An Indian Journal*, ed. John Radford (London and New York, 1994)

Scott, Paul, *The Raj Quartet* [see pp. 138–39] (London, 1977)

Seton, Grace Thompson, '*Yes, Lady Saheb*' (London, 1925)

[Sherwood, Mrs], *The Works of Mrs. Sherwood*, vol. 3 (New York, 1855);
          and see Darton, F. J. H.

Shope, Bradley, 'Masquerading sophistication: fancy dress balls of Britain's Raj',
          Journal of Imperial and Commonwealth History, 39:3 (2011),
          pp. 375–92

Sinha, Mrinalini, *Gender and Nation* (Washington, DC, 2006)

Smailes, Helen, *Scottish Empire* (Edinburgh, 1981)

Smith, Margaret, *A Different Drummer* (London, 1931)

Spear, T. G. P., *The Nabobs* (London, 1932)

—, *Twilight of the Mughals* (Karachi and Lahore, 1973)

Stanford, J. K., *Ladies in the Sun: The Memsahibs' India, 1790–1860* (London, 1962)

Starr [Mackesy], Leonora, *Colonel's Lady* (London, 1937)

Steel, Flora Annie, *The Garden of Fidelity, Being the Autobiography of Flora Annie Steel,
          1847–1929* (London, 1929)

—, *On the Face of the Waters* (London, 1896)

— and Gardiner, G. *The Complete Indian Housekeeper and Cook*, new edn
          (London, 1898)

Stein, Elizabeth Gertrude [Morton, Eleanor], *The Women in Gandhi's Life*
          (New York, 1953)

Surtees, Virginia, *Charlotte Canning* (London, 1972)

Swabey, Hilda M., *The Chief Commissioner* (London, 1912)

[Symington, David] James Halliday (pseud.), *A Special India* (London, 1968)

Temple-Wright, Mrs R., *Flowers and Gardens in India: A Manual for Beginners*,
    4th edn (Calcutta, 1898)
Thomas, Nicola J., 'Embodying imperial spectacle: dressing Lady Curzon,
    Vicereine of India 1899–1905', *cultural geographies*, 14:3 (2007), pp. 369–400
Thompson, Edward, *An Indian Day* (London, 1927)
Tilt, Edward J., *Health in India for British Women and on the Prevention
    of Disease in Tropical Climates*, 4th edn (London, 1875)
Tottenham, Edith Leonora, *Highnesses of Hindostan* (London, 1934)
Trevelyan, Humphrey, *The India We Left* (London, 1972)
[Tytler, Harriet], *An Englishwoman in India: The Memoirs of Harriet Tytler, 1828–1858*,
    ed. A. Sattin (Oxford and New York, 1986)
Wallace-Dunlop, Madeline and Rosalind, *The Timely Retreat; or, A Year in Bengal before
    the Mutinies*, 2 vols (London, 1858)
Washbrook, David A., 'Orients and occidents: colonial discourse theory and the
    historiography of the British Empire', in Robin Winks (ed.), *The Oxford History
    of the British Empire: Volume V: Historiography* (Oxford, 1999)
Webb, W. T., *English Etiquette for Indian Gentlemen* (Calcutta, 1915)
Wernher, Hilda, *My Indian Family* (New York, 1943)
Whitehead, H., *India: A Sketch of the Madura Mission* (London, 1897?)
Wilkinson, Theon, *Two Monsoons* (London, 1976)
Wilson, Anne C., *After Five Years in India* (London, 1895)
—, *Hints for the First Year's Residence in India* (Oxford, 1904)
—, *Letters from India* (Edinburgh and London, 1911)
Wilson-Carmichael, Amy, *Things as They Are: Mission Work in Southern India*
    (London, 1908)
Wolpert, Stanley, *A New History of India* (New York, 1979)
Woodruff [Mason], Philip, *The Men Who Ruled India*, Vol. 1: *The Founders*
    (London, 1953); Vol. 2: *The Guardians* (London, 1963)
Yeldham, Walter: see Aliph Cheem
Young, Miriam, *Seen and Heard in a Punjab Village* (London, 1931)
Younger, Coralie, *Wicked Women of the Raj: European Women who Broke Society's
    Rules and Married Indian Princes* (New Delhi, 2003)
Yule, Col. Henry and Burnell, A. C., *Hobson-Jobson: A Glossary of Colloquial Anglo-Indian
    Words and Phrases, and of Kindred Terms, Etymological, Historical, Geographical and
    Discursive*, 2nd edn (London, 1903, repr. 1985)

LIST OF ILLUSTRATIONS

Abbreviations used:

BBC   BBC Hulton Picture Library, London
IOL   India Office Library, London
NAM   National Army Museum, London
RCS   Royal Commonwealth Society, London

ACKNOWLEDGMENTS

I should like to thank the staffs of the following institutions for their assistance: the Bodleian Library in Oxford, the Cambridge South Asian Archive, the India Office Library in London, the Metropolitan Toronto Reference Library, the National Archives of India in Delhi, the New York Public Library, and the Ryerson Library in Toronto. I am particularly grateful to Dr Richard Bingle of the India Office Library for his advice. My employer, Ryerson Polytechnical Institute, gave me research time which helped to make the writing of this book possible.

Diana Barringer, Sheelah Ogilvy, Dr P. F. Griffin, Mrs J. E. Manning, Mrs W. T. Atkins, and my grandmother, Lady Olwen Carey Evans, once memsahibs themselves, made the Raj come alive in their reminiscences. My thanks are also due to those women whom I never met but who left their impressions in the Cambridge South Asian Archive (Lady Anderson, Emily Barrett, Evelyn Battye, Mrs D. Curtis, Mrs V. Downing, Miss E. Ferar, Isabel Gross, Mrs O. U. Hamilton, Mrs B. M. MacDonald, Mrs Saunders, and Nancy Vernede). The Bibliography and Notes acknowledge those others, too numerous to mention here, whose memoirs, diaries, novels and histories contributed so much to this book. In addition I should like to thank Charles Allen for material from *Plain Tales from the Raj* (London: André Deutsch, 1975), Sir John Lawrence and Audrey Woodiwiss for quotations from *The Journals of Honoria Lawrence* (London: Hodder and Stoughton, 1980), Owen Lawrence for *Indian Embers* by Rosamund Lawrence (Oxford: George Ronald, 1949), and Jane Vansittart for *From Minnie, with Love* (London: Peter Davies, 1974).

A number of friends offered invaluable help. Without Dr Joshua Sherman this book might well have remained a mere sketch. Drs Thomas and Evelyn Rawski gave me much needed technical advice. Dr Thomas Barcsay and Dr John Stratton kindly read parts of the manuscript. Finally I should like to thank the members of my large family, without whose encouragement and (if they will forgive me) nagging I would not have finished this book. I am especially grateful to my sister Ann MacMillan and my brother-in-law Peter Snow for their unstinting hospitality and help, to my late parents, Eluned and Dr Robert MacMillan, and to my former husband, Bob Manson, whose patience must have been sorely tried but who never showed it.

MM

INDEX

Numbers in *italic* refer to illustrations